Three Wars but not a Hero

LtCol Bud Barbee

TRAFFORD
PUBLISHING

USA . Canada . UK . Ireland

KATE

WITH YOUR
PERSONAILY
YOU'LL DO WELL
WHEREVER YOU
ARE AND
WHATEVER
YOU D.

Bud Barbee

Note for Librarians: A cataloguing record for this book is available from Library and Archives Canada at www.collectionscanada.ca/amicus/index-e.html

ISBN 1-4251-0966-7

Printed in Victoria, BC, Canada. Printed on paper with minimum 30% recycled fibre. Trafford's print shop runs on "green energy" from solar, wind and other environmentally-friendly power sources.

PUBLISHING

Offices in Canada, USA, Ireland and UK

Book sales for North America and international:
Trafford Publishing, 6E–2333 Government St.,
Victoria, BC V8T 4P4 CANADA
phone 250 383 6864 (toll-free 1 888 232 4444)
fax 250 383 6804; email to orders@trafford.com

Book sales in Europe:
Trafford Publishing (UK) Limited, 9 Park End Street, 2nd Floor
Oxford, UK OX1 1HH UNITED KINGDOM
phone +44 (0)1865 722 113 (local rate 0845 230 9601)
facsimile +44 (0)1865 722 868; info.uk@trafford.com

Order online at:
trafford.com/06-2724

10 9 8 7 6 5 4 3 2

Three Wars but not a Hero

There must be a lot of us out there.

Yeah, I flew aircraft in all three:

WWII, Korea, Vietnam. Never dropped a bomb on innocent people, never shot down another aircraft, never killed anyone face to face.

Counting a few years in the Air Force Reserve after the end of WW II, I retired with thirty years, 3 months, and ten days service.

So, why should anyone be interested in my life? Well, I wanted my grandchildren to know something about who I was, what I did. In so far as they know, I have been an old man all my life. They can't believe, for instance, that I was ever a teenager. Impossible. *Their* children are now teenagers. I could never have been like *that*.

Perhaps this exercise may encourage others to keep, make, a similar record. I know, it's long, but it is a cheap book. And you might learn something..

APOLOGIA

We find ourselves reaching back for a past that really never was and hoping for a future that never will be. We dull thus our enjoyment of the present..

There are so many things that one can think of when there is no opportunity to write them down or to do something with them — ideas, thoughts, cherished moments, sad occasions, periods of exhilaration and despair, impulses, whatever. So, keep a diary — but, not having done so over the allotted three score and ten, then compose as best you can, and as only you can, those remembrances, flavored by the years and by the retelling, and set them down as truthfully and accurately as possible and with only that considered amount of embellishment allowed by your sensitivities and conscience. When it comes to writing about yourself, where you came from, who was responsible, where you are going or have been, and who those are who have been along with you for the ride, for better or worse, for fun or sorrow, willingly or otherwise; when it comes to that, that writing about those people, the "mishpocha," places and things, even the minutiae which assume unwarranted prominence, the memory is challenged, and is often freshened, by the *effort.*

This is my effort.

"Ah, si la jeunesse savait,

et si la vieillesse pouvait."

And keep in mind:

"Es ist besser ein junger Alter zu sein,

als ein alter Junger."

INDEX

      My Lovely Women – The Mixer -

       The Stroke – My Sorrows & Failings

Epilogue

PREFACE

Why write a biography? Many reasons, and sometimes, just because - because this year (2006) I will be 88 years old, and time grows short. I was a pilot in three wars – WWII, Korea, Vietnam – thirty years - but not a hero. I did not kill anyone. I did not bomb any cities or oil refineries. I did not shoot down another airplane. Nothing heroic.

There are some indications that our daughters can imagine that we, the parents, grand-parents, and great-grandparents - Kathryn Jarrell Hampton Barbee and Bud (NMI) Barbee,— that we were once young, and maybe a little foolish. That may be a possibility to our children, both now way, way over forty where life begins, but it has nothing to do with the attitude of our grandchildren, now in *their* forties. Mommy Kay and Pop (I'm Pop) could never have been young — not teenagers (ridiculous) and certainly not little kids. (Inconceivable). Never happen. We were always old — especially Pop: because he is inclined to be cranky, difficult and a little irritable. (I'm really not that way at all. Strict? Yes. Perhaps a little impatient. Probably don't smile enough.)

That's part of the reason for the biography and the family genealogies. Some day the great-grandchildren might want a little insight into our generation's growing up. During the past few years, I have managed to put a few remembered periods on paper. There are now more of the little incidents — those harbingers of memory failure — when you go from one room to another for a specific purpose and forget halfway there what that purpose was. I know, it happens to everyone, but more often and with greater regularity as the days dwindle down.

And, my dear wife died and left me rudderless almost four years ago. It is hard to put a lifetime on paper. Who knows?? Maybe something can be learned from the successes and failures of the past.

Dedicated to

The most beautiful woman I have ever known –
My Wife - who made my life worthwhile.

CHAPTER I

Nashville Years

"It was the best of times, it was the worst of times, it was the age of wisdom, it was the age of foolishness, it was the epoch of belief, it was the epoch of incredulity, it was the season of Light, it was the season of Darkness, it was the spring of hope, it was the winter of despair."

Yes, there were similarities with Dickens' *A Tale of Two Cities* in many cities of the United States in the months preceding the end of World War I. Many were the young men who had gone to war. Some were in trenches and foxholes not far from romantic sounding, if pronounceable, French cities. Some were nearer home in war related industry. Farms and country towns in the U.S. were decimated and the cities were swollen. Temporary accommodations, over-crowding, inadequate sanitation facilities. Influenza: Pandemic! Diphtheria: Epidemic! Too late recognition of early symptoms, doctor shortage, hysteria, easy contagion. Hundreds died, thousands died; too few burial facilities, no room at the undertakers, the dead were piled in wagons and carts awaiting their transition to the Elysian Fields.

And this was the time I chose to make my entrance into this world. April 10, 1918. Not the best of times. But, I must have been born a survivor like my mother: during my first year of life — and this is all hearsay since my recollection of that early time is somewhat dim — I suffered from or through the "flu," diphtheria, measles, mumps, and the whooping cough. In all likelihood, I was a veritable breeding ground for assorted anti-toxins. There was great concern in the household, but I survived and their fears were eased and some of the present readers' existence was made possible. (Doesn't that make you feel warm all over?)

Thus I was born, survived, nurtured, and began to grow.

Several photographs of early childhood have also survived the years. The earliest seems to be one with my brother when I am possibly two or three — I am depicted holding a baby's milk bottle. I appear to be a little too old or too big to still be using a bottle (there are many indications that I matured slowly but successfully), but I am wearing a little dress of some sort. Another, a little later, and I am sitting on my father's lap. I am now wearing little boys' clothing. My father has a very serious look, pince-nez glasses on a string, and my mother has cut out part of herself from the photo. Last picture from that era: I am wearing full bib overalls and holding my father's .38 calibre pistol. My head is a mass of red curls. This photo was printed on a saucer-sized metal plate.

Panhandling

According to all reports and oft-repeated narratives, I developed into an accomplished panhandler during the period when I was three to six years old. Our house on Fifth Avenue, just down from Church Street,[2] was right next to the side entrance of the Princess Theater, a movie-vaudeville house. (The main entrance was on Church.) My usual and favorite ploy was to station myself just before the ticket office and accost young couples with the plea "Gimme a nickel, please mister." Only young couples, and only for a nickel. A nickel is larger than a dime, and I reasoned at that time that it was worth more. (Neither seems to have much worth these days.) Who could refuse this charming little beggar? And the local patrolling policeman rarely caught me in the act. (Aside: our back porch was adjacent to the side doors of the theater which were opened for ventilation during the warmer months, and we could watch the movies. No sound or air-conditioning in those days.)

Smoking

Surely it must happen in all lives...that time or times when temptation is too great to overcome, when the apparent sweetness of the forbidden fruit must be tasted regardless of the penalty. My friend, Snooks, and I — both about four or five — were caught smoking cigarette butts under the back porch projection. Mother was shrill. My father was man to man:

"You boys shouldn't be smoking cigarette butts that some stranger has thrown away."

"But daddy, it wasn't a stranger. It was Mr. Shoemaker.[3] We watched him throw them away and we ran and got them."

---

1 Mother always cut people out of photos, herself included, when she did not like the person or the picture. She marked my picture with an "x" in every publication, yearbook, that it appeared.

2   Just about the center of "downtown" Nashville.

3   Shoemaker was one of Mother's "roomers." He always called her "Highpockets," because she was close with her money.

This approach was not getting the desired result.

"Son, when you want to smoke, smoke a pipe like a man." My father smoked a pipe. "The next time you feel you want to have a smoke, come tell me and I'll fix you up a good pipe."

Before too long, the urge was great, I needed the pipe. Daddy prepared it for me, helped me light it, showed me how to "puff," sat me in a rocking chair on the front porch, and went inside to observe this rite of passage.

In less than five minutes I was changing color, mainly toward green, and not feeling at all well. What followed would be indelicate to describe. Suffice to say, I did not smoke again soon. It was many, many years before I was even tempted to try a cigarette. And during those smoking years which are happily behind me, I was never very comfortable with a pipe, many times that I tried.[4] Manhood promised to be a difficult achievement.

I told you my brother was nine years older. He spent a lot more time with me than I believe he really wanted to, but he and his friend Gordy Canter had occasion to appreciate my value. They were just not the age to be able to pull off the panhandling at which I was so adept. The solution was to find me with a fist full of nickels, tease me till I flared, then stand by to pick up the coins I would throw at them. In fairness, I was allowed to share in what was bought with my ill-gotten gains. That's brotherhood.

Can dogs swim? How can you find out when you live in the city? If you're a curious four year old (or thereabouts) you get your friend Snooks (same age) and the young puppy that was left over from the litter of six and go down to the Cumberland River.

Only about a mile from where you live, and just under the bridge there's a raft tied up so you can walk out on it and throw the dog in the deeper water — and he paddles back a couple of times and proves that dogs can swim.

Gruff voice demands: "What are you boys doing here?"

Dumb question. He could see what we were doing.

"Trying to see if this dog can swim." We now see it is a policeman.

"Where do you live?"

"157 Fifth Avenue North and leggo my arm."

---

4   During 1969-1970, in Thailand, during the Vietnam War, I quit cigarettes for a while and smoked the pipe, trying to accustom myself to it. I would "light up" the pipe after take-off and keep the furnace belching for an entire mission, sometimes as long as four-teen hours. I went back to cigarettes when the dentist told me that I was burning up the inside of my mouth. Nasty stuff, that tobacco..

Safely home, mother wants to know: "Bud, weren't you afraid when Officer Carney found you and Snooks under the bridge?"

"No 'cause he's just a man like Daddy, except he wears a badge and carries a gun and he was hurting my arm."

Officer Carney and providence, presumably separate entities, hovered over me like protecting angels.

157 Fifth Avenue North and surrounding area was a parking lot when last I saw Nashville. The "old" Country Music Hall of Fame on the east side of the street and just south of where I lived, is a museum piece. The old church on the southeast corner of Fifth and Church was still standing. Presbyterian, I think. It's a busier city than when I knew it. What I didn't know at the time: my future wife's father had a business right around the corner – Oscar Perry Hampton, father of Kathryn Jarrell Hampton, to whom I would be happily married for over sixty years.

But 157 Fifth Avenue North was where "Damma," my mother, began her many years experience owning and running "rooming" houses.

And now I must go back to an earlier time.

CHAPTER II

Rose Palestine Overton Hooper (my mother)

Rose Hooper was 25 or 26 years old when she arrived at the railroad station in Nashville, Tennessee, having ridden on an employee widow's pass from the small town of Dickson, thirty-eight miles to the west of the capital city.

The tall, big-boned, slightly reddish-haired, attractive young widow, breaking away from scores of in-laws, left behind her father and step-mother, brothers and sisters,[5] nieces and nephews, and countless cousins. She also left behind, in the little rustic cemetery on the tree-bordered hillside above the old Rock Church, the body of her beloved husband and childhood sweetheart, who had worked for the railroad whose mournful whistle echoed through the hills and valleys of the surrounding countryside.

With very little in the way of worldly possessions, but holding fast to her young son, Presley Freeman Hooper, now about five years old, she brought along her strong constitution, sharp mind, a fierce independence, and a bold determination to take care of herself and her own. She needed to make a living and she needed a job.

Childhood

Rose Palestine was the twelfth of fourteen children born to William Thomas Overton and his wife Amanda, née Larkins. Amanda died in 1895, having spent most of her almost twenty-eight years of married life in a hopelessly repetitive process of pregnancy and childbirth. Grandpa, sometime after the death of Amanda, married Annie (Nettie) Sylvia Hildebrand, a widow, whose grandson John F. Hildebrand of Nashville died about 1988.

Tom Overton, my grandfather, inherited a "good parcel" of land from his father, but the Civil War ending slavery changed some of the expected advantages of many landowners. He wasn't really much for farming, he did teach school for awhile (my mother always told me), but he somehow managed to lose most of the extensive holdings. I have some vague recollections of my grandfather as a tall and lanky old man with a scraggly beard who did

---

5   See Appendix for genealogy.

not seem to do very much when we visited him. In proper perspective, I must consider that he was seventy-eight years old when I was born. He did drink, according to some of the older natives, the ones who knew "Uncle Billy," who relate as how his faithful old horse would stand perfectly still, in place, if "old Tom," (as William Thomas, he was interchangeably "Uncle Billy" or "Old Tom.") on the way home from a not infrequent stint of over-imbibing, should slide out of the saddle and fall to the ground. But "aye godlins

Rosie" (as he would say) staunchly defended her daddy as "a good man" whenever such historical happenings were mentioned.

Grandpa, born in 1840, served in the Civil War, died on the 28th of September 1928 "at his home, four miles east of Dickson, at the age of 88." Loving daughter "Rosie" had sent him "a comfortable chair" from St. Louis by Railway Express, but he died before the chair arrived. According to the numerous cousins, there was a "whole passel" of acreage still left in the estate and number two son, William Richard (Uncle Dick), graciously bought out all the other children for a "fair price" (some called it stealing).[6]

Rose Palestine, possibly named for Rosie Cox and Pallie Larkins who "birthed" her, was the next to youngest of quite a family. Hattie, who was born next, had a twin (Jimmy) who died at birth. Rose and Hattie had brothers as much as twenty years older who had married and started their own families. Growing up on the farm, as virtual indentured servants to their father, they yet seemed to have an idyllic existence — as my mother Rose frequently reminded me.

They could milk the cows, saddle the horse, find the best patches and pick the best blackberries, go down to the spring and drink the cool buttermilk kept there.[7] And they could go everywhere barefoot. They had shoes for Sunday, but carried them to and from church.

---

6   Uncle Dick's son Hugh (Hugh-boy) inherited the land from his father, sold off some of the acreage, farmed much of it, and when he died (1981) it passed to his widow, Nellie Nicks Overton. They had no children, so to the dismay of the surviving Overtons, the land will no longer belong to an Overton, but to a Nicks. The Nicks and Overton families have been associated for many years. Nellie never learned to drive a car and, at last report in 1981, had never traveled beyond Dickson, less than 10 miles from her home on the farm.

7   My wife and I found this spring when we last visited, at the time of mother's death in 1981.

I always wondered if they wore shoes in school, but Mother would change the subject and insist that she did not go beyond the third grade. If true, she was a mathematical whiz: figuring mortgages, when buying or selling houses (I can remember living in ten different houses while growing up), she could come within a few dollars of establishing the monthly payments on differing loan percentages, over varying terms. But grammar and syntax were different matters: Mother was overly generous with capitalization, had no use whatsoever for commas, was stingy with periods, and entirely unconcerned about verb usage.

According to her recollections, she worked as a "mother's helper" from about the age of ten. And couldn't go to school during harvest, or during the winter when she didn't have warm clothes. But her daddy, who had been a schoolteacher, was a "wonderful man who had been very good to his children."

Marriage

The sparse county records, and statements made by her shortly before she died, tell us that Rose Palestine Overton married her childhood sweetheart, Earlie (Early Lee) Hooper, when she was twenty years old.[8] She had become a very attractive young woman, hairdo perhaps slightly severe, but that was the style of the day and accounts for the austere look of women in the photos and tintypes of that period around the turn of the century. Her high cheekbones were supposedly due to Indian blood in her background a few generations earlier.

Earlie was considered a handsome young man, just a little above average in height, trim in figure, with a full head of hair worn parted in the middle and a strong wave on either side of the middle of his forehead. He was maybe three or four months younger than she.

Hoopers and Overtons "was thick as fleas" in that particular rural area around Dickson, Tennessee, but when I came along, a Barbee, I had Hooper aunts and uncles just like my brother, who was a Hooper.

---

8   Rose Overton Hooper Barbee Isaacs Ammerman was always quite free with choosing the date of her birth: it varied by marriage and the age of her husband, insurance purposes, social security, and other considerations. Examining various records, deciphering through erasures, considering birth and marriage licenses, and her own statement, shortly before her death, that she had been a "little" older than Earlie, her first husband, we can, with some degree of certainty, fix her year of birth as 1888.

My brother — actually a half-brother — Presley Freeman Hooper was born to the young couple June 10, 1909, ten months after Rose and Earlie had taken the buggy to the county seat and got themselves married without telling anybody except a couple of friends who stood up with them. The date was August 16, 1908.

I never found out why they did it this way, but have a hunch it was to escape from Grampa.

Earlie worked for the L & N Railroad and they lived in a little house on a relative's property in the country not far from Dickson. In November, 1913, just as he turned twenty-five, Earlie "took to his sick-bed and died." The probable cause was typhoid fever from contaminated water. Not much thought was given in those days to ground water infiltration of wells or springs, which provided drinking water. The doctor very likely had misdiagnosed the illness, but just as likely could have done nothing to change the course of events. Mother never trusted "medical" doctors the rest of her life.

But that is another tale. And now Rose P. (she did not like her middle name) Overton Hooper came to the big city of Nashville to get on with her life.

CHAPTER III

Bud Barbee Sr.

She rented a room, made arrangements for Freeman to be looked after while she was working, and took a job with the National Biscuit Company on their cookie assembly line. After a couple of non-eventful years and several promotions — a consequence of her ability and willingness to do a good job — while on an "outing" with some of the other "girls" from the company, Rose met this older man, thirteen years older in fact, who had been divorced some years before. She found him to be attentive and congenial, a soft-spoken gentleman. He seemed quite attracted to her, she envisioned better security for herself and her son, so on May 2, 1917, Rosie, the survivor, became Mrs. Bud Barbee, wife of the "stationary engineer" at the Tulane Hotel, she age twenty-eight, he age forty-two.

Not a marriage "made in Heaven" necessarily, but one at least of mutual advantage and convenience. He needed a woman and she needed to get her life turned around in order to provide better for her son who was one month and eight days shy of his eighth birthday. There was an understanding that she would handle the discipline of her son. No assistance was required, no interference desired. Similar proscriptions were not applicable to me, Bud Jr., when I made my appearance, in due course, eleven months later on April 10, 1918.

I was born at home, 207 N. 8th Ave., Nashville. Christened Bud Barbee Jr., but mother always insisted it was supposed to be Bud Junior Barbee. Attending physician was W.L. Dumpter of 155 8th Ave. N.

Exemeldefonso (Exum. was the name recorded in the 1880 census of Stewart Co. TN., showing age 5.) Barbee - that first name was certainly gleaned from the bookplate, as ex libris, found in an old volume once belonging to the family of a Monsieur El Defonso — in any case, however, that mentally coruscating appellation was dispensed with in early manhood to be replaced by what is universally accorded as a nickname: BUD! Bud Barbee (18 Apr 1875-10 Apr 1946) was one of the "Clarksville Barbee boys."[9] (There were two others: Ed and Finis, his half brothers.)

---

9   The mother of one of Kay's friends warned Kay that she had known the "wild Barbee boys" in Clarksville and that she had better be careful about marrying me.

Riley Bartlett Barbee, born c. 1846, married Virginia J. Bowers, December 14, 1868, and had three children: Ida, Emma, and Bud (neé Exum.). When Virginia died ("from a blow on the head with an axe accidently by her husband."), Bart married her sister Frances Bowers in 1875 and they had three children: Finis, William Edward, and Carrie. The 1870 census of Montgomery County, TN., shows Bart 23, farmhand, and Jennie 22, Tillie (Ida?) 3/12. The 1880 census has the ages as: Bartlett 33, Francis 26, Ida 10, Emma 8, Exum 5, Finis 8/12. Bart was buried in Blooming Grove Cemetery, near Dover, Tennessee, presumably with one or both of his two wives.[10]

I have no memory of ever having seen my paternal grandfather or grandmother. Bart was the son of Augustine Barbee, born c. 1800, of Montgomery County, who married Sarah Wynne on 24 October 1844. Bart appears in the census in 1850, 1860, 1870, and 1880. "Bartey" is 4 in 1850, and "Bartlett" is 15 in 1860. The census indicates that Bartlett and his father were born in Tennessee, his mother in Virginia. There is a vague recollection that my mother once asked me, when I was a small child, what I thought of my Aunt Emma (or was it Ida?). My reply reputedly was "Yes, I like her, but ain't she mean?"[11].

Bud Barbee came to Nashville because of the greater opportunities available in the big city. In the Nashville City Directory of 1916 he is shown as single and as a fireman at the Tulane Hotel. In the 1918 directory he is listed as the Assistant Engineer of the Stahlman Building and living at 207 8th Avenue with wife, Rose. He progressed to stationary engineer at the Maxwell House Hotel, the home and origin of the coffee that is "good to the last drop"; he was responsible for all the operating systems at the hotel: heating, lighting, plumbing.

It was the heating "wot done 'im in." It happened while I was a small child. A young Negro (nobody was called a "black" in those days), stoking one of the large coal-burning furnaces, which heated the hotel, managed to get the long poker stuck in the furnace grating.

My dad, reputedly a strong man who once had swum the Cumberland River with one arm tied behind his back, was called to help, snatched the

----

10 Marriage records show that R.B. Barbee married Virginia Bowers on Dec. 14, 1868. Bartlett Barbee married Frances Bowers in 1875-6. Map of Montgomery County in 1877 shows Riley B. Barbee living on road toward Dover. Dover is about 37 miles west of Clarksville.

11 See appendix for what is known of Barbee family.

poker from the furnace, fell against the back wall and broke his hip. That effectively ended his days as a stationary engineer.

No accident insurance, no workmen's compensation, no job, no income. Mr. and Mrs. Bud Barbee rented a large house at 157 5th Avenue North and rented out rooms to people who paid by the week. (1922 Nashville Directory). Bud Barbee had a metal pin, which held his hip joint together (the pin occasionally "worked out" and had to be reinserted), and wore a built up shoe to compensate for the shortening of his leg. He was able to walk without a crutch, but had a decided limp. And he was physically able to do the required small jobs around the rooming house. And bootleg.

It was just at this time that the Volstead Act, the Eighteenth Amendment to the U.S. Constitution, took effect. Occasional bits of income could be managed by transporting a few bottles of the illicit product of some of the fairly numerous "moonshiners" flourishing in the hills of Tennessee. (Generally, this required a little bit of "taste testing.") Rose did not approve of this activity, including the "taste testing," but accepted it as a fact of life and said little.

What she could not accept was his "fooling around" with some of the female roomers. She later admitted that she was partially to blame for allowing conditions of great temptation to exist. Expecting him to show contrition and plead for another chance, which she was prepared to give him, she told him she wanted a divorce. (They were legally separated on May 14, 1924 and divorced May 11, 1925 by order of the Second Circuit Court of Davidson County.) He did not contest the action and Rose Overton Hooper Barbee, to her dismay, regained her status as a single — now with two boys, one almost sixteen and one seven.

Bud Barbee never remarried. A few years after the divorce he moved back to Clarksville, the familial locale and the scenes of youth and young manhood. Neglecting medical attention, the crippling effect of the fractured hip worsened over the years, but he managed to move about quite capably using a crutch. He could hitch up his horse to the wagon, pull himself to the seat, and drive into town from his little house on East Franklin Street, alongside the railroad tracks, just outside the city of Clarksville where he had grown up. A ramshackle house, permeated by the heady odor of curing tobacco, he shared it with the long-time retired Sheriff Collier.[12] A little

---

12 Sheriff Collier, a lanky, acerbic individual, was the father of my father's first wife, Miss Willie Collier, mother of my half-sister Mary Buford who was mother of Mary Wilmath, my niece, who is about one year older than I.

pinch of land was sufficient to grow some tobacco, have a small garden, and graze the horse.

During my growing-up years, my stepfather, Walter Ammerman, would make it possible for me to visit my natural father while my mother and step-father visited relatives in Kentucky and Tennessee.

At the insistence of a cousin, Willie Smiley, I would sleep at her house in Clarksville instead of in the house by the railroad tracks. Willie was a snuff-dipping, prematurely old, "maiden lady" who lavished affection on me and my father. She corresponded, more faithfully than I, to keep me informed about my father's health and activities. Her house had a tidy little parlor, every piece of post-Victorian furniture provided with carefully placed antimacassars, and that characteristic pervasive mustiness of disuse and ban-ished sunlight.

Daylight hours I would spend with my father, talking, playing cards, riding the wagon in to town to chat with cronies at the courthouse. When we played rummy, he somehow managed to have me win. I knew this was hap-pening, but I could never see how he did it. Maybe I inherited my fondness for and ability at card-playing from him.

Evenings, with smoke pots going to keep away mosquitoes, we sat on the front porch, talked — he always inquired of my mother's health, our family activities, my progress in school, and always admonished me not to be a "smart-alec" — he smoked his home-grown and home-cured tobacco in his pipe, we listened to the cat birds and mocking birds. All talk and bird calls were suspended for the passing trains...

Our lives were only barely tangential during my formative years. Each visit was hard to end and full of sorrow...

Bud Barbee Sr. died eight days before his seventy-first birthday, on my twenty-eighth birthday, April 10, 1946, and is buried in River-view Cemetery on the edge of Clarksville, Tennessee.[13]

---

13   Many years later, when I saw the tombstone with the name "Bud Barbee," I decided I should put the dates of birth and death. Kind of an eery feeling, seeing your name on a grave marker.

12

CHAPTER IV

Meet Me In St. Louis

Widow and divorcée, mother of two boys, 15 and 6 years old, Rose Overton Hooper Barbee married again and moved to St. Louis with a new husband, Joe Isaacs. (I cannot find the date of this marriage in any of my mother's papers, but the divorce was recorded in St. Louis County Courthouse December 21, 1926.) A short and reportedly unhappy union.[14]

We first lived in Mrs. Modglin's rooming house on Morgan Street, (now Market) just east of Grand Avenue. (The area is completely changed now, what with street widening, re-routing, and new construction.) Memory is dim on this point, but it seems that Mrs. Modglin was a French war-bride whose husband was "no longer around." She had a daughter about the age of my brother, seventeenish. Quite by accident, I happened upon them in "intimate relationship" and later related the innocent observation to my mother. I could not understand why they were resting in bed in the middle of the day..... Anyway.........

We moved to a small apartment on Olive Street, just a few blocks away, upstairs over a small bar. I wasn't happy about the move because it had been so much fun to watch the construction of St. Louis' finest new theatre just one-half block away on Grand Avenue at Morgan.

The Grand Theaters

The theater 'palaces' of the 1920's and 1930's were something quite different from the movie houses of the fifties through today. (1993)

Of course, there were the neighborhood movie houses, showing second run and B pictures, seating 300 to 500 people. Bear in mind that sound and color had not yet come along...The neighborhood movie[15] had a piano player, sometimes a violinist, possibly on week-ends a trumpeter.

---

14   I cannot recall that Mr. Isaacs ever crossed our paths again. There is a picture in my mind of having a pet squirrel and a pet guinea pig. The squirrel lost part of its tail when I tried to pull it from a drawer. This stirs a memory that Isaacs worked in a hospital where there were experimental animals.

15   Admission to neighborhood "show" was 10¢.

The big "city" theaters featured complete orchestras, thirty or more musicians, to provide suitable accompaniment to the screen action: soft and melodious for the tender romantic scenes, staccato and brassy for the "Perils of Pauline"[16] who is lying on the tracks of the approaching train, and crescendo to herald the arrival of the hero or a cavalry charge. Oh, it was exciting!

The new St. Louis Theater was representative: The lobby, which you entered after buying your ticket, was over 100 feet wide, length about three hundred feet, a massive crystal chandelier hanging from a ceiling maybe four stories high. To one side, large curtained double doorways gave entrance to the orchestra or ground floor that seated probably two thousand people. Maybe more. To the left was an ornately balustered, plushly carpeted, marble staircase accessing the lounge area leading to the first balcony seats, the loges and boxes. Placed along the walls were comfortable chairs, statues, and paintings on the walls. Here also were the "Men's Lounge," the "Ladies' Powder Rooms" and inner stairways leading to the second, third, and fourth balconies. Vast! This upper lounge area curved at both ends as passageway to the boxes, tiered on either side of the balcony. Uniformed ushers could light your way to a seat.

The orchestra pit, almost as wide as the stage, could be raised and lowered mechanically, allowing the musicians to enter and take their places out of sight of the theater patrons. The powerful organ was on a separate platform, rising from mysterious depths to fill the cavernous area with popular melodies and lead the audience in song as the bouncing ball touched the words "Come a-way with me, Lu-cille" on the screen. Orchestra and organ paired to accompany the action of the stage show, which might feature Eddie Peabody and his banjo, always a drawing card and a thrill, acrobats, singers, dancers, animals, and comedians!

Vaudeville! Sometimes the feature picture, not to mention a comedy or cartoon and the newsreel, was only the added attraction to the stage show. What glorious entertainment![17] As early teenagers, several of us would walk there from South St. Louis, about two miles, to see the Saturday matinee at one of these entertainment palaces. Admission 25¢.

But back to our small apartment on Olive Street. Mother was working at the University Club, washing dishes and occasionally waiting tables at

16   "Pauline" was a weekly "serial" that always ended an episode with Pauline in some precarious situation.

17   The union requirements for large numbers of stage-hands and musicians were the cause, at least in part, of the demise of these grand "movie palace" theaters.

large functions. (I would be attending some of these functions only a few years later.) My brother was beginning his lifelong occupation in automobile parts at Fred Campbell Auto Parts Company. And I was at Eugene Field Elementary School progressing from the second to the third grade where I was hopelessly in love with the teacher. (Can't recall her name.) Aside from my infatuation, the most persistent memory of the time is that of Christmas 1926. My brother spent his entire paycheck, about twenty-five dollars, to buy an electric train for me.

New Husband and Stepfather

While we had been living at Mrs. Modglin's, and following the unrecorded departure of Joe Isaacs, mother had met a man who lived next door and who was recently divorced from a woman who drank to excess. Today, we would call her an alcoholic. He continued his attentions, approved by me and my brother, and married Rose Overton Hooper Barbee Isaacs on the 28th of December 1926. Mother's uncontested divorce from Joe Isaacs, who did not appear, was final on December 21, 1926. One week wait to remarry was sufficient.

We moved — with our new husband and stepfather, an honest, faithful, loving, intelligent, and industrious man, for the next forty-two years until his death in 1968 — we moved to a house on Cook Avenue, some distance to the north of where we had lived.

Two particular memories: gathering around the radio to listen to the historic Dempsey-Tunney fights of 1926-7, and my dog Jackie who died and was buried in the backyard. When we lived on Olive Street, Jackie would slip into my bed, something not allowed. Once when mother was out of patience, she sent the dog to the basement and said I could go down there if I wanted to sleep with my dog. I went. In a short while mother called to see if all was well. I answered that we were okay "but aren't the cockroaches terrible?"... Mother said I could come back upstairs.

Soon we moved to 2624 Park Avenue that my parents bought or were buying in South St. Louis. Located about one-half block west of Jefferson Avenue, ours was the last house on the west end of a series of identical row houses sharing common walls. All were torn down some years ago.

CHAPTER V

Walter Helm Ammerman

Walter H. Ammerman, "Dimpo" to some of you, "Honey" to my mother, "Daddy" to me, and a paragon of a stepfather, was born June 13, 1890, in Cynthiana, Harrison County, Kentucky, about 20-25 miles northeast of Lexington, the first child of Edward Wesley and Mary David Ammerman, tobacco farmers. Two sisters were born later, Edwina and Lynne. Over the years I lost track of Edwina, but stayed in fair contact with Lynne Ammerman Boxley who died in 1987, at the age of 78, in Winchester, Kentucky. Lynne had one child, Mary Lynne, from her marriage to Ashley Boxley, was for many years the librarian of the Winchester library until retirement. Mary Lynne married at least twice, had two sons, and probably returned to Florida where she was living when her mother died.

Ed and Mary David Ammerman were both small people - about five foot three or so, the daughters were diminutive, and "Dutch" Ammerman, as he came to be called in college, was about five foot six.

Sometime around 1912 he graduated from the University of Kentucky with a degree in Mechanical-Electrical Engineering. I never knew the exact date, but a letter dated 7 June 1955 stated that he was "retiring after nearly 43 years of service with ALCOA." Both sisters also had university degrees. Although farmers, Ed and Mary Ammerman were well educated and wanted the best for their children. Mary was a writer and had at least one book published.[18]

It has been many years since they lived, and even more since I last visited with them, but I am sure that they had affection for me. There was no other grandson. But, as I recall, 'Mama,' Mrs. Mary Ammerman), had not much love for the other Mrs. Ammerman, Rose, my mother. The feeling was

---

18   The White Rose of the Miami is almost certainly no longer in print. The copyright is 1911, published by Broadway Publishing Co., 835 Broadway, New York. This historical novel of Kentucky by a Kentuckian, was to be the first of a series to interest young people in the early history of their state. I find it interesting to read it again today, especially the historical incidents relating to Daniel Boone, George Rogers Clark, settlers' brushes with the Indians, and the early patriots' clashes with British troops and loyalists.

mutual. She wanted more attention from her son than his wife was willing to allow. (And I do mean "allow.")

It was difficult, to say the least, to find time during a two-week vacation each year, to visit relatives in Kentucky (my father's), and relatives in Tennessee (my mother's), when 35 miles per hour was considered a pretty fast speed on many of the roads, and 250 miles was a two-day trip.

I can recall one trip when we had 14 (fourteen) flat tires. Stop, jack up the car, remove the wheel rim, remove the tire, remove the inner tube, find the hole and roughen the area, put on a glued patch, light the vulcanizer pad, insert the tube in the tire, put the tire on the wheel, replace the rim, pump up the tire, release the jack. Back on the road.

Only in later years[19] did I learn that my stepfather had worked somewhere in the northeast, Maine I think, after graduation, and possibly before starting with Alcoa, the Aluminum Company of America, where he worked nearly 43 years. There is a letter from C. B. Fox, General Superintendent of the Aluminum Ore Company, dated September 19 1917, at the time of my Dad's enlistment in the Army in World War I, stating he "...has been in the service of this Company in an engineering capacity for a number of years."

He never talked about experiences during the "Great War," but he attained the rank of Sergeant, and at this time I still have many of the hundreds of letters and postcards he sent to his family from places in France, Belgium, and Germany. He was a dutiful son, affectionate brother. (And wonderful step-father.)

There were numerous other memorabilia, but it was all lost or discarded along the way of many houses and many moves from one section of St. Louis to another, and from St. Louis to California (and several places in California), to Pittsburgh to California to St. Louis to Tennessee to St. Louis and back to Tennessee and back to California and finally to Florida. I remember Dimpo's (that name started with Kit when she was small) helmet from WW I, a captured German helmet, some uniform items, various shells — most of them disarmed — a pistol, and a leather-bound copy of Milton's "Paradise Lost," with fine engravings by Gustav Doré. And remembering hours spent perusing that grand poem and the awe-inspiring etchings. Would love to have that volume today.

---

19   When my dad heard me refer to Hank O'Connor, he remarked that he had worked with a big Irishman named Hank O'Connor just before WW I up in Maine. Turns out it was the father of my friend. Grace O'Connor, Hank's widow and since remarried, still lives on Cape Cod.

"Dutch" Ammerman taught me a lot. If I have any degree of patience, it must have come from watching him — making drawings, blueprints, building new additions to a house, revising existing structures, installing new plumbing and replacing old plumbing, putting in new wiring and replacing old, taking things apart and rebuilding a Model T Ford, remodeling a garage to provide inexpensive living space for rentals during depression years. 21 And reading — some of my love of reading had to come from his example. He taught me to play chess and occasionally he let me win, but not obviously enough that I could discern his moves.

A Gentle Kind of Man

His sister, my Aunt Lynne, said he was henpecked. It may have been that. Or not. Mother was a strong personality, a shaker and mover, and she did make demands upon this versatile and seemingly pliant and acquiescent man, but I have come to believe that the things that he did, apparently upon order, were either things that he wanted to do anyway, or possibly an escape from my mother's incessant talk.

It seems that wherever we lived Mother wanted a "summer kitchen," a place in the relatively cooler basement to escape St. Louis' summer heat.[20] No, air-conditioning would not suffice; she did not want that cold air blowing on her. So Dimpo would build a complete kitchen in the basement, a kitchen that would be used less than a half-dozen times. He already would have constructed a shower in the basement because the older houses that we bought did not have showers in the upstairs baths. All would not be lost, however, for these additions or modernizations were later to become additional facilities for rent, for "light housekeeping."

---

20   To the best of my recollection, during my school years (and college), we lived in the Park Avenue house, two different houses on Lafayette Boulevard, an apartment and a house on Compton, on Wilcox, Shenandoah, Juniata, and back to Shenandoah. After Dimpo retired, they lived in three different homes in St. Louis and three different homes in California, and Pittsburgh when the company called him back to work. After he died, in 1968, Mother moved to Dickson, Tennessee, bought two houses, moved back to an apartment in St. Louis, bought a house on Pestalozzi, moved to an apartment in Duarte, California, bought a house in Monrovia, back to Tennessee to live with a relative, to a nursing home in St. Louis for one day (!), back to a relative in Tennessee (disastrous), back to St. Louis to an apartment in the Saum Hotel, the Pestalozzi house in St. Louis, back to a low-cost apartment in Monrovia and finally to a retirement and then nursing home in Florida. I may have overlooked some of the moves.

18

Growing up entirely in middle America, far away from the shores I now know so well, there was never confusion about the spelling of that particular word, as I am now aware that there is a difference between "light housekeeping" and lighthouse keeping."

"Damma," the name given by Kit when she could not clearly say "Grandma," liked the idea of "rental property," because it gave her money that she did not have to account for. Dimpo paid all the bills, from his salary, but Damma collected the rents. His money was theirs, her money was hers.

We, my parents, my brother and I, lived on the first floor and the basement of the Park Avenue house, four rooms were rented on the second floor, two rooms rented on the third floor. Everyone paid by the week usually $5 a week for a room — when they paid. There was always someone like Hazel Huddleston, with her son Leroy. But I'm getting ahead.

Walter Ammerman, with a degree in mechanical-electrical engineering, was effectively employed as a draftsman. He frequently said that the company could hire engineers for a dime a dozen. What was needed were people who could design equipment, or a plant, and put their ideas on paper. During his over 40 years with the company, he designed and drew the plans for bauxite processing plants all over the world.

He was not what could be called an "ambitious" man. He liked the job he had, and he was good at it. Men he had trained went on to become top executives of the Aluminum Company of America, but they all remembered him on special occasions and holidays.

At the height of the depression years, the East St. Louis plant, making ALCOA housewares, was facing drastic reduction in sales. The proposal was to lay off some of the salesmen. Dutch Ammerman said "NO! keep the salesmen, we need them if we are to have a chance to recover." He suggested, instead, that everyone take a ten percent cut in pay. That proposal saved the plant and all the jobs in it.

Once I mentioned to my dad that there was a man named Fox who was a member of the church I was attending as a young man.

"Yes, he's the president of the company," my dad replied.

The next Sunday, when I saw Mr. Fox, I spoke and said that my stepfather, Walter Ammerman, worked for his company.

He looked me over, and with a new friendliness:

"Dutch Ammerman is your stepfather? Why, he's about the finest employee the company has ever had. I don't know how the company could get along without him."

That was nice, and had elements of the truth. In January 1956, after my dad retired, and had been living in California about a year, the company called him back to the head office in Pittsburgh for some jobs that no one else could do. They told him to "write his own ticket" about salary. They knew their man, and knew they would willingly pay whatever he asked, because whatever he asked would be reasonable.

Mother was different. She said she had to travel to St. Louis and California to take care of their property. Their answer: "Just submit your bills to us, Mrs. Ammerman, and we'll take care of them."

Sometimes in Anger

Walter Ammerman, perhaps because of his continual expenditure of energy at work and at home, was always in good physical condition. I can remember thinking how remarkable it was that he "still had muscles" at the age of 45. Of course, I was about 17 at the time, and anything over 30 was "getting up there in years."

As I said, he was a gentle kind of man, but I can remember an occasion when one of Mother's "roomers" had been giving her a lot of trouble, and when she told him to leave, he refused. She called my dad and he bodily and literally threw him out the front door and onto the sidewalk. Just a quiet, an ordinary, a gentle sort of man.... Ordinarily....

(Kit probably got to know Dimpo pretty well. When she was about twelve Damma and Dimpo took her on the train to Pittsburgh and into the northeast. And Kit and Art lived in California with them for a while. She had more opportunity to know Damma and Dimpo than Lynne did.)

Somehow it never occurred to me that my step-father might have felt at times that his married life had something lacking. When he married my mother in 1926, he had a ready-made family: I was eight years old, my brother seventeen. Eight? Maybe not too bad, but seventeen? We all know that some teenage years can be difficult, perhaps impossible. Dimpo was equal to the challenge.

It took a special kind of man.

CHAPTER VI

Presley Freeman Hooper

My brother was a talented individual. He had a good singing voice, could do some pretty fair tap-dancing without ever having had a lesson; he needed some training and direction but never got it. Whether he would have stayed with any kind of training program, or whether he would have availed himself of an opportunity, should one have come along, is problematical.

Tall, about five foot ten or eleven, broad and square-shoulders, slim hips and rather thin legs, size 7½ shoe, he carried himself erect, moving a fairly constant weight of about 160 pounds in what is best described as a "strut." His thick, wavy hair, brown with an auburn tint, encroached upon his forehead to a slight degree. Only in his later years did any gray hair begin to appear, but it remained thick and full. Blue eyes, an engaging smile, blessed with even, well-shaped teeth that yielded eventually to encounters with belligerent knuckles, a natty dresser, "Pres," or "Hoop," was a social animal.

I guess I mentioned earlier that he was born on June 10, 1909, which made him about nine years older than I. Thus, he was just past four years when his father died. Whether my father took any kind of active hand in his "raising" during the five or six years that he and mother were married, I do not know. It would be safe to guess that mother would not have countenanced any direct sort of disciplinary action. Judging by the amount of freedom that I seemed to enjoy, there seems little reason to doubt that my brother suffered from a lesser amount.

By the time the four of us, Joe Isaacs, mother, my brother and I, got to St. Louis, sometime around 1925, Freeman Hooper (mother and a very few other people called him Freeman) had managed to complete the tenth grade in Nashville, but went no further.

In St. Louis, Brother (I always called him Brother) went to work as a stock clerk at Fred Campbell Auto Supply where his phenomenal memory for auto parts earned him job security and promotions.[21] This was in the days before computers and microfilm. A few years later he was hired to head up the parts department at a B-O-P (Buick-Olds-Pontiac) dealership in St.

---

21   Consider thousands of auto parts for each make of automobile, each part having a number such as: D2OB-18C622AB.

Louis. Relatively specialized in his job, he seldom had to look up a parts number. He gained quite a reputation for this unique capacity.

While we were living at 2624 Park avenue, in the year 1929 when the economy began to unravel at the start of the Great Depression, he married the girl next door, Marguerite Boyle, the older daughter of a staunchly Catholic, Irish family. They had been dating for several months, but when it became apparent that they should marry, they eloped and did so. My brother was nineteen, Marge was twenty-one. Less than nine months later, August 29, 1929, Ronald Eugene Thomas Hooper was born. I was eleven years old and an uncle, and, I might add, a handy, built-in baby-sitter.

Ronnie Hooper played no significant role in my life, so I will dispense with him in a short paragraph. He took money from my mother's bank account, when she went into a nursing home in St. Louis (for one day), put it in a joint account, and later refused to account for about four thousand dollars. This action could have been partially attributed to his mother. I had called him several times on the telephone, had Northcutt Coil, my lawyer and friend, write him a nice letter requesting a reply. In any event, he never accounted for the money, Mother changed her will pertaining to a house on Pestalozzi Avenue in St. Louis, which she had intended to give to him, and the house later sold for over $20,000. I had occasionally thought I would write to his employer, Anheuser-Busch (the brewery), and give them the particulars, but never did because I figured he had already lost enough, even if he did not know it; Ronnie died around 1998. I never told him.

Back to my brother and Marge. Mother had a room which she could let them have, but she thought they should have a place of their own, gave them some furniture, and set them up in a little apartment. This lasted only a few months and Marge was homesick for her mother. (She later admitted that she should have broken the "strings" when she got married.) But she came home to her mother (next door) and Brother came home to us — this was not the end, but surely the beginning of the end of the marriage.[22]

To the best of my recollection, there followed several years of on again, off again, separated but dating, and eventually divorced. Meanwhile, Ronnie

---

22 After the divorce, Marge stayed single for a number of years, later married, name not known, and seemed quite happy. Marge's sister, Joan, married my cousin, Bob Marable, who drove a Greyhound bus, soon after my brother's marriage, and they had a daughter. From what I can remember, Joan learned little from her sister, divorced Bob and moved back with her mother. Both women later married again. Bob Marable married again, no children that I know of, and is buried in Riverview Cemetery in Clarksville, Tennessee, with the Barbees, the Colliers, and the Fowlers.

was growing up, attending parochial schools, becoming thoroughly Catholic and thoroughly indoctrinated against his father who seemed to find some solace in his friends down at the corner pub (read saloon) Jimmy Pelican's. Very sad in that he could not hold his liquor very well, and when inebriated became bellicose and quite touchy of differences in opinion.

He was light on his feet, with some skill in boxing. The fundamental problem, however, lay in the fact that he seldom challenged anyone his own size, nor managed to antagonize just one individual. His altercations seemed regularly to involve several others against one, him. The damages to his physiognomy, and dental work, seemed frequent and sometimes rather severe. It took some years of ageing and physical suffering to bring about learning and subsequent lessening of such encounters. The temper still flared brightly and suddenly but did not involve as much physical response...

Eventually divorced from Marge, sometime around 1940-42 he went to California, either with or followed shortly by Genevieve Jones and one of two sons by her first marriage.[23]

For a while he traveled the west coast for a large auto parts manufacturer. He visited us (Kay, Kit and me) in Mountain Home, Idaho, in 1945. Later he covered the greater Los Angeles area, establishing a following of customers who liked him personally and appreciated his professional ability to anticipate their needs and solve their problems.

A few years after the war (WW II), he incorporated his own parts company; with limited financing and poor cash flow, he was forced into bankruptcy by creditors when the companies to which he sold were slow in paying; he was hired by one of his former competitors. Not long after, he began to work for himself again, operating from his home, buying and selling auto and truck parts, refurbishing and repairing used and broken air tools, serving as a middle-man or distributor, going between the buyer and the seller. This was especially true in the case of companies using large earth-moving, grading, or quarrying vehicles, who could depend on him for locating large and unique parts of machinery.

At sometime around the age of forty, he was afflicted with severe rheumatoid arthritis that made the use of his hands and feet excruciatingly painful. Doctors prescribed complete rest, but he said he had to work and em-

---

23   Brother and Jenny (b. 23 Feb 1913) later had three children. The younger of her first two sons died of muscular dystrophy (about age 18), as did one of the next two sons. Two children, Earle and Presli Jo, are still living in California. Both have children. Mother left a few thousand dollars to Presli Jo's two boys.

barked on a systematic program of exercise that heightened the pain but prevented complete immobility of his joints. His almost complete recovery was regarded by the doctors as extremely rare.

He always managed to make a living, to have money in his pocket. He spent money freely, with help from his wife, played the horses, also with help, and both would always claim that they and Santa Anita racetrack were about even as for money invested and money paid out.

When his daughter, Presli Jo, (now married to Ken Gester, a policeman) presented him with a grandson he seemed to change. He would take Scott (1/1/1969) with him on business calls, sleep with him, never ceased giving him attention. A most loving and doting grandfather. But, sadly, he almost completely neglected her second son, Eric (10/23/1970), who came along almost two years later. It was as if he had invested all his love in one bright little boy who had a phenomenal memory for baseball statistics[24]

When we returned from Japan and Hawaii in 1957 we visited my brother in California — my mother was living there, too, at that time — and when we were stationed at McClellan AFB in 1970-72 we visited several times.

In 1978 began a tumultuous series of moves made by Damma. She prevailed on my brother to drive her back to Dickson, Tennessee where she intended to live with her niece Ida Overton. I'm sure it was a difficult trip across country for both of them. Neither in good health and in an ailing automobile. The sojourn at Ida's was short, but not sweet. Ida loved to have her grandchildren around her and the house was full and noisy. So Damma prevailed upon my brother to bring her to our house in Florida. It was good to have my brother visit in my home, but mother was quite sick. The doctor gave her some medicines but insisted that she should be in the hospital for the kind of care that only a hospital could provide. Mother refused. I was adamant. My brother took her back to Dickson where she was to stay with a young couple — grand-nephew or something, but immediately went into the hospital for about two weeks. During much of this time my brother was visiting with our cousin Dorothy Smith in Nashville.

While at our house he had asked Kay: "What would happen if you took nitro-glycerin tablets if you didn't have heart trouble?" He evidently suffered at least one attack while in Nashville, principally from the stress

---

24 At the date of this writing, January 29, 2004, I have no contact with my brother's children or their children. Phone call, letters, no response to any of these. An occasional phone call to Genny provided some little bit of information as to their well-being until she died about 1995. Lynne was able make contact with Presli about a year ago.

caused by trying to find a home for Damma and feeling the need to return to California.

Arrangements were made for mother to go to a nursing home in St. Louis. This was when Ronnie got into the act. He started the arrangements, but refused "to put a nickel of (his) money into this." I wired $1000 to him, and he withdrew about $2500 from mother's Dickson account. Brother drove mother back to St. Louis to the nursing home. He stopped to see her the next morning as he was leaving for California and she managed to convince him that she could not stay in the home. She had been there for one night. So he took her back to Dickson where she would stay for a short while with Lucille Overton, wife of her nephew Locke Leach.

My brother's health deteriorated rapidly, and he died on the 15th of February, 1979, the following year. He would have been seventy in June of that year. I blamed his death on the physical and psychological stress he suffered in trying to find some place where mother would be happy. Bitterly, and cruelly, I told her so.

CHAPTER VII

Friends and Roomers

Somehow or other, with all the moving we seemed to do during my school-boy days, I guess I grew up without any tremendous load of complexes from the process. 2624 Park Avenue was a focal point,[25] perhaps because it had the longest tenancy connected with it, perhaps because it was the place of making childhood friends — although there weren't a whole bunch of them: "Those friends thou hast, and their adoption tried, Grapple them to thy soul with hoops of steel." (Shake.) Herman Beede next door, Jackie Beers across the alley and up a coupla doors, and Roemer Wilbas whom I came to know in McKinley High School.

Trying to put down certain dates, when this began, when that ended, when there are no records at all, becomes a process of reconstruction. When Damma married Dimpo, just after Christmas of 1926 (and I have had that re-cord), we moved from Olive Street to Cook Avenue — so that was probably early 1927. I know that I started the 7th grade in the fall of 1929, and it was the third grade at Eugene Field school where I fell in love with the teacher, so it was the fourth grade that I skipped, starting the fifth grade in the fall of 1927 at Hodgen School..

Now, that process leads me to knowing we moved to the Park Avenue house in 1927, I started the 5th grade at Hodgen School and stayed there for the 6th. Hodgen was in what would be considered a middle middle-class district, an area where many homes were owner-occupied. Just a short dis-tance to the west and south were some areas of fine homes, definitely upper middle-class or better. About twelve blocks (close to a mile) to the south was Buder elementary school in a quite poor neighborhood of small rental houses and apartments. It was from the "Buder gang" that trouble would come to the Hodgen playground during the summer months when activities would be in full swing. They were the "tough guys," but we generally man-aged to hold our own — or run for cover if outnumbered.

Our "gang warfare" did not compare with the extreme violence of today, but we had some pretty rough and tumble times with the

---

25   Some years later, after extreme degradation of the neighborhood, the whole 2600 block of Park Avenue was torn down.

Buder gang. One particular time remains clear in the memory: we had heard they were coming, got organized, and repulsed them. One big intruder (big for us kids at that time) came with brass knuckles and I hit him between the shoulder blades with a regular brick while he was roughing up one of our guys. He never returned on any subsequent "raid."

One summer — I must have been about twelve — I was pitching horseshoes with a guy I didn't know very well. We were playing "ringers," where only the ringers counted. I got lucky and beat him, and he was so mad he slammed one his horseshoes down squarely on my left big toe. That smarts, I tell you. I managed to hobble home, but didn't tell Mother because she could get pretty upset about such things. Coupla weeks later she noticed the discoloration and swelling and took me to the doctor. He felt the upturned toe, affirmed that it had been broken but was now partially healed, and opined that nothing should be done at that late date. Since then, I always wear a hole in the left sock because that toe points upward and rubs against my shoe.

"Frankie" was a tough kid. His brother had been sent to prison and his parents didn't seem to keep very close watch on Frankie; he had a reputation for fighting and being a "bully," even though he was not overly large for his age — he was one year older than I. I avoided him. Sometimes I would cross the street to avoid him. My brother got into fights and mother did not want me to fight. I was ten or eleven when it happened. The Nation Wide grocery store up the street from my house was throwing away a real good box that I had a use for. A wooden box. Frankie snatched it from my hand. I said, "That's my box." He sat on the box and said, "It's the box of the guy who's sitting on it." Some of the older guys, the "drug-store cowboys," started urging us to fight for it. I told them that I had to go home and change from my good school clothes. Mother was curious as to why I changed clothes and hurried right back out, and followed me back to the store where Frankie and I had started sort of sparring around. She made me stop. The big guys yelled at her and said I was a sissy, afraid to stand up for myself. Mother gave them a scornful look, turned to me and said, "All right then, whip him, Bud."

A kind of "red flash" went off in my head and the next thing I knew I was on top of Frankie, beating his head on the sidewalk. They said I was trying to kill him when they pulled me off. Somebody took Frankie home, and he never bothered me again. Whenever he saw me, he crossed to the other side of the street.

I learned early that I did not have a "quick" temper, as my brother had, but that I could be quite violent if sufficiently aroused. Don't bother me, I won't bother you. My generally mild manner might lead a person to believe he could try a tentative punch. My response is likely to be quite violent — an over-reaction, it has been called. Hardly a problem any longer, at my age.

The Beedes lived next door, a single storey flat, part of a duplex. Herman's father worked in a wood-heel shoe factory. I never knew what he did, exactly. Mr. Beede was tall and slender, Mrs. Beede was short and dumpy. They were Catholics and Herman went to a parochial school where the nuns would hit the kids with a ruler. I guess that kept them in line.

But what was important was that the Beedes would "go out to the river" on weekends. They would go fishing and swimming in the Meramec River, just south and west of the city limits..And they took vacations in the summertime. My family seemed to be working all weekends, and in the summer we visited relatives in Kentucky and Tennessee instead of taking a vacation. I got invited to go to the river with Herman a couple of times, and I could see that the Beedes had more fun than we did. It took some years for me to understand that we owned property and they didn't. We lived and ate better than they did. We drove better cars than they did. And the depression did not affect us financially the way it did the Beedes. Herman did not go beyond high school, became a truck driver, and died when he was about sixty.

Mother "took in roomers." Actually, Dimpo had converted most of the house into housekeeping apartments, with stoves and ice-boxes — not refrigerators, ice-boxes. Several tenants would share a bath.

We had one regular roomer: Mr. Wise, a quiet, conservative Jewish gentleman. He lived in the back room on the second floor. The back stairs were between his room and the bathroom. The front stairs were between the bathroom and the middle room. Mr. Wise owned a small farm on the outskirts of the city to the northwest. I must concede that we did on occasion drive out to his little farmhouse for a relaxing weekend. I can recall there was a pump organ that I liked to pedal and make noises on. And Mr. Wise ate a lot of All Bran.

Damma was a sucker for a sad story. Hazel Huddleston was one of them. I never knew what had happened to her husband, if there ever had been one. She and her son, Leroy, were a combination — no man could have taken that combination for very long. Hazel could never quite manage to pay her rent on time, was always behind, and mother would carry her. When mother finally had enough and told her she had to pay or move, Hazel left owing several weeks of rent.

And thatsonofabitch Leroy. I had a fairly new B-B gun, a pump Daisy, and one day it wasn't where I had left it. Mother would not believe me when I said I was sure that Leroy had stolen it.

"The poor boy hasn't had many things, but he wouldn't steal your gun." Good hearted mother.

I told Leroy that I knew he had taken it (I really didn't know for sure.) and that he had better give it back or expect big trouble. Herman and I started watching Leroy and saw him drop the gun in the big trash container on the alley behind the house. I was bigger and stronger than Leroy, and mother would be upset if I did anything to him, so I told Herman to beat him up. And he did. Hazel and Leroy moved away shortly after this little episode and we had the good fortune to never hear from them again. Some people are just no damn good.

Herman and I were good buddies throughout grammar school days. We stomped on tin cans so that they would fasten onto our shoes and then we could walk in the rain without getting our feet wet. I guess boys don't do that anymore. Our parents were congenial, played pinochle every week or so, but generally led different sorts of lives. By the time of high school, we had moved away and I saw Herman only occasionally when I accompanied my parents to check on the Park Avenue house and collect the rents.

Jacques Beers was another buddy. Not as close as Herman, but the three of us got along together. Jackie's father was a nice looking man. Never knew what he did for a living. He had married a French girl at the end of World War I when he was in France, and they spoke French at home and at the dinner table. I learned to say "Est-ce qu'il y a du beurre?" They had a tin-roofed garage with a dirt floor, and it was a great place to play with our little cars when it was raining. Sometimes his little sister, Jacqueline, wanted to play and we had to humor her or she would go crying to her mother and then we all had to stop.

Once when we were playing we heard fire engines and Jackie and Herman wanted to go see where the fire was. I tried to talk them out of it, but when the sirens stopped pretty near, we all ran to see the fire. MY HOUSE! I was supposed to sort of "stoke up" our coal-burning furnace when I came home from school and I had sorta "stoked it up" pretty much so that I could play a little longer. There was a lot of smoke, but the only damage was some scorching of the sub-flooring in the area just above the furnace. Close call. Never "stoked it up" too much again.

It seemed that Mrs. Beers was not real happy in the United States. She did not have many friends and no relatives. Other women, according to my mother, thought Mrs. Beers was kind of "fancy" and "had an eye for the men," whatever that meant. Mrs. Beers was younger and prettier than most of the other women. Not too many years later, we learned that Mr. Beers had killed himself. Depression days were hard on a lot of people.

On the subject of mother's roomers: one character must have been years ahead of his time: he played the guitar and sang what we would probably call country-western. His favorite was "The Red River Valley." There were times I thought I would go nuts listening to him twanging that guitar and nasally giving out with song. I sure wished he could go back to that Red River Valley and stay there.* Today when I hear some the country-western people and their ballads, I believe that our old roomer was probably as good as any of them. He may have been the one that Dimpo literally threw down the stairs and out. Dunno.

Some of the roomers who prospered when times got better remained mother's friends all her life: Pal and Pearly Clauson, and their daughter Dolores, who used to tease me until I was almost mad enough to hit her, and she would come around singing or making noise when I was trying to read or study; and a Mrs. Morton's daughter, Geraldine, who conspired with Dolores to see how they could irritate me; Mr. and Mrs. Dorsey and their sons (one of them, Eddie, went on to be head of the Teamsters Union in St. Louis); Wallace and Pearl Snyder who later raised mink and gave Damma a mink stole — they now raise dogs and we exchanged Christmas cards for a number of years; Violet (Beckman?) who worked in a laundry about two blocks away was a young girl (19 or 20?), became the supervisor at the laundry, had the back room on the third floor and later the front room also.

* Not really a bad song:
From this valley they say you are going,
We will miss your bright eyes and sweet smile,
For they say you are taking the sunshine
That brightens our pathway awhile.
Come sit by my side if you love me,
Do not hasten to bid me adieu,
But remember the Red River Valley
And the girl who has loved you so true.

And "Ace." If I ever heard Ace's last name, I can't remember it. He was always just Ace. Dimpo had partitioned off the back end of the basement and made it into a light housekeeping room. Ace lived there. In the front, or furnace end, there was a small bedroom and a shower stall. Ace made hot tamales. He bought all the ingredients, corn meal, ground meat, and corn shucks, cooked them and put them together, loaded them in his shoulder box which held several dozen and went out into the night singing out "Ho-o-ot ta-MAL- ee-ees." During the warm summer nights in St. Louis in the early '30's people sat outside on their front steps where it was a little cooler. Ace had some regular customers. Ace would help Dimpo on construction projects and always paid his rent on time. My mother and dad liked Ace. I liked him too, and he would sometimes give me a leftover tamale.

CHAPTER VIII

McKinley High School

McKinley High School was home to me for six years, 1929 to 1935. I covered all the floors, from the basement to the third floor, had classes in just about every room in the building - excluding the principal's office (I never had the requirement or opportunity to see his inner sanctum) and the administration room - knew my way around the auditorium, the first floor and basement shops and the gym, and finally learned to make a loud whistle while going down the stairs from my third floor history class to my second floor Latin class.. After my first year, I was aware that the location of certain lockers was important for the safety of the contents — end ones in the basement were frequently bashed in and raided.

Before straying too far into some of the survival realities, I must point out that McKinley had been a four year high school until 1929 when it was changed into a junior high with grades seven through nine. In 1932 it reverted to a four year high school, so that my residence there was continuous - grades seven through twelve - with the exception of a few days at other high schools when we moved from the area and I had to get special permission to remain at McKinley. I can, therefore, unashamedly state that I spent six years at McKinley High School.

In My Mothers Houses

Keeping the Park Avenue house, which was fully rented, we rented a duplex on Lafayette Avenue that had extra rooms, which we could rent out, which we did. My only memory that remains of that place, where we stayed about one year, is of reading and studying one night while my parents were not at home and drinking a little bit too much of the wine that my dad made.[26]

---

26   About the middle of the nineteenth century the making and sale of intoxicating liquors for use as beverages was declared illegal in many of the northern states. This gradually faded until only Maine, Kansas, and North Dakota were "dry." Many states retained laws prohibiting sales on Sundays, election days and others. When the U.S. entered World War I in 1917, ostensibly in response to German action against "neutral" shipping, the "prohibitionists" succeeded in getting legislation that stopped the sale of liquors to soldiers and sailors. In 1919 the Volstead Prohibition Enforcement Act was passed over the President's veto, prohibiting the sale for beverage purposes of liquor

It was a much handier house for school because it was several blocks closer and only one block to the library.

The library, on the southwest corner of Jefferson and Lafayette, was a squat, square, mixture of architecture whose front was much too massive for its one-storey height, but it was delight to me because then, as now, I kept at least two books going all the time. I could replenish my supply each night on the way home from school. I then specialized in mystery, western, and adventure - are there others? S.S. Van Dine, Ellery Queen, Edgar Rice Burroughs, H. Rider Haggard, Zane Grey.

We next rented a small apartment on Compton Avenue, farther from school and library, farther from the Park Avenue house. I had to ride my bike to school and it was not convenient to the bakery where I had been accustomed to stop on the way home from to school to buy a sponge cake that I would eat with a quart of milk and a half-dozen or so bananas to hold me till dinner. It was not convenient for mother to collect the rents — and there was no one to talk with. We stayed there but a coupla months before we moved back to the Park Avenue house. Nobody ever seemed to know why we moved to Compton in the first place.

Before long we moved again, this time about 4 miles farther south, to a nice little bungalow on Wilcox Avenue, a half-block from the intersection of Morganford Road and Gravois Avenue, the location of the Bevo Mill, a popular German restaurant in the form of a Dutch windmill. Another good, solid "Dutch" neighborhood of compact bungalows, rectangular spots of lawn in front, leading up to white stone steps (scrubbed faithfully each week), a small window in the center of the roof peak looking out from what might be a small attic space; inside two bedrooms and a single bath, a full basement with a coal-burning furnace. In the rear, a fair-sized, fenced-in back yard.

Now I got a ride to school with my dad who had to drive most days because he was no longer on his old car-pool route. (His convenience never

---

containing over one-half of one percent of alcohol. The country tired of this experiment by 1933 and passed the 21st Amendment repealing the 18th Amendment. Prohibition led to smuggling of liquor from Canada, speakeasies, and is credited with the increase in a great range of gangsterism that flourished in an atmosphere of disregard and violation of the "law of the land" by even the most substantial and generally law-abiding citizens. Many homes, ours included (sometimes to the dismay of my mother), produced "home brew," a light-alcohol content form of beer for consumption in the home — not for sale. I never cultivated the taste for it. But I did like many of the wines that Dimpo made: elderberry, dandelion, grape, blackberry, among others. Mother would have a sip of wine occasionally, but she monitored very closely the consumption of wine or beer by my dad.

seemed to be a consideration in our peregrinations.) I was in a different high school district, but because of transportation difficulties, I was able to get permission to remain at McKinley High School.

Wilcox was one of the houses where Dimpo had to install a 'summer kitchen' in the basement. A complete kitchen, nevertheless: sink with hot and cold water, gas stove (Dimpo did all the piping and testing), refrigerator, etc. As best as I can recall, mother used it three times- say la gare and the Parisian taxi will take you to the railroad station. (Don't worry about it, it's a pun.) There may be a photo around someplace showing this house.. Maybe the Juniata house. Anyway...(Boy, having a rum and tonic before dinner and while writing doesn't seem to brighten my recollection of events. But, whatever.)

One Girlfriend

Final move while I was in high school was to a large house on Lafayette, just east of Grand Avenue. We rented it and then rented out rooms. This was where we got to know the Dorsey family who rented from us.

Across the street, and occupying two large square city blocks, was the reservoir which served as a holding tank for much of South St. Louis' water supply. A few years earlier the city had paved over the top of this great tank and tennis courts were installed on part of it. These were hard surface, of course, and complemented the clay courts which were below in a park-like area. McKinley High School had only one small, non-regulation court at the side of the school building, so we used the reservoir courts as our home courts. My girlfriend at the time, Jane Powell, lived about one block away on the west side of Grand Avenue and would come by for me to play tennis during the summer of 1935, following our graduation.

I don't know why I said "girlfriend at the time," because she was the first and only girlfriend I had in high school. I did have sort of a crush on Esther Buschbaum who was a year ahead of me in school, but she regarded me as just a pest — which I surely was. Back to Jane: We got to know each other during the senior play, "Dulcy," in which she played the leading role and I was her brother. Aside from a school dance in the gym (and she was trying to teach me to dance), I don't recall that we ever had what you would call a real "date" until after we were graduated.

Our group at Second Presbyterian Church got together at someone's house for a New Years' Eve party and I had to take Jane to a midnight mass in the midst of our festivities.

34

Jane was Catholic and somehow that may have been the reason we broke up: her parents did not like the idea of her attending our Sunday evening young people's group at the Presbyterian church. I say "broke up," but that seems to sound "sudden." We just sort of drifted apart. We did have different outlooks — I think she anticipated a life much like her father and mother had, a quiet, middle-class existence in a nice little bungalow on a nice little street in a respectable neighborhood in South St. Louis. While I had not as yet formulated a precise plan for my future, I knew that I wanted something more.

Now I am ahead of myself again.

Athletes?

I tried various sports in school, none with any conspicuous success. Too slow for backfield, but too light for the line, I nevertheless survived some bruises as a third-string blocking-dummy tackle before I got wise and tried something other than football. About the same in track. Made the team in tennis, but not good enough for inter-school competition. Ben Butler fit almost the same mold. We got tired of painting the bottoms of our feet with that red stuff (tincture of benzoin?) that looked like iodine and was supposed to toughen the soles and prevent blistering. I think it really was to protect our feet against those sweat-stained and cracked-leather shoes that were passed down year after year to the second and third stringers. So Ben and I started competing against each other in the gym: jumping rope for endurance, working the rings and parallel bars for strength. And we were active in organizing and participating in new clubs: horseback riding, ice-skating, fencing, chess. I was the best left-handed fencer - I was also the only left-handed fencer.

Perhaps because I was the last boy to wear knickers to school when everyone else wore long pants (not jeans - no one wore denim to school) I was "pantsed" several times. A group would gang up on me, just before the start of a class and pull my pants off. I suffered silently until I could encounter those responsible individually and take persuasive action. My reputation as a "sissy" persisted, though, until the day that I knocked the first string quarterback completely off the gym floor and into the parallel bars stored along the side wall.

Enough was enough. I had no more problems with any of the athletes. One of them was heard to say: "Don't fool around with Barbee. When he gets mad he's dangerous." I guess so, but I don't get "mad" very often.

Teachers

Since I always kinda liked school — more accurately, perhaps: I have always liked "learning," both the process and the result - it would be natural that there would be some fond memories of those teachers who helped me along the way. Prominent are Zeppenfeld, O'Reilly, Marchessault and Mehl.

Mr. Zeppenfeld was my homeroom and biology teacher. Of all the things I learned from him, like dissecting frogs and observing the contractile vacuole of paramecia, one thing persists: he impressed upon me that one mark of a successful man was clean fingernails. Josephine K. O'Reilly taught English and sponsored the senior play; to that spunky, little Irish spinster I owe my interest in the English language and literature and theatre. Charlie Marchessault tried to get Latin in my head — once when called upon to translate a passage in Caesar's Commentaries (or was it Cicero's Orations? - whatever) I began to read from a translation that I had inserted in my text. After class he congratulated me for my translation of material that was not in our text and suggested that I might want to let him have my "crib." In later years I came across Charlie Marchessault when he had left teaching for some endeavor more financially rewarding and we reminisced briefly about McKinley.

Helen Mehl taught math. She was tall and slender and pretty in a plain, clean sort of way, and maybe all of twenty-seven years old. I liked her and I liked math. She seemed always to have chalk on her hands and clothing. I worked hard to do well in her classes — averaged over 99%, and one year had 100% on all class work, tests, and homework. A few years after graduation I met her niece at a church outing and it was revealed to me that Helen Mehl was a very nice person — but not a goddess. Perhaps the iconoclast serves a purpose, but I dunno.

Many girls took the Commercial Course, which accented typing, shorthand and something called 'Business.' Some of the boys were in the Industrial Arts Course and spent a lot of time in the wood shop, the metal shop, and Mechanical Drawing. A few students are listed in the Nugget (year book) as Fine Arts, some in the Classical Course. Most of us took the General Course. This led to satisfying the college entrance requirements and allowed a few selected electives.

Generally, colleges required two years of math, science, history and a language — which was generally Latin — and four years of English. In grades nine through twelve, as nearly as my memory allows, I had the requisite four years of English, (grammar and rhetoric, grammar and world literature, American literature, English literature), four years of math (algebra, plane geometry, solid geometry, calculus and trigonometry), four years of science (general science, biology, botany and zoology, chemistry), two years of Latin, two years of history (European and American). Four years of "gym" was required of all. I recall one semester of woodworking, one of metal shop, one of printing (we actually 'set' type by hand and printed the school news), and probably the most valuable course of all: one semester of typing.

These were good years, interesting years. I can't recall any period of particular anxiety, greatly depressed feelings, extreme rebellion or resistance to authority — that of home or society in general. In retrospect, these were relaxed, formative years, years of what can now be perceived as slow maturation.

During these years, from the time I was eleven until I was seventeen, a significant influence was the Lafayette Park Presbyterian Church. But, churches deserve their own area.

CHAPTER IX

Churches

Lafayette Park Presbyterian

Churches were a significant influence on my life. During the years from the time I was eleven until I was seventeen, it was the Lafayette Park Presbyterian Church, on the west side of the street, across from the oldest park (1836) in the city. There I went to Sunday school and church, and it was the meeting place of the local Boy Scout troop. Several names flood back: Roemer Wilbas, Kermit Fisher, Melvin Morrissey, others.

There was a small basement room, concrete floor, which was our basketball court — about one-quarter size — and contained a ping-pong table. I became fairly adept at ping-pong, or table tennis as it is now called. There was a side door, on the north side of the building which opened to a long hallway, on the right of which were the offices and the kitchen.. To the left was the large meeting or Sunday School room. Small alcoves along the side of this room partitioned areas for small classes. The Boy Scout troop met in one of these. As I recall, one had to pass a swimming test in order to progress to First Class in Scouting. I never learned to swim at all until after I had left the scouting program, so I remained a Second Class scout. No one enjoys being second class.

The sanctuary or main church room was on the second floor. There was an outer hallway, with benches for latecomers, where some of the ushers seemed to stay during the entire service. Inside, the pews were in an arc, about one-eighth of a circle; the floor sloped gently down to the pulpit which was elevated about four or five steps and was centered on the dais which also held three large "bishop" chairs. Behind and above the pulpit was the choir loft and organ, accessed by stairs on both left and right.

Surely the organ was late 19th century, with an array of pipes ranging from the tiny arm-size-small to the largest bass. A small, dusty closet-like area allowed passage to the area behind the organ for maintenance.. It was an excellent hiding place, too. I sang in the youth choir a few times. Miss Scheske said I gave "added volume," but she knew as well as I that it was near impossible for me to stay on key. (Whatever that is.)

Viola Scheske was something else. She was a "maiden lady," a more polite term, occasionally more nearly accurate, than "old maid." Hard to say how old she was at the time - late thirties, maybe early forties. She taught a Sunday School class, sponsored and chaperoned our young peoples' group, was a thoroughly dedicated Christian woman. She had some kind of book-keeping job with Brown Shoe Company.

There was no doubt but that the church was her significant, if not mag-nificent, obsession. For some period of time, she allowed me to drive her Model A Tudor Ford on Sunday mornings picking up children and bringing them to Sunday School. There was a slight hiatus when she learned that I was not yet sixteen. Well, I have done some mean things in my life, but one regarding Miss Scheske is bitter in remembrance.

Chief among her admonitions to her adolescent charges, and there were many and frequent (admonitions and charges), and not altogether unde-served, but foremost in memory is:

"Don't do anything you can't do to the glory of God."

You just know that such a stricture seemed impossible and brought on the quasi-humorous response that is the refuge of self-conscious youth. It must have been about 1932-3, place a summer church camp in a rural area of Missouri, I was working as a waiter, serving tables, in order to defray some of the cost. I was pouring some coffee for Miss Scheske. She dearly loved her coffee. Probably her only indulgence. I had this fiendish thought, had to have come from the devil, and said to her:

" Miss Scheske, can you drink coffee to the glory of God?"

She paused, looked up at me in exquisite anguish and replied:

"No, Bud, I can't," turned her coffee cup over and never drank coffee again.

As I said, I have done some mighty mean things, but I never want to hurt someone like that ever again. We remained friends, but it was never the same for me. It was over sixty years ago, but to this day my Psyche retains the scars of such a mean, petty, thoughtless moment.

Second Presbyterian

During one of those summer church camps, this time at Lindenwood College, on the outskirts of St. Louis, I met some of the people from Second Presbyterian Church, which was in the "Westend" section of the city. We had moved from the area close to Lafayette Park Presbyterian Church and the people from "Second" were a lively, interesting bunch, so I started going there along with several others from the "Southside": Ben Butler, Charlie Knaus, and Roemer Wilbas. If we were not "regular" in attendance at the morning services, we were steady attendees at the evening young people's meetings (the Tuxis society?) and fairly frequent at the evening church service.

Dr. MacIvor, bustling, stocky Scot, could hold the congregation in rapt attention with his peppery, often acerbic sermons. Raising the annual budget resolved into a matter of a few remarks by him directed to specific unnamed individuals who had no doubt they were the subjects of his focus. The assistant minister, Dr. Euwer was the one the young people turned to. He was admired and beloved by all.

Sally King, Anne Moore, Frances Bradley, Billie Ruth Mechling, Janice Wightman, Jean Browning, Knox Taussig, Tom Kirkpatrick, all attending or graduated from Soldan High School, and Charlie Knaus, Roemer Wilbas, Ben Butler, and I, all attending or graduated from McKinley High School.

Perspective: these were the years 1935 to 1940. We were still reeling from the Great Depression which began with the stock market crash of 1929. Lesson in ancient history, right? Right. You felt that if you ever made a salary of $5,000 a year that you would have it made. Bread was never more than ten cents a loaf, fresh. Day old, two for ten. A nice apartment, not sumptuous but nice for a young married couple, might be $37 a month.[27] Milk - eight cents a quart. Tuition for Washington University, for those who could afford it, was $125 a semester — town students, living at home, not dormitory people. Evening paper was two or three cents — I got one-quarter of a cent per paper when I sold them on the northeast corner of Jefferson and Park a few years earlier, sometimes a little more if the streetcar moved on before I had time to make change. Adult admission to the picture show was twenty-five cents. Coke (Coca-Cola, that is) at a drive-in restaurant was ten cents.. After a movie date, two cokes and a nickel tip — two bits. Beginning to get the idea?

Back to our group at "Second Pres." We generally gathered at about six o'clock (eighteen hundred hours) in the church basement for 'tea.' This was a social hour with servings of tea, coffee, cookies, and ice cream. Ten cents. At seven we met in a sedate oak-paneled room — fireplace going in winter

---

27   Mother charged her "roomers" $5 a week, $7.50 if they had two rooms. Many preferred to pay by the week, not knowing from one week to the next whether they would be working or moving on.

months — just off the chapel, for short inspirational messages and discussions of topics of vital interest. Our sponsors, or chaperones, were a middle-aged couple almost thirty years old. The Magnusons. Great people.

Sometimes we would stay for the eight o'clock church service, but more often we would all take off for someone's house where we would play some games, but mostly sit around and talk. Many of our families had been substantially affected by the depression.

Tom Kirkpatrick had to drop out of Washington U. after the death of his father. He and his mother, a woman of breeding and great dignity, lived in a small, ordinary apartment. Tom had gone to work for his brother who operated a tailoring firm in downtown St. Louis. Knox Taussig's family had suffered less financially and he was attending Washington U. as was Frances Bradley, whose father was the head administrator for Barnes Hospital, the university's medical center. (Lost touch with Knox Taussig after primary flying school at Thunderbird Field, Arizona, in 1941.) Can't recall what Sally King and Billie Ruth Mechling were doing after high school.

Janet Wightman was one of the two youngest of the group and still in high school. A very sexy little girl she was, and an accomplished dancer — except that she was too stiff for straight ballroom dancing. She and I became quite good as a waltz team and at one time had thoughts of becoming professional dancers. She eventually did. Her family was very "comfortable," on her father's income as the Vice-President of Purina Mills. They lived in a magnificent apartment on Lindell Boulevard renting for over $600 a month, more than our fathers' salaries. During the war years, WW II, while we were home on leave, Kay and I were at the Jefferson Hotel night club when Janet and her husband were the dancing feature of the floor show. Janet pulled me from the table and we did a short bit of an old routine.

Jean Browning was the other "young" one of the group, just finishing high school and studying music. Nothing comes to memory about her father, but I do remember that Mrs. Browning kept a very tight rein on Jean. Jean was a musical prodigy: she had made a guest appearance as a piano soloist, playing Beethoven's C Minor Concerto, with the St. Louis Symphony when she was twelve years old. When the soprano of the church quartet was absent for some reason, Jean would fill in, joining a much older trio, to the great enjoyment of the congregation. After a short stint at Washington U., Jean was accepted at Juilliard to study piano, and when her piano professor heard her singing as she practiced, he encouraged her to switch to voice training. Jean Browning Madeira became the world's leading Carmen — she received more curtain calls for her performance of that leading role at the opera house

41

in Milan, than anyone else in the history of La Scala. I heard Jean sing the role at the outdoor theater in Washington D.C. in 1962 and went backstage, stuck my head in the door of her dressing room and said "Hi! Jean." She exploded: "Bud Barbee! whatever happened to you and where have you been?" We reminisced awhile, and she said that she had had a 'crush' on me but that I had avoided her — I reminded her of her mother's watchfulness that successfully guarded her from anyone who might interfere with her carefully planned future. About six years later, Kay and I heard her sing excerpts from "Carmen" at a musical festival in Boston, and we have the opera, with her singing the title role, on LP records. Jean Browning Madeira, wife of a well-known conductor, died a few years later.[28]

Billie Ruth Mechling (6/16/1918 - 6/2/2001), tall, rather thin, blonde, excellent features, sort of quiet, from conservative family of moderate means. Married Roemer Wilbas. A note (9/24/2001) from Roemer about her death: "She was never in robust health since we moved to Florida in 1985, but from a slow decline I noticed an acceleration in 1998 when she was diagnosed with Alzheimer's."

Frances Bradley, slightly overweight, possibly the least attractive of the girls in our "group," went on to graduate from Wash. U., married a Johnny Alderson, had three children, died sometime in the 1970's.

Annie Moore. Slight, vivacious, life of the party, very attractive, probably the most "natural" of the group. Married Tom Kirkpatrick in late 1941; he was in the early draft for World War II. We exchanged Christmas cards until early in the '60s and then lost track of each other. A letter from Billie Ruth Mechling Wilbas in 1976 said they had lost contact with Tom but they had heard that Anne was quite sick, and mentioned their two children, Curry and Edwina. Tom's brother was named Curry. Have noticed in recent years that a Curry Kirkpatrick is with Sports Illustrated.

---

28   A press release in 1967: "JEAN MADEIRA ...There is magic in the name. Comparable to no one, she is Madeira — a rich and special talent — a voice that excites, soothes, and overpowers — a stunning beauty — a brilliant actress. Madeira is the captivating diva of every leading opera house in the entire world. Madeira is "Carmen," gloriously, devastatingly, and "Carmen" is Madeira! But Madeira is other things. Madeira is a spine tingling "Azucena," a sultry, irresistible "Delilah," a poignant, compelling "orfeo." In Wagner's "Ring" cycle, Madeira is the power of thunder and lightning. In recital she displays a penetrating musical understanding and a voice capable of the greatest refinement, as well as deep passion and intensity. Jean Madeira is, in fact, the most powerful personality in the vocal world today."

Sally King, a rangy, rather angular, good-looking blonde, independent to the point of haughtiness, from a family that had suffered substantial financial reverses in the stock market but managed to retain a beautiful home and their social position.[29] I remember her saying once: "We always dress for dinner," and Tom Kirkpatrick countering with: "Yeah, and come down and eat hash." But all in good fun. Sally's older sister — was it Betty? — was a real beauty but lacked the spark and spontaneity of Sally. Their mother was the epitome of the socialite of poise, beauty, dress, and breeding. Once when we had congregated after our young people's meeting, Mrs. King said: "Look, why not learn something useful instead of just chattering?" And she began to teach us to play bridge, contract bridge because auction bridge was just going out of fashion. She moved among the three tables pointing out how the "count" was made and all the fascinating facets of the game. Mrs. King gave me a fever for the game that infects me to this day. I have played bridge for money and for fun, read the bridge columns faithfully. Fond memories. About the time of WW II, Sally married a tall, handsome ego named Jack Heitman. Nobody thought the union would make it - it didn't. She has married again.

Charlie Knaus, one of us "southsiders," never really fit in and dropped out of the group after a year or so. Charlie was killed in WW II.

Ben Butler, nice looking but with a slightly too-large nose, curly hair, a nice guy but nauseatingly polite to females. Within a few years, he married a girl named Jules Vollmer whose father had an Oldsmobile agency where Ben began working. She was an over-made-up, over-dressed, over-catered-to girl who required constant attention. She did not fit into our group at all. Ben and Jules were divorced after a few years, and information comes that Ben married again.

We were a "group." We never paired-off or dated individually with the other members. Not all of the "group" was always present, but we still were and acted as a group. Finally, exceptions arose: Tom and Anne, as I had already mentioned, and Roemer and Billie Ruth started pairing and eventually

---

29   The King home was the finest I had ever seen at the time. To the left of the entry hall an enormous living room with several seating areas, grand piano and all the accoutrements of taste. To the rear of the entry hall a spiral staircase and beyond that the dining room and the butler's pantry, something I had never seen before in a house. The spacious kitchen seemed almost rudimentary: we had a more modern kitchen in our home. But ours was not designed for hired help. Most surprising about the King house was the garage: we had a New Year's Eve party there (was it 1935 or 1936?). The interior, floors, walls and all were of spotless white ceramic tile, and over the four-car automobile area were living quarters for the maid and chauffeur.

married. At this late date, I can't be sure of some of the facts and chronology, but I think it was just about the time of high-school graduation for Roemer, January 1934, that his father died leaving his widow with one young son and two younger daughters. I can't be sure that Orchard Paper was Roemer's first job, but he certainly was with that company for many, many years, even after it was taken over by larger companies. Around 1975 or so, he was hired away by the St. Joseph Paper Company and made an officer of that company before he retired in 1982. The company called him out of retirement, and I don't know when he finally retired and they moved to Florida. Both he and Billie Ruth have had some rather serious health problems in recent years.(But much improved according to Tony on 10 Oct 1989.) They have three children: Tony (Roemer Anthony Jr.), in St. Louis; Carol in Ohio (b. 1942) married to professor of psychology, has two children, boy (with GE) and girl (soph at Gettysburg College); and Gary, somewhere in the Air Force (back in England again flying F-111 in October 1989). Roemer`s two sisters, Gloria and Adele, still living in 1989.

A stimulating, varied group. A few of us were starting to smoke. There was no sex, no drugs and very little alcohol. We weren't angels, but we had wholesome good times together. Bygone days!

CHAPTER X

College and University

Jefferson College

After high school, I had no idea whatsoever of what I wanted to do. Starting up at that time was a new school offering a work-study program. Work six weeks, school for six weeks. Presumably the work would be in connection with the studies which were in the field of commerce and finance — business in other words. Practical experience and application of the course work (although it didn't quite work out that way).. This sounded interesting so in the fall of 1935 I enrolled at Jefferson College whose classrooms were in the Downtown YMCA.

After the first session of classes, my first job was stock clerk at Rice-Stix Dry Goods Company, wholesalers of dresses, sweaters, blouses, materials, watches, hosiery, etc., etc..I learned about the various types of materials, even dotted-Swiss, and the most popular sizes of men's sweaters and women's blouses. I became adept at a method of saving time by filling several orders simultaneously, making me about 25% more productive than other workers who had been there longer. It also made me unpopular, especially when I did not go along with the practice of taking a nap during the afternoon in the middle of a sweater bin.. "Quota busters" are not well-received.

Brown Shoe Company

My second job was at Brown Shoe Company, maker of Buster Brown, Airstep, and others. Also as a stock clerk during the first time around. And this time it was the foreman that got after me. He told me that I came to work dressed too well — coat and tie. Reasoning: workers in nice clothes would be careful about getting dirty and would not do as much work as workers in old clothes. Problem: I filled more orders than any other clerk and managed to stay neat. That really bothered him. The supervisor, Mr. Paul, called me into his office to say that he was pleased with my performance and that I could dress any way I wanted to. That kinda ticked off the crotchety old fart – uh - foreman.

After one and a half years at Jefferson College I came to the realization that I was not cut out for business. Certainly not for accounting. I had made no errors on any of the assigned homework, had a 100% average in class work and examinations, but I was not sure of the difference between a debit and a credit. You can't go through life "lucking-out" on the fundamentals. Besides, I was running out of "pigeons" who would play me at ping-pong (for money) during the lunch hour — I depended on them for my lunch money. Ah, well.

I stayed on at Brown Shoe after the Christmas break. And that created a problem: the college claimed I was "taking a job away from the school," but Brown Shoe was happy to have me. I was making $12 a week — but that was what they were paying some of the men who had been with the company for some years. I began to fill in on the wrapping, packaging and labeling line. Orders filled on the upper floors would travel down the conveyor-roller tracks to the wrapping line. Small orders, 1 to 3 boxes, were taken off the track by 'wrappers' who used precut sheets of brown wrapping paper, taped the package and pasted on the order sheet. Orders of 4 or more pairs rolled to the next station, went into appropriately sized boxes, were stencilled, and sealed. Stencils had to be cut for new customers. Filled orders kept moving to the shipping room.

"Old Mike" had been with Brown Shoe for years. He swept the floors where orders were filled and packaged. While I was working on the packaging line, one of the other workers went on vacation. Old Mike said he could fill in. So he swept floors until packaging got behind, then would step in and wrap or box as needed. When the regular wrapper returned from vacation he was assigned to another job and Old Mike kept sweeping floors and wrapping and boxing. When the man who made the stencils and stencilled the boxes went on vacation, Old Mike said he could fill in. So he swept floors, wrapped small orders, boxed big orders, cut the stencils and stencilled the boxes.. The regular stenciller never returned. Sometimes the orders would get stuck between floors. Old Mike knew how to climb up the tracks and clear up the jam. Meanwhile, he swept floors, wrapped small orders, boxed big orders, made stencils, stencilled boxes, and kept the orders rolling on the tracks. Now doing the work of three and one-half men, Old Mike continued to earn $12 a week. Old Mike was busy as a bee and happy as a lark.

Mr. Paul knew of my tentative plans to return to college. One day he called me into his office to tell me that he thought I could apprentice as a shoe salesman and make a lot more money, but he did not want to try to talk me out of going back to college. It was tempting, but I left in the fall to enter Washington University.

Washington University

September 1937 — I entered Washington U. It would change my life, but not in the way imagined or originally intended. My year and a half at Jefferson College translated into about one year of credits at the university in the College of Liberal Arts. I now knew that I was going to be an actor.

Several stints as a "spear carrier" at the Little Theater of St. Louis, a coupla short speaking roles, a walk on role in "Night Must Fall," with the visiting star Burgess Meredith, of course the senior play in high school, and two summers as an usher at the Muny Opera, mixing with "theater" people, I was nineteen and had decided my life's calling.

The two principal theater activities on campus were Thyrsus and the Quad Show. Thyrsus produced several plays during the school year, generally some sort of Shakespeare adaptation, and some one-act plays written by students in a playwrighting course. The Quadrangle Club produced the annual Quad Show, a musical comedy, also student-written.

I managed to have a part in practically all the productions of Thyrsus, and one year received an award as the only student to have performed in all the productions for the year. (Greater quantity than quality.) I was the most active, if not the most talented. My first year with Quad Show was backstage doing makeup — my experience at Little Theater had given me good training in this area. The second year I continued to supervise makeup and had a small part as a member of a comedy singing and dancing male quartet. Kay Galle, leading lady, would come up with fluttering eyes "How is my makeup,Bud?" Kay Hampton was ready to slap her face. In my senior year I was the production manager of the show.

These were quite professional performances — we even went "on the road" to Missouri U. for performances. As I said, these plays and musicals were written by students. The most successful has been Aaron E. Hotchner, also of the class of '40, who became quite friendly with Ernest Hemingway and wrote the definitive biography of that famous author. Hotchner now partners with Paul Newman in their food enterprises. A few of the actors went on to get roles on Broadway. But the most important event happened before I started these activities.

Newcomers to the university were invited to the freshman mixer — even if they were not entering as freshman. (I was accorded a sophomore.) Select seniors were appointed to the freshman mixer committee which made all arrangements for the dance and the festivities. The second girl I danced with was a willowy honey blonde wearing a black wool dress topped with a little leather "dog" collar. After that dance I did not dance with anyone else. Back in those days if you saw someone you wanted to dance with, you "cut in."[30] The understood protocol was that you did not cut in on the person who had cut in on you. So you had to wait until someone else cut in before you could come back and dance with the same girl. So this willowy honey blonde in the black dress found herself dancing with me every third partner. Obviously quite sophisticated, she wore a subtle perfume, was no doubt a "big woman on campus," had great legs, danced beautifully, following my not terribly experienced steps, and seemed somewhat, well, almost embarrassed by my persistent attention.

"What are you doing? You're supposed to be mixing, not dancing with me all night."

"I'm just getting acquainted with the girl I'm going to marry."

"You're crazy."

What she did not know was that I had decided right then and there that I wanted to spend the rest of my life with her — she was what I had been looking for. But I soon found that getting a "date" with Kay Hampton was not an easy thing to do.

She had started dating this guy, Byron Herbert, back in University City High School, continued through college, and at this time he was a sports reporter for the St. Louis Post-Dispatch newspaper. Several weeks went by as I kept trying for a Friday or Saturday night date with no success at all. She and Byron seemed to have a permanent arrangement for those nights. I managed a football game a few times when Byron was evidently working.

After I pledged Phi Delta Theta I found out that he had been a Phi Delt and all the brothers informed me that I was trying to break into something that could not be broken into, and some of the others who had already graduated were quite obviously and openly resentful of my even trying.

A coupla breaks came through for Sunday evenings and Kay Hampton was a big hit with the Second Presbyterian church bunch. Christmas came and she had a party at her home. She invited me, the guy she had told her parents was a much older man she had met at school. I sent a dozen long-stemmed red roses. Good move! Byron's friends had heard I could play

---

30 "Cut" was not used in other geographical areas - it had a sexual connotation.

ping-pong so they set me up with the brother who had been the fraternity champion. I proceeded to clean his clock. Aha! Not such a pigeon as they expected.

Initially I had accepted a bid to Sigma Nu fraternity, but after a few weeks, I saw that I did not fit in with that group — they seemed immature. When the word got around that I was dating (pretty infrequently to my chagrin) Kay Hampton, Big Woman On Campus, president of Delta Gamma sorority, etc, etc, the Betas and Sigma Chis started giving me the rush. Northcutt Coil, a friend from South St. Louis, was a Phi Delt and that was the determining factor as I decided to pledge Phi Delta Theta. Good bunch of guys — even Byron Herbert the alum.

By the following summer, 1938, after her graduation, I had made some inroads. I was free of commitments when the Hamptons were going to Michigan for their summer vacation. Mr. Hampton had to delay his departure and I was available to drive Mrs. Hampton there from St. Louis and bring the car back for Mr. Hampton. Doesn't hurt a bit to get in with the family. Make points that way.

When school started in the fall of 1938, Kay began working in the university bookstore, and I found I had to spend a lot of time there. Now things were beginning to tilt my direction. Northcutt Coil (Cutter) was dating "Pepper" (Esther Lincoln) Throop, daughter of the chancellor of the university. This was a foursome for bridge. Cutter's dad was a minister, not much money, so we two south-siders had to stick together. Some nights we played at the Hampton's, some nights at the chancellor's residence, called the "Shack." Girls, of course, furnished the refreshments. (Actually, the girls' parents.) How two guys from the "other side of the tracks" ever got into this position, with two girls from the affluent "west end," I'll never understand.[31] Just natural talent, I guess. As for the game of bridge, I was improving. To the detriment, sometimes, of my studies, I played bridge in the afternoons for money — just enough for spending money, you know. (Gotta go for dinner now.)

My mother once said — actually she said it many times — that after I had met Kay Hampton she was the only thing I could ever think about. I had always said that I was going to marry a rich girl. Mother said "Bud, how do you know that you will fall in love with a rich girl?" My answer was simple: "I'm not going to meet any girls whose parents don't have money." And here was this exciting BWOC, best-dressed woman on campus, drove her own

---

31   Pepper once said that she was a freshman in college before she found out that not every family had a full-time maid.

car, father an executive with a big department store, two brothers who were doctors. But mother had been right: I fell in love before I knew all these things. And later I learned that all those things were not what they seemed to be to me. I was in a different, unfamiliar environment.

I managed to pass my courses — later I would wish that I had spent a little more time in studies, but I suffered no ill effects. During 1937-1938 I had six courses: English, French, Geology, Psychology, and two classes of Political Science. The next two years required only five courses, and I ended with majors in English, French, Political Science and Psychology. Some of the courses were selected on the basis of using textbooks and class notes that Kay had from when she had taken the courses. With all that, she had better grades than I ended up with. I spent a lot of time with the "theater" and I began to work in radio, doing, among other things, a regular news broadcast for United Charities. The radio station donated the time and I donated my services.

Some of us did some crazy things. Like the time there was a "social" on the Quad with servings of cookies and punch. The punch came in big five gallon milk cans. A couple of us snitched one of those cans, took it to the fraternity house, mixed in some grain alcohol we bought at the corner drug store and had a pretty wild party. Some of the fraternity brothers did not approve of this sort of thing and disapproved of drinking in general — years later, some of the college teetotalers became the heaviest drinkers.

In retrospect, however, these were idyllic years, halcyon days. The camaraderie and "in" feeling of the fraternity, the exhilaration of intramural sports, the widening of intellectual horizons, the pleasures of the social affairs, particularly the fraternity and sorority dances, and the many wonders of the rite of passage into adulthood. And, of course, being in love with a wonderful woman. What would one change of those times?

CHAPTER XI

Off to Work We Go

Part-time jobs

During the college years there were a number of jobs, part-time, summer and incidental. These were sufficient to provide a little spending money, aside from ping-pong and bridge winnings, and gasoline for the family car which I seemed to have pretty free use of. One summer I drove the bus for Sebago Day Camp, picking up kids from their homes and delivering them to the camp and back again in the evening, and serving as a junior counsellor during the rest of the day.. Two summers I ushered at the Muny Opera in Forest Park — a much sought after job that I got through the good offices of Tom Kirkpatrick. The performances of light opera and operettas were enhanced by the appearance of well-known Broadway, Hollywood and Metropolitan Opera stars in the major roles. Local talent, primarily, auditioned prior to the beginning of the season for parts in the dancing and singing chorus and many of the minor roles.

The Municipal Opera of St. Louis is one of the foremost outdoor theaters in the U.S. It was the first to have a revolving stage that enabled the next scene to be put in place during a performance and then rotated into the forefront in less than a minute. The amphitheatre seated ten thousand with standing room and seating on the grass for two thousand more non-paying spectators. Some of the best seats for viewing dance routines and patterns were the upper 25¢ seats - yes, I said twenty five cents! Then there were a number of rows for 50¢, more for $1.00 and $1.50, the closest seats and the boxes were $2.50. Actually, the view of the stage from the box seats was quite poor. Most desirable locations for ushering were the $1.50 and $2.50 seats.

After a week of performances, *The Mikado* (and other Gilbert and Sullivan productions) began to tire somewhat, but *The Desert Song, The Student Prince*, Showboat, and others remained a delight to see and hear.

Out Into The Real World

June 1940 and the college graduate[32] with essentially no practical training was informed by the radio stations that a year's experience on a small town station was necessary prior to the granting of an audition. Meanwhile, a job? Retail Credit Company, engaged mainly in investigations for insurance companies, could hire and quickly train an investigator in the nuances of interviewing neighbors and acquaintamces regarding the drinking, social habits and morals of those applying for insurance of various sorts. My trainer led me to believe that it was OK to fabricate some comments when it was difficult to find someone to question regarding the applicant. That didn't seem honest to me. I found that I could handle a lot of cases by skipping lunch, returning to the office just at closing time to begin dictating my research to a Dictaphone in order for typists to complete the report the next day. I would close the office after all others had gone.

My work must have impressed the bosses. After about two months on the job, I was offered the territory of southern Illinois, covering the area south of East St. Louis. Shook up a number of people in the office there in St. Louis who were sure that one of the men with a lot of seniority would be given the job. It was a promotion and more money.

Working out of Carbondale, where I had rented a room, I would be on the road just before seven, work my way back to home base by about seven in the evening, type a draft of my report, and leave it for final preparation with a secretary who worked primarily for a lawyer. The reports constituted a form of piece-work: the more reports I turned in, the more money I made: I averaged about $80 a week, equivalent of about $35,000 a year today. Weekends I would hurry back to St. Louis to try to maintain my position in the affections of Kay Hampton.

WJPF The Voice of Egypt

On one of my trips through Herrin, Illinois, I saw notices of a radio station about to begin operations. The manager told me he had brought his announcers with him from a Springfield (Illinois) station, but agreed to let me audition. He hired me at what he said he was paying the others: $80 a month. About one-fourth of what I was making with Retail Credit, but it was the opportunity to get the needed year's experience on a small town radio station. I gave Retail Credit two weeks notice, cleared up all the accounts, and began a short career as a staff announcer around the first of October 1940.

---

32 My parents surprised me with a 1937 Ford coupe as a graduation present.

As I said, the pay wasn't great, but times were different. There were two hotels in town — I stayed at the old one in a small one-person bedroom, shower down the hall, for $5 a week, 25% of my pay. The hotel restaurant offered a meal ticket for $5 that gave reduced meal prices and saw me through a week. I still had $40 a month left to squander as I saw fit. Of course, I took my laundry home each weekend. And I carefully limited my losings at eight-ball and nine-ball pool. (Sometimes, however rarely, I did win.) A few dollars went for gasoline — pump prices for regular about 12¢ a gallon, or lower during a "gas war." Still had a few dollars left for Kay Hampton and a not too lavish weekend date.

Soon it was apparent why the networks wanted people with small town experience: country (read small town) announcers do everything: news, sports news and live sports coverage, commercials, interviews in the studio and on the street, disk jockey stuff, programming, and even sales. During the high school football season, we would occasionally have a Saturday afternoon live broadcast from the stadium. I did the first live radio broadcast in the United States of a bowling tournament, to the accompaniment of crashing pins and commentary, highlighting ultra-modern overhead score screens and pin-setting machinery. The other announcers were married so it naturally fell my lot to do the 'late' night stuff and close the station for the day. Ordinarily, the standard day went something like this: arrive a little before noon, check the local news and select stories from the United Press teletype machine that seemed always to be clattering away, announce fifteen minutes of the news from twelve until twelve fifteen, music or local color until 1:00 pm, lead into the Cardinal baseball network sponsored by Hyde Park beer or a classical music program for the same sponsor[33] when there was no game, "disk jockey it" until 6:00, tear off more UP news for one-half hour of national and financial news, play records introduce studio performers or interview celebrities, sometimes a remote from a local dance hall if someone like Fats Waller would be performing, do fifteen minutes of late news from 10:00 to 10:15 and then sign-off and close "WJPF, the Voice of Egypt, Herrin, Illinois" for the day. That part of southern Illinois was known as "Little Egypt" because it included Cairo in the southern part. After locking up for the night, I would sometimes stop off at the local pool (billiards) parlor for a lesson in eight-ball or nine-ball by the son of the proprietor (at my expense), and then to my hotel for a bowl of soup before going to bed.

---

33   The small, remembered, times: when I was reading, on the air, one of the commercials extolling the taste pleasures of Hyde Park beer, I had the hiccups so bad that I'm sure the listening audience, if there was one, was sure that I was imbibing the product.

Fred was the oldest and most experienced announcer. He generally opened the station in the morning with a "farm" program, covering local conditions, including the weather, and the market prices: wheat, corn, pork, etc. Doug was the other announcer that came with the manager from Springfield. His wife worked as the secretary at the station. Doug was "the" disk jockey of the station — covering some news, but mostly chatting, answering calls and requests, and selecting records. We called them "transcriptions," but they looked just like oversize records.

Weekends a little different: sign-off on Friday night and head for St. Louis — distance about 140 miles. That little 1937 Ford coupe (black, of course) came to know every bend in the roads between Herrin and St. Louis.[34] I say "roads" because U.S. Highways 57 and 64 did not exist and my route was either 148 to 14 to 51 to 154 to 13, or 148 to 14 to 51 to 154 to 3.34 There were other ways also, but most of them proved a little longer than the ones I listed. Fifty and sixty years ago the state of Illinois probably had more total miles of highways than any other state — so many little towns not too far apart.

Came June 1941 and I told the manager it was time for me to get back to St. Louis and try to get ahead; he agreed that there was no future for me in Herrin. There were no openings in St. Louis, but the stations put my auditions on file, and I took a job as a ticket-reservations agent at the TWA office in the

Jefferson Hotel in downtown St. Louis. The pay ($125 a month) was not exactly munificent, but more than my job as a radio announcer. Also the advantage of living at home, no hotel or meal bill, no long weekend drives.

Warclouds (and a little history)

Germany had attacked Poland on September 1, 1939. Under the guise of protecting White Russian and Ukrainian minorities in eastern Poland, Russian forces moved into Poland on September 17, and the end of Polish resistance came on September 28 when Germany and Russia signed a friendship treaty, dividing Poland for the fourth time in history. Secure in the east with the Russian treaty, Hitler launched his attack on The Netherlands and Belgium on May 10, 1940 on the pretense of protecting them from the Allies. British forces on the continent were forced back to Dunkerque and evacuated by

---

34 Knowing the roads did not keep me from dozing at the wheel on one occasion and slamming into a bridge. Couple hundred dollars damage that Kay — at the time my girlfriend — lent to me. Can't remember that I ever repaid her. .(For so many things.)

June 4 — leaving many men and much materiel behind. France's "impregnable" Maginot Line was outflanked and taken from the rear. The French asked for an armistice and capitulated to the Germans on June 24, 1940.

Great Britain was standing alone. On June 4, Winston Churchill, reporting on Dunkerque, told the House of Commons:

"We shall go on to the end, we shall fight in France, we shall fight on the seas and oceans, we shall fight with growing confidence of strength in the air, we shall defend our Island, whatever the cost may be, we shall fight on the the beaches, we shall fight on the landing grounds, we shall fight in the fields and in the streets, we shall fight in the hills; we shall never surrender, and even if, which I do not for a moment believe, this Island or a large part of it were subjugated and starving, then our Empire beyond the seas, armed and guarded by the British fleet, would carry on the struggle, until, in God's good time, the New World, with all its power and might, steps forth to the rescue and liberation of the old."

Summer 1940 and 1941: Russia invaded Latvia, Lithuania, and Estonia. Germany cut up Rumania, Hungary, Yugoslavia, Bulgaria, and Greece.

The German air assault on Britain began in August 1940, the Berlin-Rome-Tokyo-Axis was formalized in September, British possessions in North Africa were under attack by the Italians and Germans, and the Japanese were moving forward in their conquest of Asia, which had begun in 1931 in Manchuria.

June 22, 1941, Hitler, now feeling secure in western Europe, attacked the Soviet Union, abrogating their peace treaty. Russia, which had safely attacked Poland, Finland, and other small countries, now appealed for help from Britain and the United States. The final German defeat in Russia would not have been possible without British equipment and American Lend-Lease supplies to make up for the Red Army's losses. The Soviet government was reluctant to give publicity to Allied assistance. Our statesmen and politicians should be required to read Machiavelli's "The Prince."

Recognizing the imminence of involvement in the war, the U.S., on September 16, 1940, passed the Selective Service Training Act. More than 16,500,000 men between the ages of 21 and 35 were registered on October 16, 1940. I registered in Herrin, population about 10,000. By the summer of 1941, I knew my number would soon be coming up in that small town. The idea of being in the "walking" army had little appeal for me.

CHAPTER XII

YOU'RE IN THE ARMY NOW

Jefferson Barracks

When I returned to St. Louis, and before taking the job with TWA, I knew I had to do something about that low draft number from Herrin. In the summer of 1938 some of my classmates at Wash U had taken the exam given by a traveling Aviation Cadet board. The storm clouds over Europe were an encouragement to many at the time. My friends easily talked me out of taking the exam — remember, I was going to be an actor. Now, in early June 1941, I thought I might be facing the "walking" army, so I joined a group of others at Jefferson Barracks, on the outskirts of St. Louis, to take the physical exam for entry into flying training.

After filling out interminable forms, I came to one of the first examiners in the "assembly line": the EENT - eye, ear, nose, throat. The candidate directly in front of me in the line was failed for a diverted nasal septum. I knew what that was — I also had that condition — so I attacked:

"Doctor, that's what I have too, but you see it doesn't affect me at all." And I very strongly blew through my nose, which I had been careful to have completely clean.

Doctor: "Yeah, I can see it doesn't bother you. Pass."

And I moved on through the examining line. Soon, standing in shivering complete nudity, another doctor tells me I cannot qualify because of flat feet. I use reason:

"Doctor, I can see that flat feet might be troublesome in the infantry, but can you see any reason why it would make any difference flying an airplane? And besides, my feet have always been like this. I don't have fallen arches, I was born without any."

Doctor: "I see your point. I agree that there is no reason this should affect flying an airplane. Pass."

That did it! I was told that I would be notified when to report for training. Now all I could do was wait.

St. Louis is generally pretty warm in June, July and August, and into September, but the TWA ticket office was nicely air-conditioned, located in an air-conditioned hotel, when very, very few homes were air-conditioned. So I was not uncomfortable while I waited for "the call." And I had learned the technique of the nickel pin-ball machine in the drugstore of the hotel and managed to win about two dollars during each lunch hour.

Around about the end of July I heard that one of the men who had taken the exam with me had got his orders to report for flying training. I sent off an indignant letter to the War Department (I didn't know that one doe not do such things if one is to come under the jurisdiction of same) telling them in no uncertain terms that I should also be called. In a few days, the return mail brought the news that I was to report to Thunderbird Field, Phoenix, Arizona, NLT (Not Later Than) 31 October 1941. Whee!

About the first week in August, Kay took off driving with Helen Burcham to California, but we kept up some correspondence; she wrote regularly and I sent letters to widely-spaced general deliveries. (Now, over sixty years later I still have her letters.) Still it was a lonely time for about a month.

After we had reported to Jefferson Barracks for induction into the Army in October, Charles Armstrong, Richard Antrim and I (that put us pretty close together alphabetically) agreed that we would drive to Arizona together in Charlie's car and split expenses. This was my first trip out west and when we hit the White Mountains in Arizona, Charlie scared the hell out of Dick and me. Just too fast around those mountain curves with no guard rail and steep drop-offs that ever so often revealed bits and pieces of rusting automobiles at the bottom. But spectacular scenery for midwesterners!

Thunderbird Field

Report NLT 31 October 1941. Not knowing any better, we reported in a day early.[35] Hoooo-boy! You learn quick! Charlie parked the car outside the gate, and upperclassmen greeted us and offered to help with our luggage.

---

35 42-E was the last cadet class to go directly into primary flying school. Following classes went through what was called "pre-flight," which gave them some military drill, and some testing for physical reaction to the stresses of flying. Class 42-F, with which I graduated, started their pre-flight training, at the same time that we in Class 42-E started primary flying training. 42-F came to Thunderbird with regular GI uniforms, while we were still in flight suits and civilian clothes — before the start of the war (December 7, 1941, Pearl Harbor Day) we could wear civilian clothes into town — on those rare times when we had permission to leave the post.

We didn't have much, but we were wearing and had brought civilian clothes — no war yet.

We thought that was nice of them to help us — until we stepped inside the gate — WHAM!

"Come to attention! Brace, mister!" (We soon learned that a brace meant an exaggerated form of attention, with the chin pulled in, the head erect, eyes straight ahead, and the stomach flat.) Pick up those bags! Eyes straight ahead! What's your name mister?"

"No it isn't, mister. It's 'Aviation Cadet Barbee Sir,' mister! Now here's your barracks number, mister. You will double-time to your room. You will double-time every place you go, mister. Do you understand, mister? Then why are you standing here?"

I start to leave.

"MISTER! Did I give you permission to leave, mister? Mister, get this through your thick head: when an upperclassman is talking to you, you wait until he is finished and gives you permission to leave, mister." And so on and so on and so on.

It was just the next day that we learned that those SOB's had just become upperclassmen the day before upon the departure of their upperclass. Well, our time would come, but I did not figure that it would seem to take so long. They gave us slips of paper that told us where we were to live. Our barracks were four long buildings, one storey, laid out in a sort of squashed diamond shape, like two "V"s with the wide ends together, a grassy area between the two rows, and a large space in the middle, with the flagpole gracing a circular center area. At the bottom of one of the V's was the ground school building, at the other end the dining hall and recreation room. There were other buildings, and hangars, as shown in Appendix C, but the barracks, ground school, dining hall and recreation hall were the confines of our daily lives.

The "barracks" were somewhat like motel rooms, minus the amenities, but not really like the standard enlisted pre-war barracks. Thunderbird Field was a civilian contract school, owned by a group of Hollywood movie people. The instructors, both flight and academic, were civilians. The relatively plush accommodations, and the frequent visits by movie personalities, gave Thunderbird the well-earned name of "Country Club of the flying schools." We were only six men to a room with adjoining bath. But this was better than we had in basic and advanced flying schools which were run by the military. The upper class were grandly ensconced in two-man rooms.

58

In our barracks rooms we were shown how to store our clothes, precisely, how to make our beds, precisely, and how to proceed to supply, precisely, to draw our flying gear, etc., etc., etc. Our issue was: coveralls, flying, two sets; helmet, flying, one; goggles, flying, one pair; scarf, neck, flying, one; and permanent issue: shoes, black, low- quarter, two pair, and socks, black, short, six pair. It seemed to be accepted that we had our own underwear and handkerchiefs, which I believe we did — I couldn't answer for the others. Until we went "off-post," or into town, we wore coveralls for all activities except athletics.[36] Provision was made for the purchase of athletic shorts.

Before we had a chance to "settle in," we were hustled out for a formation. The formation was for the purpose of telling us what and when the next formation would be: a supper formation. Cheez! And, Oh yes! The instruction that we would double-time (run) at all times when we were not undercover. (That means outside of buildings.) BUT! We were to come to a normal pace (walking) when encountering an upperclassman (or an officer, but they were quite rare in the cadet areas) and render a salute. Of course, this provided an excellent opportunity for us to be instructed in the nuances of a proper salute: upper right arm straight out from the shoulder and parallel to the ground, the forearm at a forty-five degree angle, wrist and fingers perfectly straight in line with the forearm, thumb tight against the index finger, index finger just touching the outer edge of the right eyebrow. This exciting maneuver to be executed crisply and held until acknowledged by a return salute from the officer saluted. There was a lot to learn before we even saw an airplane.

The first morning was an eye-opener! Bugle sounding and ungodly racket before it is daylight. FALL OUT ! So we jump into those coveralls, run out the door and join a horde of others, all madly dashing about, all in the dark. Confusion. Upperclassmen somehow arranged us into some sort of order, and then we all started running again. This run was to be the regular morning one-mile run (except on Mondays, when we ran two miles "to get the weekend alcohol out of our systems") that we were to enjoy throughout our training. The run ended in a formation near the dining hall which we gladly entered to have a nice quiet breakfast.

Not so fast there! Not quiet, not leisurely, not altogether enjoyable, but good. Now we learn to be gunners. Gunners pass the dishes of food back and forth down the table. This is managed so that the gunner has to hurry like

---

36 Cadets were just beginning to phase out the "cadet blues," a distinctive cadet uniform, and no decision had been reached as to what uniform we would wear.

hell to get something to eat during the allotted time. And be able to consume a square meal in the process.

(Thanksgiving 1989 has come and gone and I have been neglecting this chapter for some while. But a short aside, having mentioned Thanksgiving: Tom Kirkpatrick, back in St. Louis, had told me to look up some cousins in Phoenix, and they invited me to Thanksgiving dinner - and to bring a friend. So I invited Charlie Armstrong to go along. Lovely family that had moved to Phoenix for the climate. When the turkey was carved and the maid was serving us, my friend Charlie says:

"I don't like turkey." And I tried to disappear in my chair.

Without hesitation, our gracious hostess directed:

"Marie, bring Mr. Armstrong some of the ham."

The rest of the dinner was without surprises. Somehow that incident seems to come home at Thanksgiving. Why didn't he tell me he didn't eat turkey?)

Now we settled into the routine of flying, athletics, ground school, drilling inspections, and eating. The weather was routinely excellent, so we flew every day, Monday through Friday, reaching for the magic point of around eight hours when arrived the expected time to solo. Some did it earlier, some later, but eight hours was the average.

Ground school instructors first introduced the intricacies of engines, principally internal combustion and specifically rotary, air-cooled; meteorology, so we would know what kinds of clouds our heads were in; theory of flight (wasn't it a proven fact?); navigation (some of us would fly without a navigator and others would have to double-check how the assigned navigator managed to screw up simple arithmetic); and refresher mathematics (so we could help the navigator).

Athletics: every morning we ran a mile before breakfast, following ground school we had an hour of games (football, baseball, soccer) topped off with another mile run - on Mondays, of course, we ran the two miles "to get the alcohol out of our system." Saturdays were for inspections — no one ever passed — drilling and parade practice, and walking "tours."

A certain number of "gigs," or discrepancies in barracks inspection and/ or military discipline, resulted in a prescribed time of marching on the ramp during what would be "free time" or "open post." No one was able to avoid this form of "punishment" entirely. If the inspectors could find nothing to criticize, they would mess up your bunk and award demerits for a poorly made bed. For many of us, no such Draconian measures were required.But, I am running ahead. We march into the dining hall, position ourselves behind our chairs, take our seats upon the command "SEATS!"

In order to assure proper posture and decorum we learn that underclassmen sit only on the front two inches of the chair, back straight, head erect, eyes straight ahead, one arm in the lap at all times, except when necessary to use two hands as in cutting meat, the other using the proper implement but not resting upon or touching the table, and the food conveyed to the mouth in the fashion of a "square meal," in which the fork or spoon is lifted vertically from the dish, moved horizontally to the mouth and returned to the dish in reverse process.

"Mister!"   "Yes, Sir!"

"Have you finished, mister?" "Yes, Sir!"

"Mister, are you still hungry?" "No, Sir!"

"Since you are not hungry, you don't want your dessert, do you?"

"Oh Yes, Sir!"

"Then you are still hungry, aren't you?"

"Yes, Sir!"

"Fine, then have some more potatoes, mister."

"But, sir -"

"You must learn that a cadet is always truthful, mister."

"Yes, Sir!"

"Then have you decided, are you hungry or not?"

There was our first "Catch 22."

We assembled after breakfast to learn our flying and ground school schedules: quite simply, flying in the morning, ground school in the afternoon combined with athletics, alternating weekly. It was always preferable to fly mornings while the wind and heat currents were still not developed, and with ground school in the pm, we were able to shower and be fresh for dinner (read supper). We were also advised about the "probability factor":

"Look at the man on each side of you. One of you will not be around at the end of this training."

The prediction was close. Class 42-E, starting in October 1941 and finishing in December 1941: 140 cadets started,[37] 58 were eliminated from pilot

---

37 42-E could be called a "Mid-west" class: over 70 from Missouri, 21 from Illinois, Iowa, Kansas, Arkansas, and the rest from Pennsylvania, the Carolinas, Minnesota, Wisconsin, Massachusetts, the Dakotas, Oklahoma, Oregon, Colorado, Ohio, Idaho, Nevada, Arizona. All who completed primary successfully went to Minter for basic, and to Luke, Williams or Stockton for advanced. I got to see many of them at Williams. 42-F

training. Class 42-F, started in December after the war had begun and were treated slightly more liberally by the end of primary in February 1942: 192 started, 59 eliminated.

Of course, each was sure that he would make it, but couldn't quite make up his mind about which man on either side would not. Of our original group of three, Dick Antrim was eliminated at Thunderbird, I was held back one class (more on that later) and Charlie Armstrong made it, but was killed shortly after graduation, flying a Martin B-26 in Louisiana, when one engine failed on takeoff. Although the Martin B-26 was the AAF's fastest medium bomber, I think the Douglas A-26 was later reclassified as the B-26 and the inherently unstable Martin was discontinued.

Following that bit of unnerving prognostication, half of the formation proceeded to ground school and the rest of us marched to the flight line where we were introduced to and shown the proper way to fit our parachutes (you mean we might need these?), and marched out to a gleaming yellow machine, our parachutes banging against our buttocks with each step.

"Switch off?"
"Switch off!"
(Pull the prop through a couple of times.)
"Contact?"
"Contact!" (Give the prop a quick snap through and you have start.)

I was number two of our group given an introductory tour of the area in the back seat of the Stearman PT-17. This radial-engine biplane with open cockpits was reminiscent of the in-line engine World War I Spad. (Like Snoopy flies.) And, of course, wearing helmet, goggles, and scarf flying in the wind.

Nicknamed "The Yellow Peril," many of us came to regard this primary trainer as just that. On this first half-hour flight the instructor oriented us with the airfield, surrounding hills, fields suitable for emergency landings, and the controls of this flying machine. How simple it seems now, but how awe-inspiring then. We got to follow through on the controls during simple

---

had the greatest concentration from Texas [55], California [27], Indiana [18], Missouri [10], Oklahoma [8], Minnesota [7], Wisconsin [5], Illinois & Louisiana [4], and the rest from Michigan, South Dakota, Nebraska,Kansas,
Washington, Arkansas, North Carolina, Florida, Iowa, Ohio, Massachusetts, Maryland, New Mexico, Oregon,
Idaho, Wyoming, Utah, Kentucky, West Virginia, New York, North Dakota, Alabama,New Jersey, Nevada, and District of Columbia.

maneuvers. The instructor could speak to us through a speaking tube connected to our helmet, but we could not talk back. After all, what did we have to say? Then he said "You got it." Gulp!

Just fly it straight and level. That's all. Just straight and level. Later we realized that the airplane could do this just about alone, providing we did not give it too much "help." But we grabbed that stick (elevator and aileron control), and jumped on those rudder pedals (like brake pedals on a car, but not for stopping), and proceeded to ramble up and down and all around the sky to the obvious amusement of the instructor. He took over, returned to the home field, demonstrated a couple of landings, and the momentous first half-hour flight was over. Next student.

Following each flight we entered the time and our name in the Form 1, a flight log book. Sometime during the second or third week of flying, while filling out this form, the instructor noticed I was left-handed...

"Which hand do you use for the throttle?"

"Why, my left hand."

"And which hand do you use for the stick (control)?"

"My right hand. Why?"

"Well, that crazy Antrim is left-handed, too, and he flies cross-handed with his left on the stick and his right on the throttle!"

Poor, "crazy" Antrim got sick every time he went up. When I say sick, I mean he threw up on, over, and into the cockpit. Routinely, we met his airplane with a bucket of water to wash it down. Before he had the chance to solo, it was apparent he was not cut out for this flying business and he was eliminated from pilot training. It was a big disappointment, but it was inevitable. A few weeks after Pearl Harbor and the start of the war, Dick was sent to officer training in a ground career.

Awaiting assignment, with time on his hands, Richard Antrim wrote and directed some radio programs produced on the local radio station, and we both played some of the roles and handled the announcing. Remember, I was an experienced performer. After the war started it was permissible for cadets to be married. I remember that Dick and I went into town together to find a jewelry store that had been recommended. We wanted to buy engagement rings. It was over sixty years ago, but it seems that Dick liked and settled on a star-sapphire for Ann Clark and I found a pretty, but small, diamond for Kay. We had to buy the rings on time. Didn't finish the payments until after we were married. I lost track of Dick during the war, but we met again in St. Louis after the war and Dick became my insurance agent until the Air Force recalled me to active duty.

On toward the end of November, I had seven and one-half hours of flight instruction and was about ready for my solo flight...Then a morning reveille, still dark, I am running past the corner of the barracks, full speed, and at cross-paths here comes a

Chinese cadet (we had a large group of them), the top of his head level with and crashing into my left cheekbone. Diagnosis: fracture and frontal dislocation of left zygomatic process. He knocked me fairly flat on my tonkus. It hurt like hell. But I refused assistance, got on my feet unaided and walked to the infirmary. One of the disqualifying items for flying wa ever having been knocked unconscious. My cheekbone was crushed in, broken away from my nose and ear, and I felt some dizziness (more than normal), but I held on to consciousness. The flight surgeon dispatched me to the base hospital at Luke Field where I stayed until shortly after December 7, 1941.

Lying in bed at the hospital, I was offered two aspirin for the pain. The nurse was holding them in her hand, sort of to the right of my head. From the corner of my eye — it hurt to turn my head — I thought I saw four and said: "All four of them?" Oops! Note in my file: "Possible double vision." Thereafter, several times a day, in comes a nurse or doctor asking how many fingers she/he was holding up, or how many pencils. No more evidence of double vision. And the decision was made not to operate to try to raise the crushed left cheekbone. But if the Flight Surgeon at Thunderbird had not stayed on my case and been thoroughly convincing in his support, I would have been disqualified for flying. Dr. (then captain) G. S. Ortman. I am indebted to him.

When I returned to Thunderbird to continue my training, I found the rules governing cadets had been changed throughout the Air Corps: upon coming to the corner of a building, a cadet would stop running, walk past the corner, then resume running. So I was responsible for a form of progress. But meanwhile I had fallen behind my classmates in 42-E, and would even have to catch up on flying time with the class of 42-F.

So I would sit in on my friends in 42-E when they discussed their aerial acrobatics and other flying items, then the next solo flying day I would go out of the local area and try some of these things. Like spins. I knew how to pull up in a stall and let the plane fall into a spin, but I didn't know how to recover, so I just let go of the controls and watched the earth slowly stop spinning as the inherently stable craft recovered itself from the maneuver. Probably not a highly recommended procedure. Some of my practice aerobatics likely were maneuvers never before done.

64

About the Chinese. Their liaison officer wrote to the Chinese Cadets of Class 42-F:

"You have gained the unique honor of being in the first group of Chinese Cadets to train in America under the Lend Lease Act..." I'm sure Thunderbird was chosen for this honor because of the extraordinary facilities and the connections with the movie industry. Many of these Chinese cadets were already accomplished pilots and had flown in combat against the Japanese. On occasion one of the instructors would encounter them flying formation and engaging in "dog-fights" with each other — activities strictly forbidden for us. What sort of disciplinary action would be appropriate for young men who would soon return home to fight and die? Time magazine gave good coverage to them in one issue and I was pictured playing ping-pong with one of the Chinese. I also had the pleasure of assisting them in writing their comments about the United States and their training.

A Flying Cadet had a busy schedule, very little free time, only an occasional weekend away from training. But duty calls and the conscientious man responds. When Lt. Gilmore, Commandant of Cadets, asked me to accompany a group of "Arizona Sunshine Girls" on a donkey trek into the mountains, for a Fox Movietone Travelogue movie short, I considered it a form of military order and accepted the assignment. It was shown several months later, after I was commissioned and married (which sort of go along together), and Kay and I saw it at an on-base theater. This adventure did not cause any great commotion. But, then...

Next, I reported to Lt. Gilmore to be asked (?) to pick out "another good-looking cadet" (his words) for an escort assignment. We were to be escorts for Janet Blair, at that time a rising young starlet.

I picked Jim Conlan — not that he was so good-looking, but that he would not be any competition. The movie people, in their publicity grooming for Miss Blair, wanted about a dozen cadets to be at the Camelback Inn outside Phoenix, to gather around Janet Blair at the piano, and to be pictured at the pool with other nubile young hopefuls. Then two of us took Blair and her companion to dinner and to a rodeo being held in town. When Kay had inquired why I had not written for some while, I had responded that we were so busy there just was not time. Then Look magazine published a big picture spread of us at the hotel, at dinner, and at the rodeo. Well! Try to explain that, will you?

Back to flying. Thunderbird had no runways, but two rather distinct landing areas: one, the paved ramp (Tarmac), part of which was used for parking aircraft, and two, the unpaved, grass area. Now consider several other

65

factors: the undercarriage, or main landing wheels, was quite narrow. The wheels were close together — called a "narrow tread"; the student pilot sits in the rear seat and, while taxiing or landing, cannot see directly ahead of the plane; there were no trees around the landing field, no markings on the paved ramp. So, I have been landing on the grass area where even the rows of grass give an indication of heading and direction, until one day I decide to land on the paved ramp, I do not get the tail down soon enough, the aircraft begins an indiscernible turn, too fast, it falls off on one wing tip, and I do what is called a "ground loop." Embarrassing,. Not a great amount of damage to the equipment, but a severe blow to the savoir faire. This requires a "check" ride which I pass easily. More...

Aside from aerobatics, we are subjected to a series of "stages," when the instructor demonstrates cross-wind landings, and 90, 180, and 360 degree overhead approaches. The idea is to gain confidence in when to cut the engine in order to land in the designated area. Can be quite tricky. So this one day, at one of the auxiliary practice fields, the instructor crawls out of the plane, engine running, and tells me to demonstrate these maneuvers.

When I finally land, he tells me I have gotten a perfect grade on the stages and cross-wind landings, ahead of all the other students, that I no longer have any tendency to ground-loop, and that I should fly back home (Thunderbird) and have the next student fly over. So, I fly back to Thunderbird, now full of confidence, elect to land on the paved ramp, make a very nice landing — until the very end. The airplane gets away from me, does a severe ground loop, and tears the wing all to hell. Oh boy!...

When my instructor learns what happened, he is practically in tears, for this errant performance requires that I have a check ride by one of the military check-pilots. I report to the flight line the next morning to find my instructor with his head in his hands. There on the schedule board, next to my name, is the name of the check pilot: Lt. Dreisbach -the "washing machine." Common knowledge that no one ever passes a check ride with him.

"Do the best you can," says Mr. Chapin, my instructor, with resignation.

"Yeah, - don't worry," my answer, as I strap on that butt-bumpin' silk parasol.

I had heard about some of the things that this discontented "I wanna go to combat" 2nd lieutenant had pulled on others. No conversation as we went to and climbed in the airplane and got started.

"Go ahead, take it on out, take off, climb to 500 feet and level off."

66

I had been told that his procedure was that as soon as you varied the altitude by 20 feet, he would knock the stick out of your hand, beat on the sides of the plane with both hands, and scream into the gosport..

Drifting slightly above 500 feet, I knocked the stick forward to get back on the precise altitude, banged on the side of the plane, looked up and smiled as he was looking quizzically at me in his mirror. His surprise and astonishment faded, the corners of his mouth curled up into what might have become a smile, and:

"I got it," he said, as he took the controls from me. For the better part of a half-hour he proceeded to perform some of the most spectacular, precise aerobatics I have ever experienced. Then:

"Take it back home and land," and I took the controls again, flew back to Thunderbird, landed on the Tarmack (the paved area), stayed right on the rudders with the needed corrections when tricky gusts of wind caught us, and brought the plane into the parking area safely. Lt. Dreisbach crawled out of the front seat, told me:

"Fill out the form, I have to go to the bathroom."

In the flight line operations building, Jim Chapin, my instructor, wanted to know:

"How'd it go? Did you pass? What did he say?

"One: I made the take-off and landing, but he did all the rest of the flying. Two: I don't know. Three: Said he had to go to the bathroom."

Later, Lt. Dreisbach told Chapin it was the best check ride he had ever had!

The total flying time allotted in primary training was 60 hours, which included a final check ride, but after we had all passed our 40-hour check ride and were practically assured of graduating from primary, a tailoring firm came on post and measured us for uniforms, the "pinks" and "greens" that army officers wore. Our class had not been issued the old cadet uniforms at the start of training, and after the start of the war we had to be in uniform when we went to town, so the decision was made to give us the uniform allowance for regular uniforms. When we wore the uniform into Phoenix we were mistaken for officers and saluted by the advanced cadets of Luke Field, who were still wearing the "cadet blues" - then, as we returned their salutes and they saw the cadet wings on our hats, they seemed to say something like "sonuvabitch" through clenched teeth, as we smiled and said hello. Always some lighter moments during stressful days.

I mentioned the engagement rings a little ways back. Along with a request of "Colonel" O.P. Hampton for permission to marry his daughter, that I had been dating for over four years, I sent Kay the ring for Christmas 1941. The military authorities had recommended that we wait until the end of basic training to get married. The saying was:

If you made it through basic, you were in the Army, meaning that you would get your commission and, presumably, your wings..Permission was granted and my bride-to-be concurred.

CHA PTER XIII

BASIC FLYING SCHOOL - & MARRIAGE

Gardner Field, Taft, California

Taft, California — little town about 25 miles southeast of Bakersfield which is 111 miles north (and slightly west) of Los Angeles and 129 miles east of San Luis Obispo. For the life of me, I can't remember how I got from Thunderbird Field, Phoenix, Arizona to Gardner Field, Taft, California. Maybe it was by train — or did I ride with someone who had a car? Dunno.

Whatever the mode of transport, I was at Gardner Field from February 24, 1942 until April 25, 1942. This was the Army, not a civilian contract base. We had Army instructors, mostly lieutenants, many of whom were desirous of being elsewhere — like fighting the war, instead of risking their lives trying to teach some of us unteachables. Not the country club atmosphere of Thunderbird Field, and regular army barracks, not little private rooms for two.

The first thing that greeted us, over in a corner, as we checked through supply, was a pile of bloody flight coveralls with bits of bones sticking out. An airplane had crashed just the day before — too much bottom rudder[38] on the turn into final approach, we were told. The BT-13, "Vultee Vibrator," was especially sensitive to an excess of bottom rudder. A very graphic lesson of the dangers of attempting to correct overshooting the final approach turn. Really makes you conscious of the problem. The accident actually happened, but was the evidence placed there to immmpress us?

Well, here we were, facing a bigger airplane, one with one low wing instead of the two wings that we were used to, a lot more instruments to try to figure out, and a propeller that was controllable — assuming you learned how to control it. And a sliding canopy that closed the cockpit so you couldn't feel the wind blowing about your ears. I guess that was good. But, aside from the controllable prop, the big thing was the radio, transmitter, receiver, and interphone, the whole bundle. Well!

---

38   The left pedal in left turn.

Several of our classmates had "previous" flying time before entering the flying cadet program. Private flying time. They had no trouble at all in primary: the airplane was similar in many respects to what they had already flown. Basic was different. The ones who had coasted through primary now began to have problems adapting to this larger, more complex aircraft. The wheels came off their coasters. As I remember, practically all of those who were "washed out" in basic were those with "previous" flying time.

Flying dual, the instructor was in the front cockpit, the student in the back one. Flying solo, the student took the front cockpit. Could see better from there. The radio switch was in the front cockpit. For some unexplainable reason, I never learned how to turn on the radio. The instructor always did it when we flew dual and I could never see what he was doing up there. Whatever ground school instruction we had on the system, I must have missed. So on my solo flights I would call the crew chief and he would reach somewhere in the cockpit and turn it on. I was always too embarrassed to ask one of them to show me the switch. When our frequent admonishment was "Keep your head out of the cockpit," I followed it literally and faithfully. Of course, it was meant to apply only when in flight.

Basic was our introduction to night flying. For the first time we were going to be flying out there in the dark! Before we actually got started many of us in the lower class would go down to the flight line at night to watch the pretty red, yellow and blue lights of the runways and taxiways and ramp, the white landing lights suddenly coming to life in the darkness over the field, descending to the ground and climbing off again to disappear in the dark sky, and the flaming torches dotting the air. Flaming torches? Having seen the long flames coming from the engine exhaust, as we observed them from a distance and on the ground, still did not prepare us for the experience of seeing those bright flames just inches away from our eyes as we flew. The flames were there in the daytime also, but not so readily apparent or visible as at night. Just a bit disconcerting at first.

The remarkably memorable event of basic training was MARRIAGE!. Kathryn Jarrell Hampton drove west with her mother, Kate Greer Hampton, AKA "Mamomma," when I wrote with the information that we could be married at the end of basic training which, according to those in the know, was when you were "in the Army." That you had, in other words, successfully passed the toughest part of the flying training. Later I wondered about this. Kay's father could not come west because he had business arrangements in New York and St. Louis and could not get away. We could have delayed the wedding until I graduated in June, figuring I might be able to get a few days leave, but things were pretty uncertain now that the war was underway and we had waited a long time already. (Over four years!) There were a million things to do: get permission to be married (supposed to have that to make it official), arrange for the wedding (reserve the chapel, clear the chaplain, get bridesmaid, best man, organist, soloist, officer to give the bride away, flowers and corsages, etc., etc.), arrange flying schedule and ground school courses to allow for 3-day pass, get the 3-day pass. I'm sure there were other details. But we got the date set for April 18, a Saturday, so that we would have Saturday, Sunday, and Monday, reporting back in on Tuesday to finish the week and graduate on April 25.

The Daily Midway Driller, Taft, California, Monday, April 20, 1942, announced on page 3:

Gardner Chapel
Scene of Wedding

The wedding of Miss Kathryn Jarrell Hampton and Cadet Bud Barbee, Jr., was solemnized Saturday afternoon at 1 o'clock in the Chapel at Gardner Field with Chaplain Estes Lewis officiating.

The bride wore a soft beige frock trimmed with dark brown and matching accessories. Her corsage was orchids.

Owing to the unavoidable absence of the bride's father, she was given in marriage by Lt. Randle Bennett. Mrs. Randle Bennett, in a frock of green with a corsage of talisman roses, was the bride's only attendant. Cadet Barbee was attended by Cadet Frank Morgan of Corning.

Cadet Dick Moore sang "Because" and "I Love You Truly" with Cadet Roy Baldwin of Pittsburg at the organ. Cadet Baldwin played Lohengrin's Wedding March and Mendelssohn's Recessional. (The scripture read was from the Book of Ruth, beginning: "Entreat me not to leave thee, or to return from following after thee: for whither thou goest, I will go.." We repeat it to this day.)

Mrs. Barbee is the daughter of Mr. and Mrs. Oscar P. Hampton of St. Louis, Missouri. She attended Washington University where she was president of her sorority, Delta Gamma and a member of Mortar Board the senior women's honor society. She is a sister of Major Oscar P. Hampton, Jr., and Captain Stanley F. Hampton, members of Washington University Medical Unit, stationed at Fort Benning, Georgia.

Cadet Barbee also attended Washington University where he became a member of Phi Delta (sic) fraternity. He is the son of Mrs. W.H. Ammerman of St. Louis and Bud Barbee of Nashville, Tennessee.

71

Following a short wedding trip in Hollywood the couple will make their home in Taft until the groom's transfer to another field.

The next column relates that the Gardner cadets will present a program about Gardner Field on Wednesday, April 22, and that:

"Bud Barbee, of Class 42-F will announce the program. This will be no new task for him as he performed this job at a radio station in St. Louis before entering the air corps. He also prepared the script for the show."

It was a busy time for me. The night before the wedding, a group of my "friends" converged on my room, held me down and shaved the hair from my personal parts. Some things can get confused during such a period.

Before the wedding, Kay and her mother were staying at a motel located on a hillside in Taft not too far from the field. One day, shortly before the wedding, I flew over the motel and tried some aerobatics just to show off a little. But nothing seemed to work quite right — fell out of the loops just as we got inverted, spun out of the snap rolls about three-quarters through the turn, and the slow rolls bore no resemblance to the desired maneuver. I reported the poor handling to the crew chief when he crawled up on wing after I had landed, taxiied to a parking spot on the ramp and shut down the engine. He appeared slightly shaken and asked me:

"What plane were you assigned to take?"

"Why, this one. Number 405," I replied.

"Yeah, but this is number 450, and this airplane is redlined for any aerobatics because of control problems. You're lucky you got back safely."

Which probably accounts for Lt. Simmons, our instructor, deciding to ride with me on our last night cross-country flight on Friday the 17th, the night thebefore the wedding. He had planned to ride with Jim Conlan who seemed to have problems with navigation, but decided he could keep in touch with him on the radio if he strayed. Good thing. When we hit our turning check-point on the Pacific coast, where we were to turn north on the next leg, Conlan kept heading to the west. After some frantic radio calls, we got him back on course and the flight proceeded smoothly. He would not have made it to Japan.

Our "short wedding trip in Hollywood" was just that. We left Gardner Field right after the ceremony, drove to Los Angeles, a little over two hours, and found the nice apartment that Mrs. Anita Knight, bubba Stanley's mother-in-law, had so graciously made available to us. Seems the apartment complex was owned by Dr. Gabler, Anita's father, and one unit had been reserved for us. It was high on a hill overlooking Hollywood. The first night we found a cozy litle restaurant that served French onion soup from a big tureen brought around to the tables. Onion soup has had a special place in our hearts since then, but we have not found any quite so good as that was. And we were so young and so in love (and still are over sixty years later).

We reported back to Gardner late on Monday and left again on Friday to drive to Williams Field, Chandler, Arizona, near Phoenix, to begin Advanced Training.

Somewhere I forgot to mention that Kay had driven from St. Louis, in her 1939 Ford convertible, with her mother (Mamomma). Guess you could call it her 'dowry.'

My basic pilot time was 71:20, including 2 hours in an AT-6A, plus 5:25 as a co-pilot when another student was practicing instrument flying. With the 60 hours in primary, a total of 130 hours. Not very much from the perspective of almost 6,000 hours later.

CHAPTER XIV

Advanced Flying School

The 'dowry' that Kathryn Hampton brought to our marriage was a slick little 1939 Ford convertible with a rumble seat. Don't know what a rumble seat is? Tell you: it is a seat for two that opens, front to rear, to form a seat back and expose the seat bottom, in the area where the trunk of the car would be. The passengers are entirely in the open, subject to wind and rain, even with the top up on the forward part of the car. As you might imagine, luggage or storage space is practically non-existent. Well, the rumble seat can hold a little luggage and we had a little on the trip from Gardner Field to Williams Field, Chandler, Arizona, a distance of about 550 miles. A two-day drive, no interstates at that time.

On the way to Phoenix from Taft, California, we stopped shortly in Los Angeles where Mamomma (Mrs. Hampton), joined by O.P. Hampton, had gone to visit relatives.

In those days, there was a long stretch of open highway between Phoenix and Chandler, Arizona. Today, Phoenix has expanded so much that there is no break in the streets or houses between the two cities. Camelback Inn, of some notoriety from primary training, was in a secluded area of the desert in 1941. Now it is just about in the middle of Phoenix.

Chandler wasn't really very much in those days, but Kay managed to find a nice little apartment with reasonable rent; I was making $75 a month, less required haircut and laundry charges. This apartment was upstairs over a private garage and overlooked an automobile graveyard. There were open wooden stairs leading up to the apartment, and scorpions scurried about under the bottom stair.

May and June in the Arizona desert — hot! But our little evaporative cooler, high on the wall, made life bearable. This "cooler" consisted of a fan blowing through a panel of excelsior-like material saturated with water slowly dripping from above. In any event Kay survived it. (Our barracks were NOT air-conditioned). I had only a few weekends to spend there, being restricted to the air base all during the week and some weekends. Kay frequently met me at the base during evening free time. She was the only cadet bride and seemed to get lots of attention from the single officer instructors.

The aircraft of advanced flying training (the AT-9) were more like "real" airplanes: retractable landing gear, controllable props, full instrumentation (for those days). Williams Field was considered training for multi-engine (bomber/transport) and nearby Luke Field for single engine or fighters. As we see later, it didn't quite work out that way. Luke trained in the North American AT-6[39] while we flew the Curtiss AT-9, a low-wing, twin-engine monoplane. Our instrument training was in the AT-6 and the BT-13, as were any acrobatic endeavors. The AT-9 was all metal — no fabric covering of fuselage or control surfaces — had side-by-side seating of pilot and co-pilot and was completely electric. We thought of it as having one speed: 120 mph for take-off, climb, cruise, and landing. The instructors demonstrated a full-flap landing and told us never to try it alone: the craft seeemed to duck down and head its nose right for the ground. About like a rock. A really, really steep descent. After we got comfortable with the AT-9, most of us had to try this prohibited maneuver at least once — quite thrilling.

The emphasis in advanced flying school was on precision flying. We all knew how to fly, now every flight accented how to fly right, to fly the Army way. Smooth but positive handling of the controls. Perfect execution of climbs and descents. Maintenance of prescribed altitude within +/- ten feet. Precision spot landings. Recovery from unusual positions. All aspects of flight, both visually and under-the-hood instrument flight. We still had drill periods and military formations and academics, but the cadet "nonsense" hazing was almost non-existent. Relationship with the upperclass was more relaxed, and the instructors (all Army) did their best to bring out our best. It was accepted that we were likely to become brothers-in-arms, officers and gentlemen.

In primary, Lt. Gilmore, the Commandant of Cadets, had told me that I would probably not make a very good second lieutenant, or even a good first lieutenant, that not until I was a captain would I be a really effective officer. So I had told him that I would try to waste as little time as possible along the way. After six months as a second looey and seven months as a first lieutenant, I was promoted to captain at the same time as my instructor at Williams who was a first lieutenant while I was a cadet. More later on promotions.

---

39   After the war, the AT-6 became the T-6 and soon was used as a primary trainer. Later the T-28, with tricycle landing gear, replaced the T-6, followed by the Cessna T-37, the primary jet trainer with side-by-side seating. As late as 1966, the Brazilian Air Force was using the T-6 as a counter-insurgency weapon: drop hand grenades, fire 30-mm machine guns.

Exciting things still happened. One night, about two weeks before graduation, returning from shooting landings at an auxiliary field, with another cadet in the right seat as copilot, we lost all electric power. No lights. No radio. Our flashlights sufficed to see the instruments and the controls in the cockpit, but were of no use for signalling or landing. The most critical part was to find an opening in the steady stream of other planes, merely blinking lights like so many fireflies, in the landing pattern.

The landing procedure was to enter the downwind leg at an angle of forty-five degrees, proceed to the base leg (90 degrees to the wind) and then to the final approach into the wind. This we now had to do with no way of letting the control tower or other aircraft know where we were or where we were going. With no electrical power for lowering the landing gear, we went through the procedure for lowering them manually, but we had no way of knowing whether the wheels were down or not.

Well, we landed. Probably the best landing I had ever made. But no wheels. We slid along the runway for quite a distance, the engines stopped when the prop tips bent.

"Before you get out," I told my copilot, "let's double-check that all switches are off."

At that moment there was a "thump" on the right wing and we saw the taillight and exhaust of another plane as it bounced into the air. Later we learned that it was a student in a BT-13 who was not using his landing lights and had turned his radio down and did not hear the radio warning not to land because we were on the runway. He explained that all the "chatter" on the radio bothered his concentration, so he had turned it off.

After all flying was over for the night his plane was located by some minor damage on the underside of his left wing. He had not reported the incident because he claimed he did not know he had hit another aircraft. Thought it was just a "rough landing." Had we not delayed momentarily to clear all switches, my copilot would have been killed by that dunderhead.

I was instructed to report to the school secretary (an officer) the following morning. "You will have to appear before the Flying Evaluation Board," he said, "and we need to know whether you wish to go to navigator or bombardier training or return to civilian life and wait to be drafted."

"Nobody ever passes the Flying Evaluation Board," he told me. I said I would take my chances.

The FEB met the following day, interviewed me in great detail about the flight and all the circumstances. It was obvious that they did not believe that I had gone through all the emergency procedures for lowering the gear.

They questioned my instructor about my flying record, my military performance, my academic performance. All well above average. When he came out of the hearing, he was near tears. He had never 'lost' a student. There was not much hope.

After the Board had deliberated about an hour, and was about to make their decision, the Engineering Officer dashed into the headquarters and entered the hearing room.

He had just completed thorough testing of the landing gear, found that the control wires were cut, and that it was impossible for me to lower the gear by any means. Seems that the control wires had been cut almost completely through, with just a few strands uncut, and that those strands failed after I had finished shooting landings at the auxiliary field.

Exonerated! But had the Engineering Officer been one minute later, the Board would have eliminated me from flying, case closed.

Later it became known that there had been many acts of sabotage on training bases throughout the United States.

The last week or so of training went by without further excitement and we came to GRADUATION! and COMMISSIONING! and rating as PILOTS!

CHAPTER XV

Second Lieutenant - First Assignment

June 23, 1942: big day! Graduation from advanced flying school, *"the President has appointed and commissioned you in the Army of the United States" as 2nd Lieut. Air-Res, with serial number O-726183, and Special Orders Number 136: "By direction of the President, and having satisfactorily completed the prescribed course of instruction as Aviation Cadets (Pilot), and having accepted appointments as Second Lieutenants Air-Res.,...the following named Second Lieutenant Air-Res, is with his consent ordered to active duty," and, Personnel Orders No. 149: is "rated PILOT, under the provisions of Army Regulations 95-60, War Department, 1941."*

And my dear wife was there to pin those silver wings and gold bars on me.

For months, at times it seemed eons, we had looked upon second lieutenants as gods. Maybe little gods, but achievable gods. Now we were one. Captains and above were stratospheric figures with which we had little to do. Our goal was to get those golden bars and pin on those silver wings — one and inseparable. We had been "lower class" and were ready to step into the higher realms of officer-hood. Following promotions were always welcomed and always exciting, but this was the step, the sine qua non, the end anticipated at the beginning, and the beginnning of a new beginning. We were officers and gentlemen and PILOTS! Impossible to put into words the feeling. We had done what we started out to do. We had "reached the unreachable goal." For this day, at least, we were fulfilled.

(Slight break in this chapter for a few days. We have had a most interesting visit from our daughter, her daughter, and our great-grandson. Then we left Florida to attend my 50th class reunion at Washington University in St. Louis. Stopped in Murfreesboro TN on the way to St. Louis.

This is now May 17, 1990, and we are waiting for Kay to finish her toilet — now drying her hair — so we can go to the first occasion, the "signing in" or registration — supposed to be from 2 till 5. The Golden Anniversary Cocktail Party is from 6 to 8 at the Alumni House, which I hope we can find. It may be where Pepper Throop lived when her father was chancellor of the university. At the time we referred to it somewhat irreverently as "the shack." My wife was enticed to go shopping for shoes by her niece, Suzanne

Hampton, in whose house we are staying. Took longer than expected and we are now running a little later than I had hoped for, but no big deal. Weather here has been awful — rain for weeks, severe flooding throughout the area, but today has turned beautiful — sun shining and temperature just perfect. We must have brought this from Florida.

Found the Alumni House OK — saw no one at the sign in, but quite a few had gathered by the time of the cocktail party. Have to review the anniversary booklet to remember all who were there. Some I could not recognize, even after I saw their name tags.

Thursday night, Suzanne and Bud had Elise and Bob, Anne and Mike, Hamo and Arnie and Stephanie and later Jimmy, Hila and Dan and Dustin and Devin. Bud barbecued hamburgers in the rain on their little side porch. His rain gear was quite a sight Evening ended with strong disagreement between Bud and Hamo. So, what's new?

Up early Friday morning for robing in cap and gown and graduate hoods to march in the processonal. Continental breakfast was available, but most were too busy talking to others to eat. Some conspicuous absences from the march date. Hope some of the pictures of us in our finery are good.

All occasions were splendid! The old friends, the good friends, the well-remembered acquaintances and some not so well-remembered. Probably get back to more nostalgia later on in this rambling, but right now these quotes come to mind:

"It's true: you can't go home again. Home isn't just a place, it's a period in time, too, and while you can look up old haunts, you can't turn back the clock. And yet, if someone were to try to recover the past, he might learn something...for one does not, after all, lose one's childhood; it lives on even under the debris of years."

[Article by Egon Schwarz in WU Magazine 1988 No. 1. - writing about return to Vienna after many years.]

Day after we returned from reunion Lynne came home from Nicaragua.)

Back to the new second lieutenants -

Orders for our first assignments as officers were published and distributed early on the 24th of June: Special Orders Number 137, par 6:

"PAC in TWX, AFPMP V 3480, Washington, D.C., the following-named Second Lieutenants AAF are reld fr further asgmt and duty and WP fr this

sta on or about 25 June 1942 to sta indicated reporting upon arrival thereat to the CO for asgmt and duty."

About 30 went to Fourth AF, March Field, California, and the rest of us, about 70, went to Second AF, Salt Lake City, Utah.

Very scientific assignment:
0726181 thru 0726221 to 2nd AF
0726222 thru 0726235 to 4th AF
0726236 thru 0726270 to 2nd AF
0726272-74-76-78-80-82-86-87-88-89-90-91-92-94 to 4th AF and the missing numbers were ordered to duty as instructors at Williams Field. This was a way to disguise having Frank Morgan, 0726283, who had known the base commander (Col Herb Grills) for many years, retained as an instructor.

Those of us going to the "repple depple" (replacement depot) in Utah got together and agreed we would take the full allotted travel time and arrive there at the same time. About a dozen, however, decided they would go on ahead to get there first and get the choice assignments. By the time the rest of us arrived they had reported in, been given their orders and were gone: to Wendover Field, Utah, a place out in the "boonies" (the boondocks)—the salt flats of Utah, a miserable base.

The rest of us, along with groups from Luke Field and Stockton Field, reported in on June 29, were told that an even number of pilots were to be sent to Davis-Monthan in Tucson, Arizona, and to Geiger Field, Spokane, Washington. If we could split ourselves evenly, we could take our choice. I chose Geiger Field because I had never been to Washington state and had just come from Arizona. (Turned out to be a good choice.)

After a little "jockeying" around, we were evenly divided and orders were cut..The Geiger Field group was assigned to the Thirty Fourth Bombardment Group (H). Most of our Williams Field group were further assigned to the 7th Bombardment Squadron (H).

During the month of July I flew over forty hours in the B-24, and qualified as an instructor pilot. On 30 July, I and a couple of other pilots flew Col Eugene L. Eubank, Hq II Bomber Command, and Col Nathan B.Forrest, Hq Second Air Force, on an inspection tour of *"Army Air Base, Salt Lake City, Utah, thence to Army Air Base, Wendover Field, Utah, thence to Albuquerque, New Mexico, thence to Army Air Base, Alamogordo, New Mexico, thence to Army Air BAse, Davis-Monthan Field, Tucson, Arizona, thence to March*

80

Field, California, in connection with matters pertaining to the Second Air Force..." and return.

On the leg from Tucson to March Field we planned our route through a pass in the Rockies. In those days the aircraft were not pressurized and oxygen masks were required for flight above 10,000 feet. To avoid that, we chose going through a pass rather than over the mountains.

As I was blithely heading for the pass, Col Eubank (an old man of about 40) came into the cockpit, adjusted his bifocals, scrutinized the chart, and "suggested" that the pass we were looking for was "just a little south" of the one that was on my present course. Naturally, he was right. Takes a little wind out of the sails for a "hot pilot" second lieutenant.

There was more. Just before we arrived at March Field, Col Eubank said he would like to try the landing at March, if I didn't mind. He proceeded to "grease it" onto the runway, hauled the yoke back into his belly and scraped the tail skid along the runway, slowing the plane down until he could gently ease the nose wheel down for a perfectly timed landing. Then he explained:

"You see, son, the brakes on this plane are pretty expensive but that pad on the tail skid costs only about twenty five cents to replace, and it is a good way to help slow down initially." Yessir!

At Wendover, imagine a couple of runways, a few scattered barracks and other buildings, out in a salt desert, no town in sight, no trees, no vegetation. At Wendover I found my classmates, who jumped ahead of the rest of us to get the choice assignments, were flying as co-pilots in B-24s and had not even touched the controls because their pilots had so little experience that they could not trust anyone else. And I was an instructor flying VIPs on a tour. The moral:

Don't try to beat the system. I later learned, through a LIFE MAGAZINE article, that this particular outfit, sent to England as a unit, became known as the "Clay Pigeon Squadron," because it was routinely attacked and shot down by the Germans regardless of position in the group formation. Very few survived. Ironic about getting "the choice assignments."

Not long after we arrived in Spokane, the group which had chosen Davis-Monthan in Arizona were transferred to Geiger Field. By that time, practically all the available housing was gone. We had found a nice apartment in a good section of Spokane.

Shortly after the outfit from Davis-Monthan arrived, the new squadron operations officer, a captain, told me I was being transferred to Moses Lake, near Ephrata, Washington. Another isolated base with no housing and no provisions for dependents. Then he wanted to know if I would mind if he talked to our landlord about renting our apartment when we left. I said no.

Kay, meanwhile, had met and come to know a woman in the same building, a Betsy Rendle. While having coffee with her, Kay mentioned that we were going to be transferred — it looked as if the captain wanted our apartment — and she didn't know what to do.

"Do you have your orders yet?" Betsy asked. "No? Well, in the Army you don't pack until you have your orders. so just sit tight."

When Kay told me about this, I made the connection: Col Rendle[40] was our group commander! He evidently did not approve of selecting officers for reassignment on the basis of the desirability of their living quarters. The next day my orders to Moses Lake were cancelled.

Not long afterward, several of us were selected (properly this time) for assignment to Alaska and our names were posted on the squadron operations bulletin board. Before I went home, I ran into one of my classmates, Lt. James A. Jones, at the Officers Club bar.

"Hey, Barbee! Hear you're on the list to go to Alaska."

"Yeah, that's right."

"You're married aren't you? Do you want to go to Alaska?"

"Not particularly excited about it."

"Do you mind if I volunteer to see if I can go in your place? I'd like to go where there might be some action."

---

40   Beau Rendle was a reserve officer, called to active duty from his job as an airline pilot. Of course, he had more flying time than practically any of the regular Army pilots. A lot of this time involved instrument flying on the radio ranges. Radio ranges were the most sophisticated navigation facility of those days. The other navigational aid was the "light line," lights scattered across the country which blinked a Morse code signal identifiable by referring to the aeronautical chart of the region. The radio ranges broadcast two signals: an "A" (dot dash) and an "N" (dash dot), the A directed to the quadrants containing North and South, the N directed to the easterly and westerly quadrants. Where the A and N signals came together, a "leg" was formed which contained a solid sound in which the A and N overlapped to create a single "buzz." Directly over the broadcasting station there was a "null" or "cone of silence" where there was no sound. If an airfield were nearby, one of these "legs" assisted the aircraft in an approach to that field. By a system of "range orientation" a pilot on instruments could "fix" his aircraft on the proper "beam." Beau Rendle had the consummate skill of being able to fly through one of these legs or beams and be able to tell how far he was from the broadcasting station. I never encountered anyone else who could do that.

"Fine with me. You have my permission to try."

The next day my name was scratched and Jones got what he wanted.

Almost one year to the day later, after having been assigned in the interim to Walla Walla, Washington, Rapid City, South Dakota, and Ainsworth,Nebraska, many of us returned to Geiger Field, Spokane. Who is there but 2nd Lt. Jones, freshly returned from Alaska, who takes one look at me — I have now been promoted to captain - and just about blows his top. C'est la guerre.

That summer, Damma (my mother, Rose Ammerman), took the train from St. Louis to Spokane and visited with us a few days before going on to California where my brother lived. This was her first opportunity to see her son decked in his military regalia, but it was primarily necessary for her to check on her daughter-in-law, to see if I were being fed and taken care of properly. She approved.

My lovely bride had never been in an airplane, so that summer I had to show her how I could do it. We rented a Waco open cockpit, biplane and went flying in, around, and over the surrounding hills, helmet, and goggles, and scarf flying in the wind.. Looking back at her I could tell she was enjoying the ride.

When it came time to go home, we were up a coupla thousand feet so I throttled back and started to glide down. Every few hundred feet, I would advance the throttle, gun the engine a little, and throttle back again. After having done this a few times I noticed my passenger had a worried look on her face. Then I realized that she did not understand that (1) throttling back allowed us to descend without picking up too much airspeed, and (2) periodically advancing the power was to "clear" the engine and keep it warm. I smiled reassuringly, I hoped, and explained what had been happening after we were safely back on the ground.

During July and August I accumulated about 84 hours in the B-24D, In September we changed to the B-17F. After five landings in an hour and a half, I was checked out as an instructor pilot. We didn't waste much time in those days. Flew a total of 43:35 that September.

In the middle of the month two of us out of the original group from Williams, Luke, and Stockton, were transferred to the 88th Bomb Group, 317th Bomb Squadron: I had crew #17, and James P. Kiernan had crew #18. Many of the others in our original group were sent overseas as individual replacements. We began training for combat, and on September 29, 1942, Special Orders No. 271 ordered "...a temp change of station. Travel by privately owned conveyance is not authorized. Travel by dependents, packing and crating and shipment of household affects (sic) are not authorized..." and most of our group proceeded to AAB, Walla Walla, Wash., by rail.

CHAPTER XVI

We Train For War

Some of us flew the airplanes to the new station, others took the train, and the wives, now our camp followers, drove down in our "privately owned conveyances."

At Walla Walla we went on sustained combat crew training: restricted to the post, we lived in the barracks and BOQs, adhered to a schedule that, for some unknown reason, was changed regularly, with an unforeseen result that some of us flew only night missions for a month. We didn't know what the ground looked like in the daylight. I got lost on my first daylight flight: there were none of those friendly little lights, scattered around the countryside, blinking at me, guiding me home to my stretch of concrete runway.

We would land anytime between 0200 and 0600, do calisthenics illuminated by Jeep headlights, shower, have dinner (?), and meet our wives who had come on base to go to the picture show (movies?) with us. Then it was time for us to go to bed and get our eight hours of rest. Sometime around 2 to 4 pm, we had breakfast (?), proceeded to ground school and instrument trainer lessons, then had lunch maybe around 8 to 10 pm before getting ready to fly again.

Now, those meal hours just did not fit in with the regular mess hours. You might want eggs during the early hours of the morn, and maybe a nice meal of meat and potatoes at a normal dinner time. But you didn't get what you wanted. The only thing that seemed adaptable to our schedule was pork chops! We had pork chops for breakfast when we got up in the early afternoon, pork chops for lunch in the late evening, and pork chops for dinner in the wee hours of the morning. And fried. Over fifty years later, I still do not like fried pork chops.

Now the wives - our camp followers. Only a few of us 2nd Looeys had wives and they drove down from Spokane to Walla Walla, rented motel rooms which were just across the road from the end of the most-used runway, watched for our signals (from the cockpit we could key lights on the underside of the aircraft) as we took off and landed. After we landed, the women would drive out to watch our calisthenics by Jeep-light and we would go to the movie - sometime between 2 and 4 a.m.

Our training had begun in earnest. We flew as a crew: Pilot (nowadays called Aircraft Commander) - 2nd Lt Bud Barbee; CoPilot-2nd Lt Ralph W. Emerts; Navigator (who used maps, charts, sextant, calculators, and a drift-meter to determine our position and headings) — 2nd Lt Hilliary H. Turner; Bombardier (who used maps and the highly classified Norden bombsight to bring us over the target, flipped a switch to open the bomb-bay doors, accept-ed control of the plane from the pilot during the final bomb run, released the bombs, and advised the pilot "Bombs away") - 2nd Lt Warren J. Harris; AEG (Aerial Engineer Gunner) S/Sgt Joe Kray; ROG (Radio Operator Gunner) Sgt Shirl J. Hoffman; Gunners: Sgt John N. Knapp Jr, Sgt William L Davis, Sgt Joseph J Paquin.

The navigator and bombardier sat below the pilot and copilot in the nose of the plane and manned the 50-caliber machine guns mounted there; the flight engineer monitored all systems and operated the top turret: two 50 caliber machine guns mounted in a swiveling turret that could fire in all directions; the radio operator maintained voice and Morse code contact with ground agencies, headquarters and operated one of the side-mounted machine guns; the three gunners operated a side gun, the tail guns, and the lower ball-turret guns — the ball-turret went to the smallest of the three gun-ners. Thus there were ten 50-caliber machine guns that each aircraft could fire at attackers.

We continued our cross-country navigational missions, using celestial navigation by the navigator, pilotage (map reading) by the pilots and naviga-tor. More frequent dropping of practice (loaded with sand) bombs on des-ignated bombing ranges. Firing at targets towed by fighter aircraft. Some of these tow-target aircraft were piloted by WASPs, the Women Auxiliary Service Pilots, and whenever our gunners would move up on the long cotton/rayon sleeve tow-target and get too close to the towing aircraft, we would be treated to some very salty, unladylike comments from the female pilot. The first time this happened we were quite surprised and astonished at this female's utterances. Aerial firing at a moving target is different from firing at stationary targets.

Flying at altitude — 15,000 to 25,000 — was also different. Not only the requirement for wearing oxygen masks, and dressing warmly for the cold air, but the performance and handling of the airplane. The air is thinner and the engines require much more attention. Carburetor icing can occur before you know it, and engine power is reduced. Flying at altitude in for-mation adds other factors. Moisture inside the plane becomes frost all over the windshield. You have to keep rubbing the glass to clear a small spot so that you can see the other aircraft and maintain your relative position. Just a little more trying than formation flying below 10,000 feet, where we would form up after take-off and climb to altitude as a squadron or group of nine to twenty-five aircraft.

At one time we were issued electrically heated suits, like full-length long johns, socks, and gloves. We could wear these under our regular light weight cotton flying coveralls and be comfortable. A lot more comfortable than the heavy fleece-lined leather jackets, trousers, boots and gloves. But, it wasn't long before we realized that an electrical failure meant no heat (at minus 40 degrees), and if we had to bail out we would likely freeze on the way down to warmer zones. Back to the heavy leather clothing.

The rigors of this training were endurable and we could see the increase in our proficiency, as individuals in our own field of endeavor, and as a team becoming more able to perform our assigned function. I flew 77 hours and 20 minutes that month. The visits by the wives were like stolen moments of pleasure. And the Washington apples were delicious.

On 26 October 1942, Special Orders No. 111, transferrred our entire 88th Bombardment Group (H) to Rapid City S.D., "...so as to arrive thereat on or about 31 Oct 42, RUAT CO, thereat."[41] Again, we fly the airplanes to the new station, no shipment of household goods (we didn't have any), and the wives drove the cars. Kay made the trip over the Continental Divide accompanied by Mickey Howard, a brash, good-looking blonde. From our acquaintance with Lt. Howard and his wife, Mickey, we formed our opinion of the life style of Californians: they had an agreement that if they saw some-one else that attracted them at a party they could go spend the night with that person. Wild! My wife did not trust me around her. Sometimes I wasn't sure of me either.

---

41   RUAT CO, thereat: "Reporting Upon Arrival Thereat to the Commanding Officer, thereat." Redundancy!

CHAPTER XVII

We Train Others for War

When we arrive at the air base in the Black Hills of South Dakota, a few miles from Gutzon Borglum's awe-inspiring Mount Rushmore sculptures of Presidents Washington, Jefferson, Lincoln and Theodore Roosevelt, we find that we are now a training group, experienced enough to begin training other crews headed for the theaters of war. The new pilots have just finished a transition period of about twenty hours into B-17s from their training aircraft.

The B-17s which they have been flying were stripped down models, lacking armorplate, guns, turrets, etc., and therefore very light weight in comparison to what we fly. The performance and handling is quite different. And that causes some problems as they offer: "We learned to take off at this speed, climb at this speed, cruise at this RPM and manifold pressure, land at this speed, use this amount of flaps." And so forth and so forth. Now we have to re-educate. We have to begin to break down their notion that they know how to handle the combat aircraft.

My approach as an instructor: "Look, this is the way we do it in this plane. We know this is the best way because we have tried all the other ways. We want you to learn to do it our way, forget how you have been flying, and do it the way we tell you to. After you learn how to do it the way we show you and tell you, and you think you know a better way, then you will have the opportunity to show us how you used to do it, but until then fly the way we show you. After you have learned these new techniques and still think you know a better way, tell us. If your way is really better, we will change and do it your way." Of course, as they came to see and feel the differences in the combat aircraft from the stripped models, they never felt the need to go back to their first methods.

We began to get these new trainees, not long out of flying school, who had already been promoted to first lieutenant. It just did not seem right to me that we "older" pilots should be outranked by the trainee. And I told Captain Piper, our squadron commander so. He agreed. "Fill out the promotion papers and I will sign them." The orderly room, our administrative people, were responsible for knowing how and doing the paper work, but I felt that this was important to me, so I read the regulations, carefully typed the forms, and submitted them for signature. My friends, also second lieutenants, did

not agree with this approach and said they would follow the proper procedure and have the orderly room clerk do it. Their forms were returned for
correction several times. I was promoted a couple of months ahead of them,
31 December 1942, six months from commissioning. Not too bad.

Kay and several of the other wives had found a house with a number of
bedrooms, and a basement that could be partitioned off to give some degree
of privacy. They tried to work it out so that when a husband was able to leave
the base overnight, he and his spouse would have a little privacy. Fortunately,
this arrangement did not have to be in existence very long. The wives soon
began to have a few little differences. One wife insisted that too much toilet
paper was being used and that they would have to economize; cut down on
the showers and hot water. She did not, however, want to economize on the
liquor bill they all shared. Some decided they were going to make changes,
some structural, in the house. At the end of less than one month, Kay got
out.

Our orders came on 27 November 1942 transferring us from the 88th
Group to the 383rd Bomb Group, Special Orders No. 107, and sending us
in the newly formed 540th Bomb Sq to Ainsworth, Nebraska, where an airfield had just been completed. Naturally we flew our airplanes to this new
location, designated a "satellite" field to the Rapid City Army Air Base. Our
group headquarters and other squadrons remained at Rapid City.

Most of the wives agreed that, because Ainsworth looked like such a
small spot on the map with probably very limited, if any, available housing, it
would be better for the men to go on ahead, find a place to live and then send
for them. Kay realized the fallacy of that thinking: the men were not going
to have much time to go looking for quarters, and, because housing would
be limited, it was going to be first come first served. So she drove on down
immediately and was the first wife to arrive. Ainsworth, Nebraska, is about
250 miles southeast of Rapid City. She found that the only place available
was the house of the newspaper editor and publisher who had gone to south
Texas for the winter. Fully furnished and the price was right, after we were
accepted as tenants. Knowing our history of moving every few months, it
seemed OK to accept a "temporary" house. Two bedrooms, it was more than
we needed, so Kay invited the Fosters, Lt. James and Betty, to share with us
until they could find another. We would share the rent, groceries, and tending
of the coal-burning hot-air heat furnace located in the basement. There was
one large, about two foot square, grating in the living room that heated the
whole house. It got so hot that you could not walk on it with your bare feet.
Feeding the furnace was somewhat of a chore. Headspace was limited in the

basement so I had to assume a slightly stooped posture to remove clinkers, shake down the ashes, and shovel in some more coal. Learned to bank the fire at night fairly expertly. I guess the furnace was effective in heating the house, but I can remember once that the glass in the front door had about a quarter of an inch of frost. That was when the outside temperature got down to minus thirty degrees.

The Fosters stayed with us for a few weeks and then rented part of the house next door when it became available. They might have moved anyway. Some food items were rationed. You had to have "coupons" to buy certain things, like sugar. We had to use a lot of our sugar ration to make chocolate syrup to go over vanilla ice cream. I have a long standing addiction to vanilla ice cream. If we were having vanilla ice cream, the Fosters liked chocolate sauce over over it. Sometime later Betty admitted that the real reason they moved next door was vanilla ice cream with chocolate syrup every night. They liked it, but not every night. Why not?

About coincidental with my promotion to first lieutenant, Capt Piper was promoted to major and was replaced by Capt Wayne Eveland, a newcomer to our squadron. Wayne and wife Dawn needed a place to stay, so when the Fosters went next door, we invited the Evelands to share with us. Wayne was a little runt of a guy, smallest feet I have ever seen on a man. And what a picky eater! At the reception buffet in honor of Major Piper's promotion, Wayne said he didn't like the food that was being served and put absolutely nothing on his plate. While we were sharing the house, he had the same approach that he had had at home with his mother: if he didn't like what she had prepared, he got out the peanut butter and made himself a sandwich. Not a bad guy, really, but maybe a little stuffy.

I often thought his greatest redeeming quality was loving and tolerating his wife, Dawn. The girl seemed to have no convictions of her own. No original idea, I'm sure, was ever germinated in her brain — if there was a brain. On any subject whatsoever there was always one of two authoritative declarations from this nitwit: "I know this (whatever) is true because my mother told me," or "I know this (whatever) is true because I read it." It didn't matter what the subject was or where she had read it. A book. A newspaper. An advertisement for a patent medicine. Anything. Suffice that it was printed. Anything printed was gospel, inherently true. "People can't print things that aren't true." You can well imagine the degree of mental stimulation she imparted to those around her. A nice girl, not bad looking, but...cheez.

We didn't socialize much with the Evelands — no more than absolutely necessary with two couples living in the same house. And we did not have all that much time in the same house. They also found another place after about a month. The owner of our house was scheduled to return about April, Kay was quite pregnant with Kit, our firstborn, facilities at the local hospital were not all that great, so we gave up the house at the end of March (1943) and Kay took the train from Ainsworth to St. Louis, home to mother for the big occasion — Mamomma's "baby" was going to have her first baby.

In other ways, too, Ainsworth was an interesting time.. I said that the airfield was new. We were the first military occupants of what had been a nice farm. The three runways formed a rough triangle around what was once the old farmhouse and family graveyard. We had to actually build some of the buildings we were going to use, one of which was a small officers' club, complete with a bar of sorts. Each officer had at least one extra duty. Mine was mess officer, a traditional assignment for second johns. It was there I learned from the mess sergeant why extract of vanilla was kept locked up after meals:

"Some of these guys get addicted to vanilla and will really get drunk on it, just like alcohol."

Christmas Day we put on a show for the folks in town. I'm sure some will remember it to this day. We took off, assembled in a tight formation, and flew right down main street at roof top level. Made quite an impression on the natives. I can't recall that anyone got much too upset about this little bit of exuberance.

There was no radio beacon, no navigational facility of any sort at the field. When the weather got "down" we would use the "iron beam" to find our way home. That's what the railroad was called. Just follow the tracks until you find the base. Once I was low enough to clip a haystack with my right wingtip as I followed the tracks home. No damage. Many times we would have to time our flight very carefully from the last check-point, estimate when we were over the field, ask the tower operators to shine their biscuit gun[42] up through the overcast, and we would look for the light as it illuminated the cloud layer. Took some doing, but it worked. Then we would execute what was called a low-visibility approach. This involved taking the heading of the runway, flying a determined number of seconds, making timed turns and descending until we could make visual contact with the ground, then pulling up into a precisely timed 360 degree turn and come in for an approach. It's a lot

---

42   The "biscuit gun," so-called because of its round shape, is a high-powered search light - it could be used green to signal take off clearance, red to hold in position, and white for cloud penetration or spotlighting.

better today with ILS and GCA.[43] During the four-month stay at Ainsworth, I flew about 173 hours under occasionally exciting conditions.

Life should be an unending learning process. Many of the things I learned during the first six months of being a pilot have been long forgotten, but of all the incidents and experiences at Ainsworth, one sticks in memory. And it had nothing to do with flying or the military. It went this way: over a period of years the Army Air Corps and, later, the Air Force, had the notion that skeet shooting would sharpen our eyes and condition our reflexes as aircrew members. Thus we had shotguns available. Frequently some of the guys would take a Jeep and some shotguns and go hunting on the "reservation" which encompassed a coupla square miles. I think I mentioned that there were the remains of an old farmhouse and family graveyard inside the triangle formed by our runways. Being a city boy, and my Dad did not hunt, I had never had the opportunity to go into "the wilds" and bring out food for the table, so I joined a friend one day, borrowed a Jeep, checked out some shotguns, and went in search of "game." After bouncing around the old farm on the Vehicle, General Purpose, we flushed a rabbit, chased it into the graveyard, and I dismounted to continue on foot. Carefully cornering the small burrowing mammal of the family Leporidae, I knew I had him, and he knew it too. Caught in the very corner of the fence, this furry little creature turned, stood on his hind legs, faced me in an attitude of supplication and I blew his head off with that shotgun. Mighty hunter! Arrggghhh! Stunned by this act of deliberate murder of an animal that had done me no harm, tears welled in my eyes as I looked at the mutilation. I put the gun in the Jeep, said "Let's go home," and never went hunting again. That was over sixty years ago and the picture is still clear in my mind.

As I said, Kay went back to St. Louis at the end of March and I moved into our rather Spartan barracks at the field for a very short time until our squadron was transferred back to Rapid City. March and April brought some sieges of rather nasty weather. While we would wait for enough clearing to take-off, I got in a lot of poker playing. And Kathryn Greer Barbee was born in Deaconess Hospital, St. Louis, on April 20, 1943.

Getting on toward the end of May (1943), when Kit was about five weeks old and considered old enough to do some traveling, I was able to

---

43   ILS = Instrument Landing System - ground electronics that signal cockpit instruments which the pilot can use to fly his aircraft to runway heading and glide path. GCA = Ground Controlled Approach - instruments on the ground showing the aircraft position which the operators use to direct the pilot to the proper heading and glide path. The military has favored GCA, commercial pilots have favored ILS.

get leave to go to St. Louis to greet my increased family and move them to Rapid City where our group was training a couple of Provisional Groups. The Provisional Groups consisted of aircrews, already composed, being trained to go to the various theaters of war (England, Africa, the Pacific) to serve as replacements for crews which had been lost to enemy action or who had completed their number of assigned missions and rotated home.

It seems that we did a lot of traveling by train in those days. There were trains connecting almost every town in the United States. It was faster and easier than going by private automobile, and more reliable than air travel. Kay had checked with the pediatrician regarding a travel formula for Kit and was ready to go. Bear in mind: in those days everything got boiled. Boil the bottles. Boil the nipples. Boil the water. So traveling involved some planning and preparation. Young mother Kathryn may have more to add to this later. In any case, we got to Rapid City, found an apartment with Mrs. Hudspeth, a most accommodating gal, and Kit developed the 6-week colic. Cried all the time. Poor thing. Kay would be exhausted at the end of the day and I would take over for the evening. Rock the baby, croon a little, and read a book. Soon both of us were asleep. Was able to get all the way through The Robe. Remember the story to this day. Kit recovered and so did we.

HEADQUARTERS
RAPID CITY ARMY AIR BASE
Rapid City, S.D.
June 14, 1943
SPECIAL ORDERS)
NO.........162)

1. The 383rd Bomb Gp (H) consisting of Hq, 383rd Bomb Gp (H), and 540th, 541st, 542nd, and 543rd Bomb Sq (H) and attached units (Plummer Prov Gp, and Bowman Prov Gp) is reld fr asgmt & duty this sta and WP AAB Geiger Fld, Washington, so as to arrive thereat o/a June 20, 1943, RUAT CO thereat for dy. Auth: Confidential Ltr Hq 2nd AF, Ft Geo Wright, Washington.."

Actually, the first orders sent us to Pendleton, Oregon, but we were there for only one night; they did not know why we were there, but orders did come there correcting our assignment to Geiger, in Spokane, where we had been a year earlier. Travel by private auto was authorized. We had acquired a few little belongings by this time, chiefly a crib, a baby bed. And stuff. And it would not fit in the 1939 Ford convertible that was my wife's "dowry." Automobile production had been changed over to aircraft and tanks. This was wartime, remember. Any autos left over were rationed and hard to get. But military on orders had priority on such things, fortunately. We could get ration coupons that enabled us to travel in convoy, buy gas for all cars in the convoy on the coupon, and save our regular coupons for personal use.

To buy a new car required an application, a statement of necessity and hardship and ability to pay.[44] I had been a commissioned officer for one year and had saved enough money, along with a couple hundred from the sale of the convertible,[45] to pay cash for the car. (During the four years of the war, my poker winnings paid for all our food and some other incidentals.) We were able to find a brand new 1942 Buick Super that we could buy. Chrome "had gone to war" so all chrome parts (bumpers and trim) had been painted over - blackout it was called. Price was $1864. That's right, $1864. Four-door sedan, black, beautiful thing, and it would hold our baby crib and our luggage, and the paraphernalia needed to prepare formula for the infant. We still have some pictures of the car on a hill just outside Pendleton, Oregon.

From Rapid City to Pendleton and/or Spokane involves crossing the Continental Divide, or Great Divide, which separates the basins of streams which drain to the Atlantic and those which drain to the Pacific. In that northern area the divide follows closely the crestline of the Rockies, which means using mountain passes to cross over and eliminates straight road travel. Three national parks lie across the divide: Yellowstone, in the northwest corner of Wyoming; Glacier, which overlaps into Alberta, Canada, from the northwestern part of Montana; and Rocky Mountain, about 50 miles northwest of Denver. Yellowstone is larger than the states of Delaware and Rhode Island combined, has some of the most spectacular scenery in the United States,

---

44   My total income for the calendar year 1942 was $2165. For 1943 $1718.67. For 1944 $2130. For 1945 $2070. These are the amounts shown on my income tax return for those years. I cannot explain why I made less in 1943 when I was a 1st lieutenant and captain than I did the year before when I was a cadet for six months and a second lieutenant for six. Probably had something to do with change in reporting of flying pay, quarters allowance, and subsistence In those days, 2nd lts. were not expected to be married and received $21 a month subsistence whether married or not First lts., married, children or not, received $42. Captains, married with children received $63. By the time you reached major the children were supposed to be grown, so subsistence dropped back to $42 a month. Housing allowance rose with rank. World War II changed many things.

45   We sold the Ford for a reasonable price, I think it was $275, to an officer in the group who outbid a couple of others. The car was in good shape, we had had no trouble with it. Just a few days after we sold it, the generator failed and had to be replaced, so the buyer accused me of "unloading" a problem on him. Nothing I could say could convince him that I was innocent of cheating him.

more than 3,000 springs, pools, and geysers - particularly Old Faithful which erupts at regular intervals of usually 65 minutes - and should be visited at least once by every American.

Kit first visited the park when she was about 8 weeks old, as we traveled from Rapid City to Pendleton, Oregon, and it was not a happy time for her. The altitude, frequently over 7,000 feet, was just too much for her little tummy, considering recovery from the 6-week colic, and nothing would stay down. She would take her bottle and shortly afterward burp most of it up, to her mother's great concern and distress. When we moved on to lower altitudes she was all right again. She wouldn't have remembered much of the scenery anyway.

Changing stations, leave to St. Louis, and inclement weather, caused flying time to drop down during April-June: only 61 hours. Flew just a little over four hours in June, the last flight in Rapid City was June 20. The next flight was at Geiger on 3 July.

Back in Spokane, and having served as a first lieutenant for six months, I filled out the promotion papers once more, and on 20 August 1943 was promoted to captain.[46] It was not long after my promotion that I encountered 2nd Lt. James Jones, who had replaced me on the transfer to Alaska a year earlier, at the O. Club bar. (Chapter 15, pp 95,96). On reflection, it surely must have been a little upsetting for him.

Photographs show our first location was Hawley's Cottage Court and Florence Anderson holding Kit.

Then Kay found us a nice little house at 1628 W. Tenth. It was one bedroom, with a large dining room between living room and bedroom. Kit's crib was just outside our bedroom door, in the dining room, not a bad location. Have some good shots of proud papa and momma holding that saucy little frog of three to five months. We were attending the First Presbyterian Church, Fourth and Cedar, and Dr. Paul Calhoun, the minister, christened Kit there on Sunday, the 19th of September 1943. We had gotten to know and to like the minister and Mrs. Calhoun.

And we did a very foolish thing. Neither the first time nor the last. Regulations permitted a pilot to take his mother or wife on a short orientation flight once a year. The powers that be had overlooked this small item

---

46   Kay had given me a nice cigarette case, leather bound, when I was commissioned, with gold letters LT. BUD BARBEE. I had remarked that I could buy another one if I should ever "make" captain. Naturally, I didn't replace one that was just over a year old.

when the war started, but it was soon rescinded. While it was still permitted, I seized the chance to take my wife flying in a B-17 bomber. So, on short notice, with no planning, with no emergency instructions, we left our baby with Mrs. Calhoun and went flying in the big bird.

Only many years later did we come to the full realization that the wife of the minister had no idea of where we were from, or who to contact in event of any problem. Fortunately, nothing unforeseen did happen, Kay enjoyed the flight, and seeing our procedures, sat in the pilot's seat, would only just barely touch the controls, and talked to the tower on the radio when we thought she was on interphone. Tower operators were surprised to hear a woman's voice over the air. No harm done. Safely returned home and re-claimed child. Oh, boy!

There were dangers in our everyday flying, just as there are now, but they did not occupy our minds. We studied emergency procedures, rehearsed them, practiced them, critiqued them, were confronted with them in training without warning, but did not worry about them. I have mentioned the radio range at Spokane. It served the air base as well as the commercial airfield. The easterly leg was positioned in a valley - hills on either side were not above 4,000 feet - and was the leg used for descent for landing. When the weather turned bad, requiring an instrument approach, we had to be sure we stayed right "on the beam," the steady signal that led to the station. We had two occasions when the pilot was not oriented properly and crashed into a hillside. Jim Briggs, from our class at Williams, "bought the farm" in our first summer there, 1942, when he encountered bad weather and ran out of fuel. A couple of crewmen, who were in the rear end of the plane, survived the crash.

In September, 1943, I was given the sad duty of escorting the remains of Lt. Robert "Fergie" Ferguson to St. Louis for burial. Fergie had clipped one of the mountain tops, wide of the beam. There is really nothing you can say to or do for the parents that will ease the pain. About all there is to say is that he was your friend and that you're sorry. The trip was authorized by Army Regulation 30-1820, dated 16 Mar 31. My orders called for me to go and return by rail.

When I returned from the joyless trip to St. Louis, I was assigned as Flight Commander and Assistant to Major Jack T. Loney and his Provisional Group. Aside from Loney, myself, a flight surgeon, navigator, bombardier, and adjutant, there were thirty-five crews, ten men each, in Loney's group. Four officers on each crew: pilot, co-pilot, navigator, bombardier: out of the

140 officers, there was one Flight Officer co-pilot, one first lieutenant bombardier, and the rest were second lieutenants.

Special Orders No. 286, 13 October 1943, stated *"Crews will have completed third phase tng & will have completed all leaves & fur..."* (furloughs?) and *"are reld fr asgmt & dy AAB, Geiger Fld, Wn & WP by RR fr this sta, at the proper time so as to arrive at AAB, Grand Island, Nebr by noon 19 Oct 43,"* and *"Upon arrival 21st Bomb Wg contl pers passes fr CG 2BC to CG 21st Bomb Wg." "CAPT BUD BARBEE, 0726183, AC, is aptd Deputy Tn Commander."* That meant that I was in charge of seeing that there was sufficient food and drink, preparation facilities, sanitation facilities, etc., on board that train for three hundred fifty-six people. I had to wire ahead at one stop for a hundred loaves of bread. It also meant that I had a private compartment which would serve as my "office." Actually, I kept a poker game going there, day and night, for the six days of our travel. Added coupla hundred dollars to the kitty.

There had not been any official announcement, but it was understood that the Loney group would pick up airplanes at Grand Island and fly them to North Africa where the crews and aircraft would be stationed. In the absence of anything to the contrary, we assumed that the "supervisory personnel" would accompany the troops. Based on this supposition, Kay packed up and drove home to St. Louis, expecting to next hear from me from some sandy outpost in North Africa.

Didn't work out that way. Major Loney, the flight crews, the surgeon, and the adjutant were immediately processed for an overseas destination (never heard of them again), and the navigator, bombardier, and I were told we would not be going. We were to wait for further orders. I called Kay and told her to join me in Grand Island. We stayed briefly in the Courtesy Courts Motel, and when our orders came to report to Colorado Springs, we used our authorized 10 day delay enroute to make a quick trip to St. Louis before going to Colorado to rejoin the 383rd Bomb Gp which had moved from Geiger.

2544 Gunnison, Colorado Springs. A nice little house, just a few blocks off the main highway which led to Peterson Field, a couple of miles down the road. We were there from November 1943 until June 1944, seven months, the longest we had been at any one place. Assigned to the 383rd Combat Crew Training Squadron, we were now back in B-24s. In 1942 at Geiger we flew the B-24D. Several models and some improvements later, we now have the B-24J. This model had a nose turret instead of swivel mounted twin 50 caliber guns in the nose section, supposedly improved engines, and was equipped with a "formation stick" mounted on the pilot's left hand panel. This could replace the wheel and yoke, the normal controls, for cruising and formation flight. It was a little tricky to get used to, but once you had the feel of it, the exertion to fly formation was greatly reduced. After about five and a half hours and six landings, I was re-checked as an instructor in the B-24J. Flew about fifty-two hours in November and December.

We had experienced some bad weather in Rapid City and Ainsworth, but nothing quite like that of Colorado Springs. The street where we lived was Gunnison, not the town or county of Gunnison which is deep in the Rockies to the west and is often shown on national television weather reports. But we could have some "special" weather conditions also. When we took off from Peterson, we were already at an altitude of over 5,000 feet. This rarer, thinner air made a difference in our takeoff speed and especially the much greater length of runway required to get airborne. Training in such emergency procedures as losing an engine on takeoff was conducted after takeoff, with plenty of altitude below. Always some asshole who has to be different: one of our instructors chopped back an engine on the takeoff roll for one of the student crews. They ran out of runway before they could develop enough speed to get airborne, were unable to control the B-24 and it cartwheeled off the runway into the surrounding field. Miraculously, the most severe injury was a broken ankle suffered by the pilot. We could not believe that the crew had even survived. Needless to say, no one ever attempted it again.

We would have some fun with newly assigned weather forecasters. The new man would proceed in his briefing through his graphs and charts, the isobars, barometric pressures and conversions, and begin his forecast for the day. The pilots would sit there shaking their heads from side to side. Before long the new meteorologist would stop and inquire why we were indicating disagreement with his analysis of the scientific data.

"Go look outside at Pike's Peak." Pike's Peak was only about 15 miles to the west of us,[47] and we would then explain to him that when we could see clouds begin to "peek" over the peak, we knew they were building up on the west face of the peak, and we could predict, from experience, minimum flying conditions within four hours as the clouds rolled over the top and down into lower ground below. We knew then to schedule local training flights from which the aircraft could be recalled on short notice.

---

47   Pikes Peak was only one of fifty-two peaks in Colorado which were more than 14,000 feet.

Many times as I grew up I had seen movies and newspaper stories about blizzards. I knew we had had some pretty heavy snows in St. Louis and I had never got lost. It just wasn't reasonable that a person could get lost, completely lose his way, in a snow-storm. In Colorado I learned how wrong I was. One winter morning, still dark, after some hours of snow, I tried to get the car out of the driveway into the street so I could get to the base for my scheduled flying. Drifts just too high, couldn't make it. But only a few blocks away there was a city bus which ran along the highway from the city to Peterson Field. I knew I could make it there, so I started out. In less than fifty yards, snow knee high where it had not drifted higher, I had lost the road, I had lost all sense of direction, I could not see anything ahead of me. I turned around toward what I thought was the direction to home and was able to barely perceive a small pinpoint blur of light and headed toward it. Kay had delayed going back to bed — it was quite early — and the kitchen light was still burning to guide me safely home. It was a close call.

With weather like that, we frequently had to wait for some clearing in order to fly. While waiting, we could generally get a little game of poker going. If the game lasted past "regular" duty hours, we would sometimes have a Lt. Eby, a dentist, take a hand in the game. We really did not want him to play because he was such a poor player, he always lost, and often his little daughter would tug at him, "Come on, Daddy, Mother wants to go home," and he would say "Okay, honey, in a little while." Playing "table stakes" you could cover all bets up to the amount of money you had on the table, then you were "all in." Should you win, you won only the amount of the bet that you had covered. Naturally, you could not change the amount of money you had on the table after a hand started, but it was one way of limiting your losses on a single hand. We soon learned how to tell when Eby had a good hand: he would sneak some more money under his pile on the table. That was cheating, but if we called him on it he claimed he had "just forgot." What can you do with a guy that you feel a little sorry for because he always loses?

On one occasion in a pot limit game, I cured him. I had opened with a good hand, ace-high straight: Ace, King, and Jack of Diamonds, Queen of Hearts, and Ten of Spades. Eby raised and sneaked some more money under his pile. Eby never raised, nor added to his table money, unless he had a sure thing. I just knew that he had either a flush or a full house. I called his raise and took two cards, pitching the Queen of Hearts and the Ten of Spades. When I saw the cards I had drawn, I asked Eby how much money he had in front of him, and bet that amount to him. He pushed his money in and called with his flush (as it turned out) and I showed him my royal flush in

Diamonds: I had drawn the Queen and Ten of Diamonds to go with my Ace, King, Jack! We didn't see him for awhile after that.

Poker playing got me in trouble at home, however. I would give Kay my winnings, but she would be upset because, as she said, she never knew whether I was out there flying in that bad weather, or lost, weathered out some place far away, or what. I tried to explain that we never knew when the weather would clear enough for us to get off the ground, but she always countered that I could at least telephone. Well, she was right, and I knew it. But, you know, sometimes it just ain't convenient. It was worse after one night when we were outside looking at the stars and saw a bright flash mid-way up Pikes Peak. One of our crews had flown into the side of the mountain. Years later I knew why.

Some of our photographs show me holding Kit in a car seat that I have hooked over my shoulders. I should have developed the idea and patented it because no one had yet come out with an over-the-shoulder carrier for a small child. It seemed to me a very natural application of the car seat. We have a lot of pictures of that little rascal during those months: her first Christmas, sleeping in the playpen, sleeping sitting up in the crib, sleeping on the potty chair, being hugged and mugged by mother and father in the front yard, in her stroller, and learning to walk at about one year. More pictures in St. Louis in May, 1944, while home on leave, with everyone from both our families, including my brother's estranged wife Marge, and my Grandma Overton who was a "real old woman" at age 65.

An interesting occurrence. Kit had a small plaything made up of plastic discs and other items. We noticed one day there was just one-half of a broken disc, maybe the size of a half-dollar, and there was no sign of the missing half. We telephoned the hospital, the doctors were all busy, but we hurried out there anyway. When we told them what we suspected, all the doctors got together and started speculating whether stomach acid would dissolved the piece, or whether it would pass in the stool. They tried different solutions of various acids on other pieces of the plaything with no apparent results.

They had all been very busy, but this was a break in the routine, a different experience. Not too long afterward, the missing piece, with somewhat rounded edges, did pass in the stool. Doctors, like real people, willingly respond to a challenge.

About the middle of March, 1944, 1st Lt. Albert Boyette and I got orders assigning us to the Heavy Bomb pool in Boise, Idaho. When the base commander was told that our names had been picked from a hat, he did not approve but did nothing. When he learned that our two names were the only ones in the hat, he decided that was not fair and the orders were cancelled. In June, our whole outfit, the 214th AAF BU (CCTS(H), was transferred to the "213th AAF BU (CCTS(H) AAF Mt Home Idaho."

In my first two years as an officer, June '42 to June '44, I had a total of 1052 hours of flying.

CHAPTER XVIII

Begin Training Again as a Crew

We drive into the town of Mountain Home, about 45 miles southeast of Boise, at about nine o'clock at night, in broad daylight (!), and look for a place to stay the night. That was one small, small town. We succeeded in finding one crumby, awful-looking little tourist court that was inconceivably worse inside than it looked from the outside.

"It's always darkest before the dawn," we said. "Yeah, but it hasn't even started to get dark yet."

Fortunately, we were assigned quarters the next day when I checked in at the base. The quarters were temporary housing that had been built for the civilian contractors and their families while the base was under construction, and were scheduled to be enlisted housing. Long frame buildings that housed eight families, each unit separated from the next by wallboard. You could hear milk being poured next door. Each unit had a coal bin in front, on the street side. The coal was for the stove that was used for cooking. For heating the rooms. For heating the water. Bank up the coals at night after dinner and dinner dishes and you could have hot water in the morning for bathing, shaving, whatever. But this is summertime and we don't need heating in the house. Heads you win, tails you lose. We did have a nice grassy area between the rows of buildings where the children could play. I don't remember that we had a cat, but we have pictures of Kit playing with a kitten, chasing it, draping it over her arm. Surely it belonged to someone else.

My brother, Freeman Hooper, visited us while we were living, country style, in these Mountain Home quarters. There are some pictures of him with us and holding Kit. Seems to me that he was living in California and travelling for some large distributor of auto parts. He was not eligible for the military because of health, but I knew that he had wanted for years to be able to fly. He had had a few flights in the St. Louis area with some of the early daring pilots experimenting with air-to-air refueling. It was a big thrill for him, on one of my leaves in St. Louis, when we rented a small plane so his "little brother" could take him up for a spin.

One summer weekend we drove to Payette Lake, in northern Idaho, and rented a small boat for a lake ruise. Momentary panic when we grounded on a large rock that we had not seen sticking up in the water, but got safely off and back to shore. Got some pictures of our firstborn giving me a good, wet kiss. Have carried that picture in my wallet all these years. About fifty now. (Almost 60 in 2004.)Haven't been back in that part of the country since, but, if memory is correct, it is ruggedly fascinating.

Can't exactly remember how long we lived in this housing, but it was a couple of months anyway. One day one of our trainee crews, finishing up his flying, decided to "buzz" our housing area. He flew right down the middle of the rows of housing and he was low. I mean really low. No one got the number of the plane but someone in the housing area recognized the waist gunner who was standing in the open gunner position and later identified him. The pilot was severely chastised, but any punishment would have been less than letting him go on into combat with his crew. Never heard of him again. He wasn't the only one who did crazy things.

Crazy things... Once, doing low-level recon and photogrqaphy, in formation, I had to lift my left wing to go over a windmill — couldn't change direction because of the other aircraft. Our fearless leader on this flight was a real nut. Before our entry in the war, he had joined the Canadian Royal Air Force but was able to resign to enter our forces. As we were "terrain following," we dipped down, in three aircraft "V" formation, into the Snake River canyon. I was flying right wing. He was heading directly for a bridge, and I knew he was going to fly under it, but I knew the wing men couldn't make it. I could not turn right to climb up, so I slid under the plane on the left wing as he pulled up to climb out of the canyon. I was so close to the river that I got water in my ball turret before I could also climb out.

Later we ducked down into another canyon, scattered a large flock of geese, smashed into hundreds of the birds, suffered severe damage to the lead airplane and quite extensive damage to the others. My navigator came up from his nose position, smeared with blood, carrying a dead duck that had smashed the plexiglass in the nose of our plane. Leading edges of the wings of all three planes were dented with rivets torn loose in places. The lead plane lost one engine. We got home safely. When we all stuck to our story of flying at 5,000 feet when we hit the ducks, the group commander could only comment about "supercharged ducks" and warn us not to let it happen again.

As we increased the number of crews in training it became necessary for officers to move out of the "housing" at Mountain Home to provide room for the enlisted personnel. So we had to move to Boise, about forty-five miles away, to find any place to rent. Kay found a house at 103 West Idaho Ave., Boise, where the woman was willing to rent: we had one bedroom, a large bath, and could share the kitchen with the owner. A door from our large bathroom led to the kitchen. We could bed Kit in the large bathtub. I can remember trying to sing her to sleep with "To-ra-loo-ra-loo-ral" and "I Come to the Garden Alone." She had to choose between my singing and going to sleep. She chose sleep.

An interesting area: this was one of the areas in Boise that was served by hot sulphur springs for heating the house and hot water. Stinky for bathing, but cheap heat. Several of us formed a carpool so that we had to drive only about twice a week to the base. We could make the 45 mile trip in an hour and the passengers could take a little nap.

December 1944 and I was the oldest pilot in the outfit who had not been overseas. Oh, there had been opportunities to volunteer, but I always said: "Look, I'm trained, capable, and ready, so send me. But I'm not going to go home to my wife and tell her I have volunteered to go get shot at. Send me, but I won't volunteer." Now I was directed to form a crew and train them. Some crew members were going back for their second tour. My navigator, flight engineer, radio operator and upper gunner volunteered to serve on my crew — they knew they might have to go back again and agreed they wanted to fly with an experienced pilot this time.

Many of the crews had at least one person, a "Returnee," who had already served a combat tour, but only two of them were pilots: 1st Lt Willis a. McFadden and 2nd Lt Edward J. Zack.. Fifty-three crews were formed: aside from my crew (my navigator was a first lieutenant), six had first lieutenants as pilots, the rest were second lieutenants and flight officers. Two of the first lieutenant pilots were old friends, former instructors, from months we had spent together training other crews: Harold A. "Pete" Peterson, Jr., and Harold Hunsberger. At twenty-six I was the old man of the mountain.

We took fifteen days leave over Christmas and rode the train back to St. Louis. We decided to splurge and engaged a drawing room which would give us more room, privacy, and a place for Kit to take her nap. Well, it could have been better. Maybe the rest of the train was the same way, but we had a terrible time with bedbugs. We all got bites. It was good to get home and everyone enjoyed Kit's second Christmas.

As of January 1945 I was no longer a Flight Commander and instructor pilot. Just another aircraft commander of combat crew No. 10272, training at the 213th Combat Crew Training School, 2nd Air Force, 15th Wing. Peterson, Hunsberger, McFadden, Zack and I had the only crews that never had an instructor ride along on any of our training for the next three months during which I flew 102 hours and 35 minutes, concentrating on high altitude formation flying and bombing.

Special Orders Number 84, 25 March 1945, stated we were *"...atchd unasgd to Salinas AAF, Salinas, Calif, & WP, thereto, by rail, o/a 27 March 1945, rptg thereat not later than 1800, 29 March 1945, for overseas movement...TPA is not auth. Dependents, relatives, friends, pets and automobiles will not accompany or join individuals included in this movement."* ! Further: *"...The Gen Sup O will provide for the movement to Salinas, Calif, for five hundred fifteen (515) O & EM ordered to that sta per this paragraph & par 2, SO #84, the Hq, cs, the necessary fld ranges, cooking & serving utensils & arrange for the return of same to the TO this sta; provide the necessary ice & cleaning supplies; provide troop train rations for six (6) meals increased by troop train rations for two (2) add meals; make the proper installation of necessary fld ranges in kitchen car or cars & provide the necessary fuel. The Tr Comdr is responsible for the immediate return of fld ranges & cooking & serving utensils to proper sta. The Tr Comdr wil make accounting of his stewardship as required by WD Cir #400..."*

It took us the full two days to make the trip of about 800 miles. Salinas is about 100 miles south of San Francisco and just a few miles east of Monterey and Pebble Beach. We could never figure out why Salinas was chosen as an equipping base for crews heading overseas. Maybe we were sent there because we were intended for the Pacific theater of war, but the big push in Europe to prepare for the invasion changed that. In any event, all crews were equipped with the standard leather-covered, fleece-lined flying gear: suspendered trousers, full jackets, gloves, boots, and caps with flaps for the ears. Never could figure how to use the flaps and headsets at the same time. We were also issued the standard 45 automatic pistol. Thus arose a problem. We were issued footlockers to ship home all our civilian clothing and extraneous items. I already had my high-altitude flying clothing but I could not turn it in at Salinas. They wouldn't accept it. Salinas was in the business of issuing not of receiving. I had to take the issue clothing, but could not turn in what I already had.

Also, I had bought a good, smooth-working .45 from a pawn shop in Ainsworth, Nebraska, that someone had had during World War I. But I still had to accept a new .45 that I didn't want. So I bundled up my old flying gear, packed the old .45 and marked them for shipment to St. Louis. So as to prevent us from shipping home the items we were supposed to take with us, the authorities inspected all home-going shipments.

Thus I was notified that they would bring charges against me for trying to "steal" government equipment by sending it home. Talk about your "Catch 22"! No explanation would suffice, so, not the least bit contrite, I said: "Okay, court martial me, then I won't have to go to combat." They decided I should remain with my crew.

RESTRICTED
HEADQUARTERS ARMY AIR BASE
SALINAS, CALIFORNIA
SPECIAL ORDERS   30 MARCH 1945
NUMBER 80

2. The pers (w) B-24 Combat Crews listed on atchd annexes nos 1 to 14 are reld fr atchd 451st AAF Base Unit and fr TD at Salinas AAB, Salinas, Calif and are asgd to Shipment No FD-155-MJ, with crew nos as indicated and WP by rail to Camp Kilmer, New Jersey, so as to arrive on 7 April 1945, RUAT to the Commanding General, New York Port of Embarkation for TD, thence to an overseas destination by water. Major Oliver W. Harris, 0908588, AC is designated Prov Gp Ldr for this shipment, and will accompany pers to overseas destination on TD, and upon release by theatre comdr will ret to Salinas, AAB, Calif, USA for TD, pending further instructions. Maj Harris will ret by most expeditious means available. Captain Bud Barbee, 0726183, AC is designated Asst Prov Gp Ldr for this shipment and upon arrival overseas will rpt to theatre comdr for perm duty. This is a PCS with TD enroute. Dependents will not accompanuy nor join pers at any assembly point, staging area or port of embarkation. TPA is not atzd. Except as may be necessary in the transaction of official business, individuals are prohibit-ed fr discussing their overseas destination, even by shipment no. Each individual has been indoctrinated in matters of security and censorship of all activities of pers under movement orders; and has been instructed not to file safe arrival telegrams with commercial agencies while en route to or at overseas destination."

Special Orders 82 designated me as Troop Train Quartermaster Supply Officer. I was becoming quite experienced in handling and providing for troops travelling on troop trains.

Two weeks later, after much time spent on rail sidings while higher priority and passenger trains went past, we had reached the middle of the United States, and unloaded in Kearney, Nebraska. Didn't make it to the port of embarkation.

And now I start winding down my World War II tour of duty.

CHAPTER XIX

Winding Down World War II

Certainly it was not what we expected: unloading at Kearney, Nebraska, could not have been anticipated. We were heading for Camp Kilmer, New Jersey, and though we had been mighty slow in our progress from Salinas, California, across country, the explanation that higher priority traffic was responsible seemed reasonable. In retrospect, we could guess that the Army Air Force was trying to decide whether we should continue toward Europe where invasion aircraft losses were less than had been expected and air superiority was well-established, or turn us around for the Pacific war against Japan. In any event, there we were in the middle of the United States, and no one seemed to know quite what to do with us.

While they were making up their minds, whoever *they* were, I called my dear camp-follower, now in St. Louis, having completed another of her solo crossings of the continental divide, (not really solo, I suppose, in that she had our two year old daughter to keep her company) and told her to come on to Nebraska and bring our firstborn. We fully expected that this was only a slight delay before we got orders sending us to one of the theaters of war. Shortly came orders sending us — some of us — to Topeka, Kansas, and further placing us on detached service with the Headquarters Ferrying Division, Air Transport Command, Cincinnati, Ohio. *"Crews will remain at TAAFld, Topeka, Kansas pending receipt of Operational orders to be issued by ATC Liaison Officer."* Great! We were going to ferry airplanes to bases in the Pacific. Exactly twenty crews out of the fifty-three were thus designated, and included only the pilot, co-pilot, navigator, flight engineer, and radio operator. We assumed the other thirty-three crews, plus bombardiers and gunners, went on to Europe or backtracked to a Pacific assignment. Crews selected for the ferrying job were the first nineteen of our numbered group, plus number thirty-one. I had crew number thirty-one. Can only surmise that, being the only captain in this bunch of second and first lieutenants, they needed me to be the group leader for the move from Kearney to Topeka, for that is the way the orders read. We arrived in Topeka on 4 May, I collected the .45 caliber automatic pistols we had been issued in Salinas and turned them in to the Ordnance Supply Officer in Topeka. No flying time in April, eight hours in May, one hour, fifty-five minutes in June.

Not much to do in Topeka during the month of May 1945. Report to the field, check for any orders for ferrying aircraft, stick around for a few hours to see if any directions come through, have a drink at the O Club, go home to wife, child and motel. Every few days a crew, or two, gets orders to ferry planes to the Pacific. Actually ended with crews one through twelve being assigned to ferry jobs. Special Orders Number 154, dated 3 June 1945, sent some of the remaining pilots: *"The following officers, AC, White"* to the *"...2523rd AAF Base Unit, Hondo Army Air Field, Hondo, Texas."*

That "white" business is interesting. There was no integration. Flying in Italy, during World War II, was an all Negro group of fighters headed up by a Benjamin O. Davis who was later to become the first black general in the Air Force. I first met him in Tokyo in 1954 when he was a colonel.

Almost due west of San Antonio, about 40 miles, you encounter a road sign *"This is God's Country, Don't Drive Through Like Hell!"* You then enter Hondo, Texas, which was not our idea of what God's country looked like. We find a place to rent that has been divided into "apartments." The dividers did not go all the way to the ceilings, the bath was a common one shared with others, and the ice box (not refrigerator, but "ice-box") and a tiny kitchen sink were full of cockroaches. Enough, already. We go back to San Antonio and spend a couple of nights with Bubba Stanley - Lt. Colonel Dr. Stanley F. Hampton, Kay's brother - and Ahden, his wife.

Somehow or other we find "Little" Semrad's house. Lt. Semrad is due to return shortly but his house is available for a little while. Not the biggest attraction is the nearby 7th Day Adventist church, but that is only an occasional distraction compared to the cows next door who make noises and bump against the house during the night.

When we have to pull out of there, we find a nice garage apartment at 1611 W. Huisache, San Antonio. I say "nice" because it seemed nice after the place in Hondo. We had ants. Smart ants. (And they are driving us up the wall in Florida now.) When we found them in the sugar bowl, we put the bowl in a pan of water in the middle of the kitchen table. The next morning they were in the bowl again, and I found their trail: up the wall, over the ceiling, until they arrived exactly over the sugar bowl, where they let go and dropped in the bowl! And the flying red roaches!

Yukkk! Those suckers were over two inches long. There was a trash bin on the alleyway just outside our little apartment that was a residence for these big roaches. We did find that if we put Stearn's Roach Paste on pieces of paper, which we placed in all doorways, we could control their forays into our larders. There was a nice yard between the house and the garage and Kit had her swing there. The owner's daughter-in-law would occasionally bring her small child over and these two girls, about the same age, would play.

Back to Hondo: When we (B-24 pilots) arrived, Hondo was the Army Air Forces Navigation School. We were gathered and informed that we were going to set up a B-29 Flight Engineer School, and that the navigation school was phasing out.

Knowing what building we were to occupy, I decided to take a look at it to see if it would fit our needs, and asked Lt. Hunsberger to go along. I explained to the sergeant who met us what we were doing and he said we might like to talk to the captain who had been in charge of that section of the navigation school. I knocked on the door and we went in. The captain was looking at some papers on his desk and very obviously did not look up as we stood there. Finally, he says:

"Don't you know how to report to a superior officer?" I had to restrain Hunsberger when he was about to respond. I replied:

"We're not reporting in, captain, just a courtesy call because we are going to take over this building. As for the "superior officer" bit, I doubt very much that you are my superior in any way at all."

"My date of rank is December 15, 1943," he said with pride.

"Mine is August 20, 1943, and I think you are somewhat of a horse's ass. I don't want to see you anywhere around here next week when we take over this building," I replied, and motioned Hunsberger to follow as I turned around and walked out.

The captain's sergeant looked up as we left, smiled, and said: "Good to see you, sir." I could see that he shared my opinion of his captain.

(Hiatus here as we spend a few days in Macatawa, Michigan. Arrived here 1 Sept 1990 and today is 3 Sept. Just had the excitement of OP Hampton III getting a cat out of a tree with a broom. At first he told everyone that the cat got itself up there and could get itself down. While he is doing this, Suzanne is planning major remodeling of the "cottage." This house is really two separate apartments, living room, dining, kitchen on each side, central common stairway leading up to three bedrooms on each side. Part of the plan is to make one large screened front porch. Problem is where to put the entrance door. ....Now several days later (9/12/90) and waiting for Cecil Petty to return from post office where Marge has sent him to mail a letter. Now he is back and we are ready for a walk along the beach.

Finished all the little chores that Suzanne had asked me to do. The U.S. Tennis Open finished last Sunday so today and tomorrow I can enjoy the usual pleasures of Macatawa. Had to take the car in to the Mercury garage today to have them fix the air-conditioner. Cecil will take me back this evening. Last Thursday night we had a dilly of a thunderstorm. Lotsa lightning and thunder and rain. Had to close all the windows. Air has turned a little cooler. Seems to coincide with the departure of the summer people on Labor Day. We now planning to leave on Friday, 9/14 and drive to Martinsville W. Virginia to see Lynne. Should call the Kendalls and let them know when we will be home. Got the phone installed in the basement, but it will not "talk" with the first floor phone. First floor to second floor OK and second floor to basement OK. Can't figure. Bell does not ring loud enough in basement. May have to change instrument. Connections seem OK when Ward Dobbin called in.

Finishing up the little aside: we left Macatawa in a heavy rain and stayed in thunderstorms for several hours until we reached the Ohio turnpike. The weather cleared there but we were stopped for an hour by an accident involving two 18 wheelers that completely blocked the highway. Made it to Canton, Ohio, for the night and proceeded to Martinsville on Saturday. Spent the afternoon and evening and Sunday morning with Lynne, left for home at noon and arrived in Satellite Beach at 1230 am, Monday morning.)

Now, back to 1945

Our garage apartment on Huisache was conveniently located about a block from where Stan and Ahden Hampton lived. Kay could stay in touch with her family, she and Ahden could look after each other, and we could play bridge with them quite frequently. Which we did until one night when Stan blew his top about something that Ahden did or did not do on a particular bridge hand and she made it perfectly clear that she would never play bridge with him again. And she didn't.

In the area where the bombbays were normally located, the B-24s were equipped with engine instrument and control panels that would reflect normal and emergency conditions which an instructor could change to fit the situation. There were twelve of these panels, or stations, six on either side of the plane. Here, the men training to be flight engineers on B-29s could simulate the activities that would be required of them in the B-29 which was now being produced in increasing numbers and was the primary means of attacking the Japanese holdings and mainland in the Pacific.

Major Meech Tahsequah, a full-blooded Comanche Indian was in charge of our training group, and I was in charge of the flying training. This was the first "real" Indian I had ever known. His skin wasn't "red" but a sort of

110

heavy tan, his hair was black, and he did have a beard, but not a heavy one. We lived within a few blocks of each other in San Antonio and generally car-pooled to Hondo, some sixty miles west through the wide-open spaces of Texas. Took about an hour from home to office. The wives got to know each other and Meech and I played golf fairly regularly at various courses in and around San Antonio. I would say that we were quite compatible. This strong, chunky Indian scored only a little better than I did, but off the tee he was tremendous: I have seen him put his drive on the green from over three hundred yards away. The rest of his game, however, did not quite match up to his drive.

It was early in July 1945 before we had the aircraft and equipment to begin training. The uranium atom bomb was dropped on Hiroshima on August 6th. The plutonium atom bomb was dropped on Nagasaki (the alternate target) on August 9th. On August 14 Japan surrendered unconditionally and Emperor Hirohito announced defeat to the Japanese people. The B-29

Flight Engineer School was out of business almost as soon as it started rolling.

With the war over, it was time to start reducing the forces. Those who had a sufficient number of "points" would be allowed to take a discharge or return to inactive status. We were invited to a briefing at Kelley Field where we were told that we could sign up for immediate release or stay in until May 1946. Some of us were interested in "regular" commissions, but were told that they were "frozen."

Knowing there would be significant reductions in personnel as those returning from overseas arrived, and the information from our landlady that her son was one of the soldiers returning and would want to occupy our cozy little garage apartment, and no information at all on what would happen, I opted for release so that we could go home and begin our civilian lives.

Special Orders No. 256, 24 Oct 45, sent me from Hondo to Randolph Field "for processing to revert to inactive status." Special Orders No. 178, 30 October 1945, Randolph Field, granted me a terminal leave of one month and 24 days, plus five days of travel time, to return to my home of residence in St. Louis. My Separation Qualification Record, WD AGO Form 100, stated:

"Pilot Instructor:

He was the pilot of a 4 Eng aircraft. He instructed students assigned to him the techniques and methods used in flying a 4 Eng aircraft. He advanced until he held the position of a group operations officer. In this capacity he directed the activities of a group engaged in 4 Eng pilot tng.

He was then assigned as a mission pilot flying flight engineers. He adv. until he held the position of an operations officer. He held this position until his discharge.

He has 60 hrs in a PT-14, 70 hrs in a BT-13, 80 hrs in an AT-9, 600 hrs in a B-17, and 600 hrs in a B-24. He has 90 hrs of actual instruments and 150 hrs of hooded instrument time."

We loaded the car, Kay, Kit, and I, and went home to St. Louis by way of Mexico and New Orleans.

The end of that phase of our lives.

CHAPTER XX

Back to Being a Civilian

Well, I had made the decision to get out of the Army and I was to wonder about the decision many times in the next few years. It did seem like the thing to do at that time. To get on with our lives. Now we were back to the old cliché that the army was a home for those bums who couldn't do anything else. For many years that may have been true for some "career corporals" who had found a sanctuary in the military forces. Oh, we had some during this second "World War," and there will always be a few passing their time until retirement. Even a few of them will be captains, majors, colonels, even generals, as well as corporals. But that was done, and now what?

When I checked in with TWA, my employer before I was called to the colors, I was welcomed back as a five-year employee, sent to the home office in Kansas City to be given a gold watch honoring the occasion and assigned, in St. Louis, as a "Traffic Rep." Of course, I had been a ticket agent with the airline for only nine months before leaving for the flying cadets, but my four years and three months in the Army counted, so I was a "five-year man."

As a Traffic Representative, I was to call upon various companies, their owners, presidents, managers, traffic agents, and acquaint them with the advantages of using TWA for their business travel and freight shipping. The time-honored procedure was to convince the responsible persons to use a TWA Travel Card, much like any credit card today, to establish a credit account with our airline. This would facilitate their calling TWA for any travel by air, even if TWA did not fly to that location. (Of course, if TWA and other airlines flew to the same location, the traveler would be scheduled on TWA.) Our people, the reservations people, would make the necessary arrangements, our ticket office would issue the ticket (for any airline), and the Traffic Representative would even deliver the ticket to the customer at his office if the reservation was several days off. Jeez, I'm getting way ahead of myself.

Back in St. Louis in November 1945, with no place to live. Just naturally, we moved in with Kay's parents, the Hamptons, at 708 Radcliff, University City.[48] They had a four-bedroom house, so they had plenty of room. It did not

---

48   708 Radcliffe, off the north side of Delmar Boulevard, slightly west of Big Ben

occur to us that our living there, with a two and one-half year old little girl, would cause any problem for adults in their mid-sixties who had adjusted to being alone, caring only for each other, making plans with only a spouse to consider, having "quiet hours" as they desired, eating as they pleased. None of that entered our minds. No concern for a child drawing crayon pictures on the wallpaper, requiring almost constant attention. Certainly no one could anticipate that such a little girl would dictate that dinner dishes of various colors would have to have the cup, saucer, plate and bowl at each place setting match in color: no mixing of green and blue, for instance. Small things, yes, but try to overcome the will of a determined, precocious child and simultaneously maintain a harmonious household. As the wise man once said, "You can sit on a mountain, but you cannot sit on a tack." Very difficult. Especially when Kit was such a precious child, both to her parents and

---

Road, is in a quiet residential area of winding streets named for colleges, like Harvard, Yale, Dartmouth, with limited points of access. At the time, 708 had a wooden porch with columns supporting the roof of a small unused porch off a second storey hallway bay. An entry area, like an airlock with inner and outer doors, opened to a generous hall with a stairway angled to the second floor. Under the stairs was a coat closet with a wedge of low storage space. To the left of the entrance was an adequate dining room with a window to the front and small, colored glass windows high on the wall opposite the entrance. A swinging door led into a cozy breakfast nook separating the kitchen from the dining room. The rear door from the kitchen to a small wooden porch and stairs led to the back yard that generally had a planting of flowers and occasionally a limited vegetable garden. To the extreme rear of the lot was a garage that was not in perfect repair. To the right of the entrance door was a large living room, which at one time had been two rooms; in this room were a baby grand piano, assorted chairs, a couch, a card table and four chairs located in a bay window area. In the midpoint of this large room was a door leading to the hallway, and at the rear a door leading to a bathroom. At the other end of the bath a door opened onto a small rear hallway with an opening into the kitchen, a door leading to the basement (it was "basempt" to Kit), and a stairway to the second floor. Laundry, furnace, hot water heater, a toilet, and a ping-pong table were in the full basement. The second floor had a spacious hall separating two bedrooms on each side. Facing to the front of the house, the left front bedroom was used by Pop and Mamomma, and Kay had always had the rear bedroom on the left. The right front bedroom had once been Stanley's, and the right rear (which connected with the front) was a spare. The spare became Kit's room. At the rear of the hallway was a bath, with tub, next to Kay's bedroom, a separate toilet next to the spare bedroom, and a door to the rear stairway. A bay window seating area at the front of the hallway was a favorite relaxing place in later years when Mamomma and Pop had the house to themselves again. Kay spent many years in this house, from junior high to after college. In those days it was not unusual for a young lady to live at home when she was working in the same city.

114

grandparents. It was to be a year and a half before we would be able to move into our new "veterans" tract home.

The Tarrants lived next door, the house on the left, good neighbors, and Josephine Tarrant, the attractive mother of a pretty teenage girl, soon became a favorite of our daughter Kit. Kit could go over to see Josephine — and she called her Josephine — at will, and stay as long as she behaved, did not get in the way, and was not a nuisance. When she did something "wrong," Josephine would send her home. Kit would obey her, relating to her mother just why she had been sent home. An interesting relationship. Kit understood that Josephine was caring and fair, but firm. There were rules and consequences. And she accepted them without dissent or appeal. The same willing acceptance did not always apply at home.

To return to being a Traffic Rep for TWA: It was about the second or third day of my training by an experienced traffic representative that he suggested we go to Garavelli's for lunch. Now Garavelli's served a nice lunch, generally a selection of great sandwiches, but we were working in "downtown" St. Louis where there was a wide selection of eating places and he had suggested we drive to the "west end," a distance of almost four miles. He was the "leader" so I followed. After our sandwich, he suggested a drive through Forest Park. O.K. Then he said we should take in an afternoon movie and then write up some "calls" we had made — but which we had not made.

"Perhaps," I suggested, he "should drop me off at the office and I could go through some required paperwork."

In mid 1946 TWA initiated a position of Passenger Relations Manager at the airport and I was given the job. Purpose was to handle any problems a passenger might have, but, of course, the greatest problem always was, and still is, lost luggage. For those passengers who were going beyond St. Louis, but whose luggage was checked only to St. Louis, it meant a search of various destinations from their origin point, locating the luggage and having it forwarded. For those passengers stopping in St. Louis it meant locating the luggage and arranging to have it delivered to them; if it could not be found, then I had to get a complete description, an estimate of costs, and make out the claim sheets. As you can see, Passenger Relations Manager translated to Lost Luggage Handler.

One of the most trying incidents concerned Efrem Zimbalist (the Senior, not FBI), a famed symphony orchestra conductor. His music did not make it to St. Louis, he was proceeding to Indianapolis for a concert that evening and he HAD to have that music. He was irate, it was becoming a scene at the airport before I was able to convince him that I would definitely have his music on the next flight and that he would have it in his hotel room by the time he needed it, and I got him out of the terminal and loaded on his flight to Indianapolis.

We succeeded. Found the music and delivered it in time for the evening performance.. Boy!!

In January 1947 the pilots went on strike. All of us lowly paid employees were told to go home and wait for those overpaid throttle-jockeys to settle for an undeserved raise. Checking with the Missouri Unemployment Division I found that I could draw monthly unemployment compensation of an amount that would not feed us for a week. Those officials seemed surprised when I told them I had to have a job and that I wanted to know what was available. They said most people just wanted to draw unemployment for as long as possible before looking for another job. They did have this company that was supposedly looking for someone; they had sent several people for interviews with no success whatsoever. But I could try if I wanted to..So I did.

CHAPTER XXI

Just Not A Salesman

It was an interesting interview in a mid-town hotel[49] suite with two men from The Paraffine Companies,[50] one of whom was the regional sales manager out of Chicago. They studied the application I had filled out showing data of myself, my wife, and our daughter Kit. Some great hemming and hawing about where we lived, the fact that Kit went to Mrs. Goldstein's Nursery School, where we went to church, more hemming and hawing, until I said:

"If you are wondering whether or not I'm Jewish, I'm not."

"Oh no, it's not that. Our company president and chairman are Jewish. Oh no, we didn't mean anything like that." (I soon found out that they were the only two Jewish people in the whole company.)

They next told me that they would like for me to take "this little test."

"Oh, it isn't critical or anything like that, but the company sorta likes to see how people perform on it. You can work on it in the next room." And, "it's pretty long, but don't worry about that. Nobody ever finishes it. Just do whatever you can in the one and a half hours allowed."

I brought it back to them in about twenty minutes.

"Oh, don't give up. You've got over an hour to finish it."

"That's OK. I've finished."

"Go ahead, take your time and check your answers."

"No, really, it's OK. I've checked it over."

I could tell then that I had the job. When I went to the home office in Oakland, California, for training, everyone wanted to meet the "genius" who had not only finished the test in record time, but had all the answers correct.

---

49   The Hotel Coronado, on the northwest corner of Lindell Boulevard and Spring Avenue, a first class hotel with a posh night club - dining room with floor show, is now a dormitory for St. Louis University students.

50   The men who founded the company had come west from Pennsylvania and discovered oil in California. Although western oil had an asphalt base, they thought it was a form of black paraffin, because paraffin was the base of eastern oil, thus the name of the company.

I never told them that, as a requirement in a college psychology course in "Testing and Measurements," Kay and I had administered and corrected that exact same test over twenty five times. I knew all the answers without reading the questions. But I let them go on thinking I was something special.

My training in California with PABCO, the trade name of the Paraffine Companies, lasted about a month. I started off in San Francisco working in the main office or headquarters. This was orientation in sales, promotion, and complete background of the company. Pabco was actually number three among the large producers of linoleum and various other types of hard-surface floor coverings; Armstrong was the leader, followed by Congoleum-Nairn. The company also had paint factories on the east and west coasts, but marketed very little paint in mid-U.S. (Manufacture of paint requires very little capital investment as compared to floor covering.) Soon I moved to the factory in Oakland, just across the bay, and Kay and Kit came out to join me.

The production of felt-base rugs and yard goods is quite interesting. First comes an artist's sketch of the pattern. This is transferred to a large block of wood which has been sliced horizontally and vertically to leave standing a mass of pegs about one-sixteenth of an inch square - about like a kitchen match. Pegs not needed in the pattern are cut away. Each color in the pattern has its own block of pegs, so there may be six or eight of these blocks measuring 12 to 18 inches wide and 6, 9, or 12 feet long, depending on the repeat of the pattern and the desired width of the final print. As a large roll of heavy felt paper mopves along the production line, it is first coated with a base coat of white enamel and then moves under the pattern blocks which alternately dip into various colors and deposit the paint on the roll. It is fascinating to watch the colorful patterns emerge as the various stamping blocks deposit their paint. The product was inaccurately called a linoleum rug.

Technically, linoleum is the product of oxidized and dried linseed oil. Large trays, maybe four by twelve feet in area, but with a depth of only four inches, are filled with a processed linseed oil. The oil is allowed to dry until it forms a solid, much like the material which forms over paint in a can that is left open. This solidified material is removed from the tray and ground up into small bits that are mixed with the desired colors and deposited, under pressure, onto the backing material.[51] The large rollers which compress the linoleum bits can be made to turn at different speeds to cause a slipping ac-

---

51 Before World War II linoleum was always backed by burlap. The primary source of burlap was India. That source dried up in the war years and a shortage of linoleum developed until the felt backing was perfected. The industry never returned to burlap.

tion that will produce a marbleized effect. This process can be set to make solid colors, mixed colors, or varied squares that would then be combined to make patterns. The weight of the finished product was determined by the depth of the "mix" placed on the backing material. Naturally, linoleum was more expensive than the felt base enamel coated "rugs," and lasted much longer.

The factory also made paints, some of which were used for the coloring of the floor coverings, most were processed for various indoor and outdoor paints. Also, the company owned a paper mill which produced the heavy felt backing used for floor coverings and roofing materials. Pabco was actuallly the first to discover that the "black paraffin" (actually asphalt) of California could be impregnated into heavy roofing paper (felt) to make ideal roof coverings for buildings.

Well, lots of other technical things that interested me but would not be of consuming interest to others.

We had a good time in San Francisco, acting as tourists, eating at interesting restaurants. One incident, among others, sticks clearly in my memory: Kit, not yet four years old, was being a child and stamping her foot in water puddles.

"Stop doing that," I told her. She continued. I bent down to her level, face to face, and scolded her for not obeying. She balled up her little fist and, without warning, punched me in the nose.

I didn't know whether to laugh or cry and neither did she, now frightened at this direct assault upon the figure of authority. So I hugged her and gave her a kiss and we went on our way.

My territory with Pabco was the eastern half of Missouri and the southern half of Illinois. I travelled those areas assisting the salesmen of the distributors located in Decatur, Illinois, and St. Louis. Each distributor had about ten men who sold floor covering and other household items to the retailers of their area. Sometimes I worked with the salesmen but mostly on my own. Whenever I took an order for floor covering from a dealer, the salesman for that distributor got the credit. I was paid a salary plus a year-end bonus for the amount of company products sold in my territory. Naturally, I would encourage the distributors to stock a supply of our products and sometimes sell new items they had not stocked, necessitating an order from the factory.

Since the company made floor coverings specifically designed for commercial use, I called upon offices and warehouses, even ice-skating rinks. We had a product called Mastipave that was ideally suited for warehouses and had withstood ice-skater traffic. The stuff actually protected concrete floors from metal wheels. Skating rink floors were protected without damage to skate edges.

Really was a good selling job. Automobile was furnished and all expenses were paid, including gas, oil, maintenance, tires, washing, license, insurance, and depreciation. I would alternate a week on the road with a week in St. Louis and the surrounding areas of Missouri and Illinois. On the road was generally from Tuesday morning until Friday evening. All meals and hotel bills on the road were paid. The company expected you to stay at the best hotels and eat good meals, be honest on your expense accounts.

Pabco paid their salesmen, Factory Representatives, better than Armstrong and Congoleum paid theirs. The two leading companies spent so much money advertising that they reasoned their salesmen did not have to work very hard selling the product. As I said, a good selling job.

And in less than a year I hated every minute of it.

Meanwhile, we had moved into our own little house, 1501 Westmont. Our first home was not grand, but it seemed that way to us, and, in retrospect, I'm sure the Hamptons were as happy to have us moving out as we were to be moving in to our so-called "Veterans' housing." Builders and developers could obtain construction funds to build two bedroom houses that would sell for under $10,000 to veterans of WW II who qualified. Construction on our project began in mid-1946 and we moved in just a little over a month before Lynne was born in 1947. The basic house was two bedrooms, living, dining, kitchen, one bath, attached one-car garage.

During construction Kay noticed one house had a higher roof line. We could see that this allowed an unfinished second floor. We spoke to the builder about raising our roof the same way so that we could have the extra space, offering to pay whatever extra would be required. He passed us on to his "expediter."

"Just tell him that it's OK with me if he can handle it."

This "expediter" was the real manager, the "honcho" of getting things done, working with the unions, and checking the designs, seeing that the subcontractors were using the right materials and finishing their jobs on schedule. He was supposed to say "No" to us. But, he was about to leave for another job, said he was tired of being the fall guy for a boss that never said "No" but expected him to.

So he said, "Sure, if the boss says it's Okay, it is Okay with me."

120

So we got our unfinished second floor, with dormer windows, and almost doubled our floor space. Eventually, we put in flooring, framing and dry-wall, to create a large bedroom and a sewing room. Later, a plumber installed a complete bath. But all that took some time. Because of the provisions of the Veterans Housing program, the contractor was allowed to increase his prices slightly, to $10,200, and we were able to get the extra space at the same price as all other houses.

We had a full basement, with laundry facilities, a gas-fired furnace which we used as a blower in summer to bring the cool air from the basement into the upper house. And I had my "office" there with a big roll-top desk that mother had found at an auction house for $25. (Should never have parted with that desk when I was recalled into the Air Force.) We had an extra furnace vent put in the basement for winter heating. And that was our first big problem with a contractor.

Actually, a sub-contractor. He told us it was no big job to cut another vent into the heating duct, and that he could do it for $25. Okay. When he later gave us a bill for $125, we had Northcutt Coil, who was our attorney, write him a "nice little note." And we paid the sub-contractor $25.

Coupla things happened to sort of sour me on Pabco. The first concerned the birth of Lynne. The big furniture market of the year began on Monday, July 7th, 1947, at the Merchandise Mart in Chicago.

Our regional sales manager, based in Chicago, called a meeting of all the salesmen of the district for Friday, Saturday, Sunday, July 4th, 5th and 6th. Kay started her labor and went into the hospital on the 4th. I called the Chicago office, and explained: "I can't be there on the 4th, because I promised my wife that I would be present for the birth of our second daughter."

They told me in no uncertain terms that the sales meeting was more important than the birth of our daughter. I said that I would come when I could; Kay told me to go to the meeting, which I did on Saturday morning. Lynne, our "Fourth of July Fireworks Baby," had made her appearance the night before. At the Saturday meeting I learned that the "big, important meeting" of the night before had consisted of a steak dinner get-together at Barney's, a famous Chicago restaurant near the stockyards. I was not impressed.

The second thing came along in my second year with the company. Pabco was an essentially conservative company, always following the lead of the two biggies, Armstrong and Congoleum. After all the other manufacturers, large and small, had begun to introduce lines of vinyl tiles and vinyl sheet goods, Pabco finally tested the water. By then all the dealers were loaded with this new material and we couldn't give it away.

But the product that got me was linoleum cleaner. A year after Armstrong came out with a linoleum cleaner, a simple mixture of water, soap, ammonia, and a little pine-smelling concentrate, Pabco wanted to get in the market. We were to sell cases (12 bottles to a case) to the dealers, who would sell the bottles for 25¢ each. There was so little profit for the dealers that they used it as a give-away with the sale of floor covering. And they already had a stock from Armstrong, anyway.

So, after a few months of poor sales of Pabco Floor Cleaner, I got a call from Chicago. The Chicago region was the lowest in sales across the country and I was the lowest in the Chicago region. Push Pabco Cleaner! Sell Pabco Cleaner! Move Pabco Cleaner! Unload Pabco Cleaner! Don't be concerned with what the dealers say. Don't worry about linoleum and rugs, forget the contracts with the military and industry for Mastipave! Get out and sell that cleaner!

So I got out and sold that cleaner. I begged, cajoled, coerced. I tied in the cleaner with all deliveries of linoleum. I insisted that they take delivery of Pabco cleaner if they wanted the latest styles of linoleum. I alienated a lot of dealers, made a lot of them angry, but I sold linoleum cleaner.

In a month, I got a call from Pat, my boss, the Chicago regional manager, telling me that I was tops in the nation. I had sold more linoleum cleaner than anyone else across the whole United States.

When he finished congratulating me, I told him I was giving two-weeks notice that I was leaving the company and that my written resignation would follow. Kinda shook him up a bit.

It was a good job, the salary was good, but I knew I just was not happy as a salesman. Kay said she had known for the past year that I was unhappy.

(Harder and harder to get back to the computer and this tale. Mid November 1990, just got out of an hours worth of dentist chair with my mouth stretched open till my jaws hurt while he tried to build up a filling on a practically non-existent tooth, all the while saying "this is not going to work, the amalgam is too dry, it is impossible to do this but we can try, and it probably won't last very long anyway, well, maybe it will last fairly well, and anyway you're going to have to see your dentist to have that bridge and crown repaired, but I hope this is going to work with that partial, now how does that feel?" etc.)

122

CHAPTER XXII

The Graduate Student

Before I left Pabco, I had determined what I wanted to do — I thought. I wanted to go back to Washington U. and get a master's degree in English and be a professor — I settled for teaching. Under the GI bill, I would be able to go back to school, have my tuition paid, have an allowance for books and receive a small amount for living expenses. Of course, there was the small matter of being admitted to graduate school, considering I had not been exactly Phi Beta Kappa (ΦBK) as an undergraduate.

Admission was controlled by the Department Head, in this case Dr. Roy MacKenzie, my old professor of Shakespeare, in whose class I had not shone exactly, but I had passed. When I met with him in his office, he gave me that searching look that indicated I might not have been entirely unknown to him.

"Ah, yes. Barbee. You occasionally slept in the back row during comedies, tragedies and histories. Ah, yes."

What could I say? He continued:

"Would you like a cigarette?", and handed me his round cigarette tin.

"No thank you, sir," and waved the tin back to him.

He refused to accept the return: "Well, then, would you please secure one for me?"

And I couldn't open the damn thing.

"Here, let me help you," and explained: "You grasp the tin firmly with both hands, thumbs beneath the rim, and exert firm but gentle pressure upwards, thusly," and the top popped open.

"Now, would you like a cigarette?"

I accepted. We began to discuss possible courses of study and action. He recognized that I was somewhat older than I had been, and presumably somewhat more mature. He seemed interested in the war years, my family, and what I had been doing in general, and suggested that I come back in a week for another discussion. I was not too discouraged.

Dr. MacKenzie was an international figure in the study of Shakespeare. He was surely regarded by many as somewhat of an eccentric. He wore rather tight-fitting Brooks Brothers suits, narrow at the shoulders, ageless in style. "Mac" would not have been mistaken for an athlete by anyone, but he was tall, slim, and seemed to stride with authority in going from place to place. His hair, completely gray and wiry, was worn in what we would today call an Afro: it stood in a ball around his head. In moments of concentration he would stretch his right arm above his head, bend his wrist and elbow slightly, and with a straight middle finger reach down to penetrate the bushy growth and scratch his head. Whatever we were studying, in any class, he would enter, glare at all, the good and the bad equally, adjust his pince-nez spectacles, and begin:

"Oh, yes, Act III, Scene 2, where Juliet sighs: *'Give me my Romeo; and, when he shall die, take him and cut him out in little stars...',*" or possibly, "Act V, Scene 2, where Othello rages: *'Are there no stones in heaven, But what serves for the thunder.'*" Dr. Mac could proceed from scene to scene, act to act, quoting the lines, questioning us as to feeling and meanings, never consulting the slight text he carried in his hand. It was theatrical, and it was meant to be. No student ever took one of his courses without gaining a better feeling for Shakespeare; some of us took all his courses during the years, but they would be so much more meaning-filled today.

So, after a week of anxiety, I found myself back in the lion's den. The good Dr. MacKenzie waved me to a chair, and offered me a cigarette, handing to me the pesky round tin. I grasped it firmly with both hands, exerted firm but gentle pressure upwards with both thumbs, popped the lid, and proffered him first choice at the contents.

"Ah," he murmured, "I see that you have the capacity to learn, so you will be allowed to enter as a candidate for the master's degree. What exactly do you have in mind?"

It would not seem "rigorous" considering that I took only three courses for credit (nine hours per semester), and audited one other; but my schedule was full: classes were from eight until twelve in the morning, at one o'clock I reported to Hollander & Company to sell floor covering until five p.m., ate and slept until I went to work at the automobile club answering telephones for emergency road service from eleven p.m.until seven a.m.. I had a house, a wife, and two small children to provide for.

During the two semesters of the regular academic year, I favored Elizabethan Tragedies and Chronicle Histories, Elizabethan Comedies and Tragi-Comedies, seminars in American and English Literature, History of the American Stage (a bow to scheduling necessity and my advisor Prof. Carson), and a thorough-going audit of Victorian Prose. How dull it seemed

124

then: struggling through Carlyle's "Sartor Resartus" and his professor Diogenes Teufelsdröckh (Devil's dung), or Macaulay's dissection of Milton, or trying to coordinate Newman's "The Idea of a University" with my particular endeavors at the time. Ruskin's "The Stones of Venice" has more appeal now that I have walked upon them and considered his connected observations; his "Sesame and Lilies," speaking of learning and good books, has poignant and urgent admonition and instruction for myself, now an indulgent octogenarian: "The author has something to say which he perceives to be true and useful, or helpfully beautiful. So far as he knows, no one has yet said it; so far as he knows, no one else can say it. He is bound to say it, clearly and melodiously if he may; clearly at all events." (As to the quality of my writing, I can only borrow Matthew Arnold's comparison of Giacomo Leopardi and Lord Byron: "Non so se il riso o la pietà prevale." —"I do not know whether laughter or pity prevails.")

In summary, in 1949, Victorian prose did not excite me. Most of the lesser writers, Alexander Smith, William Morris, Walter Horatio Pater, suffered no examination at my hands, and Robert Louis Stevenson is certainly not remembered as a prose essayist. The young student today is exposed in much greater degree to the romantic poets and writers of the era and those few decades preceding: Wordsworth, Coleridge, Byron, Shelley, Keats, Tennyson, Browning (Robert and Elizabeth), Kipling, the Brontës, and Hardy. The paragraph-long sentences of the prose writers, winding and circumlocuting, elucidating, instructing, admonishing, are to the young mind like broccoli and cauliflower are to the young appetite.

Well, it was an interesting year, working two jobs, attending classes, attempting to study to maintain a 3.5 grade-point average, researching for my master's thesis, being prevailed upon to take a part in one of the student dramatic productions by Prof. Carson.

And thereby hangs a tale.

My adviser, Prof. W.G.B. Carson, picked because I had worked with him so much in under-graduate days as a thespian and he was the faculty advisor for Thyrsus, had written two books about the theatre in St. Louis: one covering the period before the Civil War, the other covering after the Civil War. Since I had not expressed any overriding interest in any specific subject, he suggested I might want to look into the possibility of bridging the gap: History of the St. Louis Theatre During the Civil War. I found a wealth of information in newspapers of the 1860's well-preserved in basement rooms of Brookings Library and spent many quiet weekends alone with those dusty files.)

Oh, that acting role in the student play? Most memorable was an incident backstage when a "sweet young thing" happened by while I was putting on makeup.

"Oh," she gushed in admiring awe, "you've got REAL wrinkles!"

Came the summer and I had two courses yet to go: Anglo-Saxon and Chaucer, more precisely Old English and Middle English. The authorities were reluctant to allow taking these at the same time: "You would be studying the equivalent of two foreign languages at the same time. No one has ever done this before. We do not think it advisable for you to attempt to do this." My argument was simply that I had to finish my course work that summer, regardless of the difficulty it might pose. Accepted. And it turned out they were right. It was tough. Kay went to Michigan with the kids, we rented the house, I stayed with my mother, but lived at the university, and struggled with the seventh century religious poet Cædmon:

"Wæs he se mon in weoruldhade geseted o_ ɸa tì ɸe hë wæs gelÿfdre ylde, ond næfre nænig lëo_ geleornade." (Translating by looking up each word in the dictionary, I arrived at something resembling an idea that the worldly old man had never learned any songs.)

The fourteenth century Chaucerian English of the Freres Tale was infinitely more comfortable:

"Whilom ther was dwellynge in my contree
An erchedeken, a man of heigh degree,
That boldely dide execucioun
In punysshnge of fornicacioun,
Of wicchecraft, and eek of bawderye,
Of diffamacioun, and avowtrye,
Of chirche reves, and of testamentz,
Of contractes and lakke of sacramentz..."

Even more aptly, Chaucer's Clerk of Oxenford who was still pursuing his studies, perhaps in preparation for his Master's degree:

"Of studie took he moost cure and moost heede.
Noght o word spak he moore than was neede,
And that was seyd in forme and reverence,
And short and quyk and ful of sentence
Sownynge in moral vertu was his speche,
And gladly wolde he lerne and gladly teche."

Yes, it was a very busy and very interesting summer. Further complicating the study of Old English was the professor's strong German accent as his guttural tones emanated from under an ice bag which he kept on the top of his head throughout the class. The classrooms were not air-conditioned, but the consensus of our handful of students was there was a reason for the strange headgear other than the heat. A grade of "B" in both courses, and I had completed the required credit hours. Tired, tired. I was always so tired.

The next steps were completion of the thesis and examinations, oral and written.

"What happens if the examiners ask me a question I can't answer?"

"They will ask you another," explained my mentor.

"And suppose I can't answer that one?"

"They will keep on until they find something you know," he assured me.

And that was just about the way it went.

You know the expression "Damning with faint praise"? After my thesis "History of the St. Louis Theatre During 1861-1865" was examined by the assigned professor, I awaited anxiously his comments.

"Very interesting. Did you type it yourself? Yes? Well, not a bad job of typing. Thank you for coming in."

And that was that. But I had successfully earned the degree, and I was offered a job as a graduate assistant to work toward a Ph D. It would pay $1800 a year.

It was just not enough to support a house, a wife, and two children, so I began to investigate teaching in high school.

CHAPTER XXIII

Teaching is Work

Maplewood-Richmond Heights High School proved to be looking for someone to teach English and Journalism. My journalism experience as assistant editor of a cadet yearbook could not be considered excessive, but was judged sufficient, and I got the job on the basis of having a master's degree and military experience. The principal seemed to think my age and experience could possibly be useful in maintaining discipline. It worked. I did not have the courses in "education" required for teaching in the public schools of the state of Missouri, so I was granted a temporary certificate for one year. More on that.

Starting salary level was $1800 a year, but with the MA degree and my "experience," I was offered $2100, with small incremental additions:

..for supervising publication of:
    the student newspaper,
    the school district newsletter,
    and the Yearbook;
..for public address system announcements at football games,
..for coaching the "B" baseball team,
..for assisting the wrestling coach,
..for being timekeeper at basketball games.

With all these additional "goodies" my first year salary amounted to about $2600, the equivalent of about $14,500 in 1990. Quite a few additional duties and, coupled with attending afternoon and evening classes at Washington U's Department of Education, and summer school, it was a fairly busy year.

To do a good job of teaching English requires a lot of dedication and time — counseling and grading papers — but can be rewarding when you see students really taking an interest in the language, its history, growth and development, and its literature. There were a few in each class, and it was gratifying to hear from them that they had been able to pass an exam that granted them credit for the college freshman course... And there were the others.

A few things come to mind — not really connected to teaching, but resulting from the attempt. Dale was a big, tall young man, considered handsome by the girls, and a good football player. He occasionally allowed himself to get out of hand as his attention wandered.

One day, after a couple of admonitions, he persisted in disturbing the class. I told him to come with me as I walked out the classroom door. He expected to be taken to the principal's office, the normal procedure. But I never passed one of my problems to the principal during the years that I taught. I figured he had his job and I had mine. I had Dale follow me across the hall to a little room, which we used to work on the newspaper and yearbook, and asked him if he had ever done any wrist-wrestling. He had. I told him I wanted to show him something and he smiled. First I rapped his knuckles on the table twice, then almost threw him to the floor left-handed. I explained:

"Dale, I've done this because I wanted you to understand a very basic idea. I'm a man and you're a boy, and there's a difference between a man and a boy. I'm the authority figure in that classroom. Keep that in mind when we go back in." He smiled, and said "Yessir." He never again caused trouble in class — but I had to wrist-wrestle practically the whole football team. With one exception, fortunately. Binky Broeder. He never challenged me and I don't know what would have happened if he had. That kid could do pushups from a handstand.

There were some characters on the faculty:

Charlie Brown: taught English, mostly juniors and freshmen, and Spanish, walked with a slight limp from an old hip injury. A pleasant individual, quiet, derived his greatest pleasure from playing piano at a night club several nights each week. Probably paid as much as the teaching. He never read assigned papers.

Anna Mae Nollner: (old maid) had been teaching English for over thirty years. Annie especially liked grammar, diagramming of sentences, had no rapport whatsoever with students. One day she came to my classroom and asked if I could help her scan "My Last Duchess" by Robert Browning. I could and did. But I tried to make the point that enjoying the meaning and appreciating the poetic expression was so much more important than understanding the mechanics of the verse. Her students never developed a great liking for poetry.

Norville Wallach: Phys Ed, but mainly assistant football coach. Weighed about 235. When I asked him if he had ever tried pro football, he said: "Yeah, but when those BIG guys started coming at me, I decided I'd try something else."

Juva Sharp, librarian, had some sort of deformity of her back and walked with a built-up shoe. Miss Sharp was a pleasant, quick-witted teacher. One day she remarked:

"I've had a run on all the books about Chaucer. How do you get these kids interested in him?"

"Why," I smiled, "I just read them a few lines from some of the racy tales, and then tell them I couldn't finish some of those off-color stories in class."

She understood.

Fred Larason, teacher of Math, General Science, Physics. A spare, energetic, extremely pleasant individual. From my first day, Fred was a helpful friend. He was a patient, understanding gentleman, and a good baseball coach.

The economic and social backgrounds of the students were widely varied but seemed to make no obvious difference in their friendships. The "other side of the tracks" people were equal to the "exclusive homes" group in their activities and scholarship. One notable difference: all the higher income, generally professional, families' children all went on to college, only a few from the "blue-collar" neighborhoods. An often heard plaint of girls from the less-advantaged: "Sure be glad to get out of high school so I can get a job and be independent." Not all felt that way. Some had greater vision. Those with inquiring minds had determined early that they would travel further, expand their horizons. They wanted not only to 'know' things, but to know the 'whys,' and asked the 'what ifs.' With encouragement, they grew. They were the editors and writers and artists for the newspaper and yearbook, the organizers and leaders of clubs.* Regardless of economic circumstance, those students who wanted more than just a grade from the teacher were those who made the profession challenging and worthwhile.

My temporary teaching certificate: to satisfy the state requirements for certification I had to complete the necessary 'education' courses. The education catchword of the day was "Education for Living." What that really translated to was training rather than education. The college Education Departments controlled the subject matter and the curriculum. Such courses as "Teaching for Life Adjustment," "Teaching in Elementary Schools," "Teaching in Secondary Schools," "Teaching English in Secondary Schools," "The Theory of Teaching," etc. My favorite: "Practice Teaching in High

School." This was the grand finale, the last of all the goodies. The aspiring teachers were assigned to a neighboring school to teach some classes under the supervision of the experienced regular teacher, be graded, critiqued, and counseled on their performance.

(Date: April 18, 1991 - our 49th Wedding Anniversary. That is today as I resume a part of this long-winded autobiography. No man could ever dream what happiness Kathryn Jarrell Hampton Barbee has brought me over the years. She is a truly remarkable woman, unique. I am sure no love has ever been quite like ours.)

Some of the courses might have had some bearing on being a teacher, but when I was told that I would "practice teach" myself because I was already teaching, I could believe that education courses were not what they were supposed to be. I had bought the texts for the courses, as required, but got "A's" in all courses except one: I had tried reading the text and got confused. It was better to use common sense. So I finished the required courses, received my permanent teaching certificate, took some of the administration courses at the suggestion of the principal who seemed interested in my work, and tried to get some momentum working on a Ph.D.

Eventually, I finished most of the course work but never did the dissertation — I knew I did not want to be a 'researching' college professor.

It was during the spring of my third year at Maplewood-Richmond Heights that the school board decided not to renew the contract of the superintendent, Mr. Adams, stating that he was not responsive to changes that the board wished to make, and hired a successor from a school district in southeastern Missouri. Some parents and students protested this action. That is almost a knee-jerk response in situations like that. But a group of teachers called a meeting of the teachers to show their allegiance to Mr. Adams. They proposed to send a letter, signed by all the teachers, to the man hired to take the position, stating that he should not accept the job. According to the leaders of the group, there could be no "fence-straddlers," we had to make a decision to be for Mr. Adams, or against him.

I was the only one to speak up:

"No one here would dare to call me a fence-straddler on any issue. For three years I have worked with Mr. Adams and the school board, publishing the school district newspaper (actually a newsletter). I have given him my cooperation and allegiance, as an employee to an employer. While he is superintendent I will continue to do so. If this new man takes the job, I will give him the same cooperation and allegiance. The superintendent hires the

131

teachers, the teachers do not hire the superintendent. The school board has that authority, not me. I cannot be a part of any effort to circumvent the authority of the school board, so I am leaving this meeting now."

A small number of others walked out with me.

Election of a new school board a few weeks later resulted in some changes and the new board voted to retain Mr. Adams and pay off the man who had been given a contract for the coming year. No one ever challenged the right of the board to expend funds in that manner.

I was called to a meeting of the new board when they instructed Mr. Adams that he was not to take any action against any of the teachers who had not signed the teachers' petition, "especially Mr. Barbee."

That was fine, and I was gratified to hear the position of the board. But I had the feeling that the atmosphere throughout the school might not be real happy and decided to look around during the summer for possible openings in other schools.

Opening in the fall of 1952 was the new Ladue High School. The school district of the City of Ladue had decided it was time to have its own high school. Ladue had schools through the eighth grade but had always paid to send their high school students to private schools or to the neighboring city of Clayton. Over 95% of the students would be continuing to college and the residents wanted to have a greater hand in exercising control over the curriculum of the high school.

Ladue was, and perhaps still is, the most affluent suburb of the City of St. Louis. Ladue, University City, Clayton, Webster Groves, Kirkwood, were the major towns of St. Louis County, mostly to the west of St. Louis which is in its own county, County of the City of St. Louis. It was noted for several decades, that Ladue had more millionaires than all of England. In 1990 there are more "developments," smaller houses and lots than in those earlier years, but still in existence are the areas of winding private roads, larger two and three-storey palatial brick homes, on one or more acres of property. (Bud and Suzanne Hampton, Kay's nephew & niece, live in one of these.) So there was the financial wherewithal for this enterprise of a new high school.

Early in that summer of 1952 I got an appointment with the man selected to be the principal of this new school. A young man, with some progressive ideas, he had been brought in from out of state. He greeted me courteously enough, but pointed out that he had a stack of applications several feet high for only a handful of jobs, and that most of them were from teachers more experienced than I. Undaunted, I pointed out that many were probably hide-

132

bound in their past experiences and not susceptible to the changes he wished to bring to this new endeavor. He indicated he was aware of the situation at Maplewood-Richmond Heights and my reason for wanting to leave there. After he listened with increasing interest to some of my ideas regarding the teaching of English, and the curriculum I proposed for the classes in junior and senior high school, he asked me: "And what salary do you have in mind?"

"I'm willing to start at five thousand," I said. (about $26,000 in 1992.)

"You think you're worth five thousand? That's more than you're making now and more than our salary schedule provides for someone with only three years' experience."

I smiled. "No, I didn't say I was worth five thousand. I said I was willing to start for that amount. I'm worth much more than five thousand but you don't know that yet. After I have proven that to you, we can discuss a more appropriate figure."

He smiled, too. "The superintendent has to approve any deviation from the salary schedule. Let me go talk to him."

The "boss" wanted to meet me.

"I understand you think you're worth five thousand?"

"No sir, that's not quite correct. As I explained to the principal, I'm worth much more than that but I have to prove that to you. When I do, you will be willing to pay more. When you and the principal are free of handling discipline problems with the students in my classes, when you see students not only learning the language and the literature but enjoying the process and increasing their SAT scores, then you will know what I mean."

"When can you start?" he asked.

"How about this afternoon?" I replied.

They were not surprised at Maplewood-Richmond Heights when I told them I was leaving. The superintendent, the principal and a few others wished me well, I cleaned out my desk, packed my personal books, and began what turned out to be my last semester of teaching English.

Ladue High School was an interesting four and one-half months. The innovative schedule: classes of one hour and fifteen minutes; bells did not ring at the end of the period, teachers were required to observe the time and dismiss classes at the proper hour; each subject met four days each week: the longer class period was to provide time for beginning any assigned homework. We had all sizes of kids in the hallways at class break: the rambling, one storey building housed grades eight through twelve.

My persistent memory is of only three students: two eleventh grade boys, frequent trouble-makers in other classes, who decided to test me. And a senior boy who was dyslexic - really could not read.

After several disruptions one day by the two juniors, I pointed to both of them and motioned for them to follow me. As I went out the classroom door, I could see their reflection as they shrugged and snickered to the other students. They were surprised when I did not turn in the direction of the principal's office but continued in the opposite direction and walked outside the building.

There we stopped. They were a little uneasy; this was something new in their experience.

"You seem to be having difficulty understanding good, plain English," I said, and proceeded to tell them what I thought of them, using every bit of gutter English I knew to describe them, their parents, and their heritage. I pointed out that if they did not like what I had said to them, or the language I had used, to bring their father or big brother to the school and I would gladly give them the same treatment.

Then I reminded them that I was the only teacher of junior and senior English.

"You cannot graduate without passing my courses. You have the choice of coming back into the class, and behaving, or going to the principal and telling him that you are not acceptable to me and would have to arrange a transfer to some private school at parental expense."

"If you follow me back to the classroom, we will start all over again with a clean slate."

Then I turned and reentered the school building. They followed on my heels, never caused a bit of trouble again, and were the planners and arrangers of a big farewell party when I was recalled by the Air Force. They were my two best "friends" at the school.

The Kid who couldn't read: the dyslexic. This was obvious from the very first day. I had to find out how he had got this far in school. Other teachers told me they let him take examinations orally. I talked with his father and mother. His mother read his assignments to him. His father, who owned a Ford auto agency, said his son would not go on to college, that he would inherit the auto business, and that he knew the business. The kid was bright enough. He just could not read. His father said that if I would work with the boy, give him some special attention, he could help me out in buying a new car. I needed a new car. So he would give me a "special deal."

When I checked with other dealers, I found I could save $200 or more buying from a dealer who wasn't giving me a "special deal." Life goes on.

After World War II, I had remained in the reserve force. For a couple of years I took correspondence courses, attended some infrequent meetings. When I began teaching I became more "active."

A unit had been formed at Scott Field in Illinois that offered regular training for reservists. One weekend a month. Saturday morning until afternoon on Sunday. Soon after I joined the unit, I was made the Training Officer. The commander liked to have a meeting with all the staff officers on Friday evening before the Saturday session, so a couple of us car-pooled to drive over on Friday afternoon.

As Training Officer I was still required to participate in the training. Obviously, there was no time on the regular training weekend to develop a training schedule, so I had to spend another weekend there preparing the schedule for the following weekend. Bear in mind that I am teaching English, assigning writing tasks which must be read, corrected and graded.

Then our reserve unit was assigned airplanes: C-46's. This was to enable us pilots to keep up our flying skills. But the flying had to be done on days other than our training days — another weekend now to go fly. And if the weather did not cooperate that weekend, try it again the following week. Meanwhile, every night that I am home I am in the basement of the house grading papers.

So my dear wife says to me:

"You go to school every day and take graduate courses at Washington U.* in the afternoons and grade papers and study every night. The reserve training was to have been one weekend a month. It became two, three, and sometimes four weekends. I hardly ever see you anymore. I think we would be better off on active duty with the Air Force and I'm ready to go."

The next weekend, just before Christmas 1952, our reserve unit colonel told me I would be recalled to active duty for the war in Korea. The school superintendent said he thought he could get me excused from this recall, but I told him that I had remained in the reserve and I felt it my duty to respond. He understood.

"Do you want to resign or take a leave of absence?" he said, "it really doesn't matter. If you ever want to come back, there will be a job waiting.

"Because people like you are leaving teaching, I have gone to the school board to demand substantial increases in our salary schedule. These increases will be keyed to what I feel would be three classes of teachers: good teachers, excellent teachers, and outstanding teachers like you. The board is going to give my proposals serious consideration."

That sort of thing makes a guy feel good, and I thanked him for the kind words.

CHAPTER XXIV

Recall to the U.S. Air Force

Headquarters Tenth Air Force, Selfridge Air Force Base, Michigan, Special Orders 9, 12 January 1953

Par 25. By direction of the President, each of the following Air Force Reserve Officers is relieved from Reserve assignment indicated and on effective date shown after his name is ordered into active military service in grade indicated and for the period specified unless sooner relieved..

On effective date of entry into active military service shown below, each officer is assigned and will proceed from his home or temporary address of record to unit and duty station indicated, reporting to the CO thereof for duty.

**MAJOR BUD BARBEE, AO726183 (USAF)(AF ResA)(DOCA 1 Nov 52)(DR 30 Jan 53)(PAFSC 7221)(DAFSC 1324)(YOB 18)(W)(FSSD 7 Dec 41)(Plt-On Fly Status) (VOL)(C) (Married, 3 Depns)(DPS USAF)(Res Asgmt: Hq, 8711th Plt Tng Wg, 2469 AFRFTC)1501 Westmont Court, University City 14, Missouri. EFF DT DY: 17 Feb 53. PD AD: Indef. DY STA & RQN: Asg PCS p/1 to 3702d Pers Processing Sq, 3700th AF Indoc Wg (ATRC) Lackland AFB, Texas, rep thereat NLT 19 Feb 53 for indoc and processing.

Did you get all that? Lots of military jargon and abbreviations. All it said was that I was to be in Texas on February 19, 1953, for processing, no family, and I could drive if I wanted to.

Lackland and San Antonio had changed somewhat since we had been there eight years earlier in 1945, but I could still find my way around. One day on the street in downtown San Antonio I encountered a former student from Maplewood-Richmond Heights High School. I could see that he was wearing a brand new Air Force uniform issued to the enlistees processing at Lackland. He popped a snappy salute, then did a double-take as he walked past.

Turning immediately, he said: "Sir, is that you Mr. Barbee, I mean Major?" I smiled and shook his hand. He stammered, "I thought it was you, Mr, I mean Major, but you were a teacher. I didn't know you could do anything else." Sad, but a lot of teachers are regarded in that light.

About a week of signing forms, listening to lectures, drawing pay, general indoctrination, and new orders:

Special Orders #38, Lackland AFB, 25 February 1953:

MAJ BUD BARBEE AO726183, USAF, prim AFSC 1231,(W) AFRes A, FSSD 7 Dec 41... plt on fly status.. asg PP 21st ADiv, SAC, Forbes AFB, Topeka, Kans. Off is place on TDY.. to Plt Refresher Crse, aprx sixty days, cl commencing 9 Mar 53, at 3304th Plt Tng Sq, Hondo Afld, Hondo, Tex. DOPF (Forbes AFB, Kans). WP Hondo Afld, Tex o/a 28 Feb 53 rep to CO thereat NLT 7 Mar 53. Upon compl of TDY Off WP Forbes AFB, Kans fr Hondo Afld, Tex RUAT CO.

So these orders told me to go to Hondo Airfield for refresher pilot training, then to Forbes AFB, Kansas. This meant I had about a week back in St.Louis to help Kay with plans for the house and moving.

Hondo, in the boondocks of Texas, was familiar from our final World War II days there. Except now there were AT-6 aircraft instead of B-24s. I had not flown small aircraft for such a long time that it was a little strange to be sitting behind a single engine again. And I had forgotten how much fun it was to fly a little maneuverable "stick" job and do aerobatics. It sorta made up for having to check out a parachute and have it bumping on my rear end as I trotted out to the plane. Like the "good ol'" cadet days.

At Forbes AFB, Topeka, I was assigned to the 815th Operations Squadron. In SAC (Strategic Air Command) in those days, the operations squadron took care of everything pertaining to flying on the base: the tower, base operations, training (ground school and simulators), flying safety, and supply. Initially, I had the job of Air Base Group Flying Safety Officer, but later Capt Lorne Whitworth took that job when I took over as Executive Officer and Assistant Squadron Commander.

The base was headquarters of the 21st Air Division commanded by Brigadier General "Smokey Joe" Caldara. Two wings of B-29 and B-50 aircraft were the main operational units under the Air Division. Most of the pilots in our squadron flew the C-47, the even-then venerable "Gooney Bird."

The Gooney was the military version, with very few changes, of the DC-3; this airplane is generally credited with the real development and growth of commercial flying. Most frequently configured to fly twenty-one passengers commercially, The Air Force use as a cargo carrier usually had passengers sitting in metal "bucket" seats or "sling" seats along the sides of the cabin. Not the greatest comfort, but the price was right. Twin engine, low wing.

Conventional gear: had a tail wheel. Very dependable aircraft. Not fast, not pressurized, but had low wing loading and could fly on one engine and glide for miles. This could, and did, lead to some interesting jackrabbit landings; sometimes called "elevator" landings (up and down).

I can recall several "interesting" flights. On my first flight to Florida, we landed at MacDill to drop off some parts, then took off to the east coast to Homestead AFB. Right in the middle of the afternoon. Going right through the middle of "thunderstorm alley." Monstrous cumulonimbus clouds rising to over thirty thousand feet. We tried to go around most of them, but it turned out to be a very, very rough ride.

Another flight was to the depot at Kelly Field, San Antonio. We were in rain all the way. Not necessarily rough weather, but wet, wet, wet. And the windshield on the pilot's side leaked — leaked in just the exact spot to run into my boot. No matter how I moved my feet, having to keep them on the rudder pedals, the rain poured into my boot. After we landed I poured the water from my boot and tried to dry my socks before returning to Forbes.

Another memorable experience occurred while flying south from Colorado Springs, Colorado, heading for El Paso, Texas, paralleling the Rocky Mountains. We were in perfectly clear air; except for a little saucer-shaped job on top of the mountains there were no other clouds; good visibility; and we began to lose alitude. Add some power, still going down. Keep adding power, keep going down — as if some tremendous weight were pushing us toward the ground. I decided to break away, while there was still some air below us, and headed to the east, away from the mountains. Almost immediately we began to climb again and regain our altitude. Sure was a puzzle.

Some years later meteorologists reported on the phenomenom of the "lenticular" cloud: seems that particular shaped cloud, atop a mountain peak, foretold of extreme downdrafts within several miles of the slopes. Several aircraft were lost as a result of this phenomenon.

Forbes was a PCS (Permanent Change of Station) which meant the family could accompany. So we rented 1501 Westmont in St. Louis to a nice couple, packed up our furniture and moved to Topeka, Kansas. We were asigned quarters (3423 Claire) at Likens-Foster housing located between the city and the airfield. This was "adequate" housing, but poorly built. When the wind was blowing from the west, dust would come into the house where the the wall met the floor.

The houses certainly deserved the nickname of "Leaky Faucet." Somewhere there is a picture of the front of the house and the carport and Lynne flying a kite in the front yard.

In my job I had to make frequent trips to the flight line and civilian autos were not allowed on the ramp. So I bought my first two-wheeler: a Cushman motor scooter. I could also use it to travel between home and the base, but it was pretty tricky at times during the winter with a little snow and ice on the roads. Required care in handling, but sure useful going between airplanes on the ramp. Can't remember exactly what happened to that machine, but the Air Force would not ship vehicles classed as motorcycles overseas so I guess I sold it to someone.

For Kit's 10th birthday we bought her a new bicycle. The first time she rode it she fell and cracked her ankle. To the base hospital and arrive just at "chow" time. Everybody out to lunch. Find a doctor who says he is going off duty but will look at our emergency, making the disclaimer that Kit will be the patient of the doctor who is supposed to relieve him. So he gets an X-ray, finds a cast and proceeds to encase her leg in what seemed to be an awful lot of plaster of paris. We can then wait for the next doctor due to come "on shift." We wait. And we wait. He is in the office and knows we are waiting. And we still wait. Finally I decide we have waited long enough and go on in to his office. He is not accustomed to such brashness, but I tell him we have been waiting long enough. Does he want to check on Kit? No? Okay, what do we do if she is in pain? Give her aspirin. When do we come back? Oh, a couple of weeks? All right. Now, can we have some crutches for her to use?

"I don't believe in crutches for children. They just try to do too much and we have to do everything all over again."

"But how can she get to the bathroom to use the toilet?"

"Well, your wife can carry her."

"Look, doctor, she weighs almost the same as my wife. How can my wife pick her up and carry her?"

Surly, dismissing me and the problem: "She'll just have to work that out. I don't issue crutches for children to use."

Now I am really angry. "Listen, you draft-dodging incompetent pill-pusher, we will see about what you will and won't do." And I storm out.

Kit is in a wheel chair and I am steaming her along toward the exit door when a nurse and an orderly yell:

"You can't take the wheel chair from the hospital!"

"Just watch me," I say, as I continue out the door.

"If you want it, come get it at my car." I had had enough of bureaucracy.

After taking Kay and Kit back home I still have a full head of steam as I return to the hospital and demand to see the hospital commander. I explain to the colonel exactly what happened. He listens. He says he just can't believe that the doctor would have that attitude.

"I know him and I just can't believe that he would do that,." he repeats several times.

I'm getting tired of this.

"Well, call him in here and ask him, or do you think I'm just making this up? I have told you exactly what happened.

"There have been many complaints about the treatment at this hospital and the attitude that the doctors have. The enlisted people and the younger officers report on poor treatment and get the runaround. I think it's time I tell my brother-in-law about the situation here."

The colonel doesn't like my tone. "I don't care what you tell your brother-in-law. I'm running this hospital. And here's a note for you to check out some crutches for your daughter."

I thank him for the crutches. That weekend we drive back to St. Louis to have Oscar take a look at Kit's injury. His comments:

"The cast is too big. It's for an adult, not a child. They have overlooked the significant injury. There is a small hairline fracture of the ankle that should have the primary attention. They have cast her foot with her toe pointed down. Should be cast with her foot flat in the event of faulty healing which would cause her to walk with her heel elevated. That would not be good."

Oc took off the old cast and fashioned a small, neat, walking cast — one with a stubby extension on the bottom.

"That will be better," he said. "What's the name of the doctor who did this and what's the name of the hospital commander?"

Two weeks later, at a dance at the officers' club, the hospital commander sees me and says:

"Who did you say your brother-in-law is? For the past week I have had people from Washington tearing my hospital apart, talking to everybody, checking everything, making changes, keeping me tied in knots answering their questions."

Dr. Oscar Perry Hampton, Special Consultant to the Surgeon General, travelled frequently to inspect hospitals, specializing particularly in orthopedic procedures and administrative practices. Having served as Orthopedic Consultant in the Mediterranean theatre during World War II, he was always concerned with the treatment and care of military personnel.

The hospital was reorganized, became more caring and more efficient. The hospital commander at Forbes was relieved of his command, and transferred. Sometimes it does matter who you know.

Several other things come to mind (after fifty years have passed) about Topeka:

Kay was assistant scoutmaster of a Girl Scout troop. Willing mothers, who want their children in certain activities, volunteer to assist in the programs so Kay was a regular volunteer. (And was a volunteer Red Cross worker at the Patrick AFB hospital until her stroke in May 1998.)

One of the mothers, from some place in the south, did not like the idea of her child having to associate with, and perhaps eat with, a little black girl on a scout outing, and issued the ultimatum to Kay that either the little black girl had to go or she would take herself and her daughter from the troop..

My dear wife, born and raised in a segregated society, and admittedly racially prejudiced, had one of her finest hours when she declared that the little black girl would remain in the troop. I was very proud of her.

The cockpits of the aircraft we flew were equipped with headsets that were uncomfortably hard on my ears. A very few of the latest and highly desirable headsets which fit around the ear with large foam padding, were only occasionally available for temporary issue to the C-47 aircrews. One day I mentioned to our master sergeant in charge of supply that it would be nice to have one of these headsets. The next day I found on my desk a brand new headset. I thanked the sergeant.

"Where did you get it?"

"Oh, major, sir, you aren't supposed to ask questions like that." I understood.

General Caldara was having the regular 4th of July reception which all officers were supposed to attend at the officers' club. This required the dress uniform — at the time a matter only of white shirt and black bow tie with the regular uniform.

One of my friends declared that he was not going to the reception: "With a crowd like that, I'll never be missed."

142

I agreed, but replied: "That's true, but I figure that if I don't go, I won't be seen." And it usually follows that you should be seen where you are supposed to be. It makes a difference.

Sometimes we had to ferry an aircraft to Lockheed-Ontario, in Ontario, California, for repairs and modifications. I seized the chance because my brother lived in Duarte, a nearby town, and there would be a little time to visit with him. That day he went into the hospital for a rather serious operation.

I was on TDY orders which called for return to Topeka by commercial air if military air was not available. Gen. Caldara was scheduled to visit the headquarters at Riverside and it might be possible to return with him if there were room on his plane. When they landed at March AFB I checked with the general's pilot (and aide) and learned they would leave at 1000 (10 a.m.) the next day. I explained about visiting with my brother in the hospital and told him I would be there at "show" time 0930..

No familiar faces at Base Operations the next day when I showed up a little before 0930. The clerk told me they had taken off earlier than planned.

Orders permitted me to fly commercially, but I realized there might be some criticism for not having returned on the general's plane. I began to check on any military flights heading east. That afternoon a message came from Topeka:

"General upset you missed flight. Ordered you be placed on leave. TDY orders cancelled. End."

That upset me no little bit. After several hops across country I managed to get back to Forbes the next day without cost to the Air Force. When I checked in with the deputy base commander to protest being put on leave, he said it was the general's order. I asked for permission to see the general. He said it would not be a good idea. I persisted. When I went in the general's office, his aide listened to my complaint and recommended that I let the matter drop.

I knocked on the door of the general's office, went in, saluted, and reported that I wished to see him about the California mixup. I told him how everyone said he was unhappy that I had missed his flight and demanded I be put on leave. He smiled:

"Bud, I haven't lost touch with humanity. When my aide told me that we were taking off earlier than planned, and that your brother was in the hospital, I thought you might want to stay out there a few days longer to be with him and suggested you be put on leave so you wouldn't have to hurry back here. That's all. I don't see how some people can get things so screwed up. How is your brother? Will he be all right?"

I thanked the general for his understanding, clarified the matter for the intermediate commanders, and reflected that it is always a good idea to get the little misunderstandings straightened out quickly. Of course, it did not hurt that the general now had a face and personality to go with my name.

There was a going away party for the general when he received orders for Okinawa. I introduced myself to the general's wife:

"Mrs. Caldara, I have never had the pleasure and soon will not have the opportunity. May I have this dance?"

She smiled: "that is the nicest way I've ever been asked to dance." Didn't cost me a thing. They later remembered me when I was stationed in Japan and flew to Okinawa on business.

One of the precepts that Polonius lavished upon his son Laertes who was about to continue his education on the continent:

"...But do not dull thy palm with entertainment
Of each new-hatch'd unfledg'd comrade..." (Hamlet, I, iii)

appears to fit a situation that arose at Forbes. The young captain in charge of the supply section was one of my golfing partners. As I remember his wife, Mrs. Martin was a nice young lady, and they had one or two young kids, but we had no social contacts with them other than official functions.

The officer in charge of the Base Communications Section, Capt. John W. Grow, had orders transferring him to another base and was trying to clear his supply account. He was short four office chairs. He came to me to explain that he had signed for the account knowing the chairs were missing because Capt. Martin had told him the chairs were temporarily in another section and that he, the supply officer, would correct the records. Now Capt. Martin was telling Capt. Grow that he will have to pay for the chairs — about $25 each.

Not to worry. I called the supply officer, my golfing "buddy," to my office and explained that he should get these records corrected, as he had promised Capt Grow. Capt. Martin acted surprised and slightly indignant.

"Why is he coming to you with this complaint?"

"Because I am his, and your, immediate superior and he says you have refused to correct the records as you promised him."

"Well, in the first place, he was stupid to sign for the account when it was short. I don't know where the chairs are now, so he will just have to pay for them."

"We know he should not have signed, but you gave your word as an officer. Your honor would demand that you set the account straight or cover the cost of replacement."

"Major, when it comes to a question of my honor or my money, my money comes first." Uh-oh!   Into my mind came:†! the hospital had reported several instances of linen shortage; I had processed some paperwork regarding a missing .45 cal. automatic pistol; some other small and seemingly insignificant incidents in the supply section. I dismissed Capt. Martin and immediately called the OSI (Office of Special Investigations) to request a thorough examination of our supply accounts.

Within a week Capt. Martin was relieved of duty, accused of court martial offenses, and ordered to stand trial. He was subsequently found guilty of all charges, stripped of his commission, and sentenced to dishonorable discharge, forfeiture of all pay and allowances, and five years of hard labor at a federal prison. His money should never have come before his honor as an officer.

(When I next encountered Capt Grow, about seventeen years later, he was a colonel and the base commander at Korat, Thailand. We played tennis together and reminisced briefly about the incident at Forbes.

"I hear Kay is coming for a visit," he said, "Where is she going to stay?"

"A hotel in town."

"Why shouldn't she stay in your private "hooch" when she comes,

rather than a hotel in town? As base commander, I have no

objection.")

In my next assignment I would write and revise regulations that would, essentially, stress financial responsibility, moral integrity, and the three words, so dramatically put by General MacArthur at the time of his retirement, that are the foundation of an officer's career, Duty, Honor, Country.

A year, almost to the day, after reporting to Forbes came orders transferring me to Korea, via the 2353rd Personnel Processing squadron at Parks AFB, Pleasanton, California.

October 1941

Most beautiful woman I've ever known

146

Newly Wed in April, 1942

Spokane, WA
Summer, 1942

Award of bronze star medal and air medal. 1970

Farewell in Thailand Nov, 1970   (Col. Jack Mitchell & my wife)

L to R   Kit, Kay, Lynne   (Kit & Lynne my daughters)

L to R   Kim, Buddy, Felicia   (my grandchildren)

CHAPTER XXV

JAPAN

Special Orders Number 61, 16 March 1954, sent me to Parks AFB for processing to Korea, presumably as an operations officer of a B-25 outfit, as provided in something called SAC Project 5008 (whatever that was).

This would be a separation of one year, so Kay and the girls drove west with me to the base at Pleasanton, California, about fifteen miles from Oakland. We had a new 1954 Ford station wagon for the trip. The color was a sort of light cream, and later we had the area around the window level painted red. An interesting combination, and attractive.

The trip was standard: Kit and Lynne in the back seat squabbling most of the time — until the driver lost his patience and cool. I stopped the car, got out and stung the girls' legs with my belt. Kay said my hand was so hard that I should not spank them with my hand. It seems that Kit's fondest remembrance of her father is that he "beat" her with his belt. There was never any bruise or blood. I know she never saw the tears in my eyes when I did this. Oh, well.

A different experience on the trip: we stopped in Yosemite National Park and spent the night in a rustic little cabin. The coal-oil lamps instead of electric lights entranced Kit and Lynne. Neat! And the young deer that came right up to the cabin.

Arriving at Parks, we asked directions of a young lieutenant colonel who was heading in our direction and he steered us to the headquarters for signing in. Cecil E. Petty. We were to become fast friends with him and his wife, Marjorie, during the next 35 years, and travel extensively with them to England, most European countries, Australia, New Zealand. For a number of years we shared favorite nephew's cottage in Macatawa, Michigan for a few days in the summer. Kay and Marj together are as giddy as schoolgirls.

Spent over a week with the 2353rd Personnel Processing Squadron at Parks before they issued orders to proceed "O/A 14 May to ...Travis AFB, Fairfield, Calif, ...pending airlift to Japan." Airlift was a little delayed: It was several days before I got out of Travis. I was required to travel in "Class A" blues, a woolen uniform, and the temperature at Travis at that time of year was just too much for that kind of clothing. One of those oh, so frequent cases: Uncomfortable, disagreeable, but not a hardship. Always important to make the distinction.

Tachikawa Air Base was the air terminal for Japan. There we filled out various forms, with information that would today be included in computers and readily accessible. The next day I was told to report to Headquarters Far East Air Forces (FEAF) in downtown Tokyo.

The motor pool furnished me a staff car and driver and I got my first look at the city of Tokyo and some of the surrounding area. Bicycles, three-wheeled trucks, large gear-grinding trucks, noisy autos, traffic anarchy. Observing the Japanese driver, and later from my own experience, it was obvious that the key to driving in this traffic was to see and be aware of all the other vehicles, but, big BUT, do not let on that you do see them. If you give any sign that you see another vehicle, that driver will take advantage of you and make you yield.

Later, when I had an old, beat-up car, bought before leaving the country, everyone would yield in recognition of the idea that one more dent or bruise would not matter to that car and driver.

So I report to Col Hinckley, a feisty little redheaded guy from Utah, Director of Military Personnel Actions. I sit while he looks through some of my records and the information form I had filled in at Tachikawa.

"How would you like to work in personnel here at FEAF Headquarters?"

"Well, as you can see from my records I have always been in operations, but I'm sure I could learn a new field." And in my mind I'm thinking: working in Tokyo looks like a lot better deal than some rice-paddy airfield in Korea, and Kay and the girls would be able to join me here.

I get the job and notice one item on my "info" sheet is circled in red: MA degree. Someone must have thought that a master's degree meant I was smarter than average. Whatever. The assignment is Chief, Officer Actions Division, encompassing all activities except commissioning and promotion. It was a real bucket of worms, but had some talented people assigned.

Mary (what was her last name?), a Nisei, was a clerk/typist who had been there since year one. She knew where everything was, and I doubt the office could have functioned without her. She could speak and understand Japanese and would help any of us who might have a problem connected with the language. Diminutive, shy, always the first one in the office, willing to work overtime as required, always pleasant. There should be a "Mary" in every office.

Staff Sergeant Keeley, NCOIC, was typical NCO: knew his job, did it satisfactorily, did additional jobs as directed, volunteered nothing.

A1C (Airman First Class) Dexter was something else. Young, impetuous, impressionable, irrepressible. Never knew what he might do next. One day, disturbed about the number of bad checks reported by Fifth Air Force, he wrote a scathing letter, for my signature, to the Commanding General of Fifth Air Force, telling him that he was not doing his job.

"Dexter," I said gently as I smiled, "Dexter we are not supposed to "chew out" a three-star general." Unpredictable? At times. But sometimes: on several occasions I had heard him talking to other young airmen about "partying" over the weekend, so one Monday morning as he came in I spoke to him:

"Dexter," I said in a very serious tone, "would you kindly explain to me what happened over the weekend and how you got involved?" (Actually I knew nothing at all about anything that might have happened, or whether anything did happen. Just pulling his leg.) He gave me this funny, surprised look.

"Major, sir," he stammered, "I don't know how you found out about it, sir, 'cause, well, the MPs and the Shore Police (Navy) said it wouldn't go in the books." With this he took a deep breath andf continued:

"But, you see, Major, sir, it was this way: me and my buddies, see, we was just having a coupla beers, at this here bar, sorta kidding with them Japanese hostesses, minding our own business, and them Marines started making remarks about the Air Force that kinda reflected on our manhood and we told them they better cut it out and they said maybe we oughta try to make them and one of them Marines looked like he was gonna take a swing at one of us and then things got kinda confused for awhile until the MPs showed up, but there really wasn't much damage and we agreed to pay for it but they took us down to the cooler for a coupla hours anyway and filled out reports and then told us to get back to quarters, and that's all there really was, sir, honest, sir."

Of course, I had known nothing at all about any of this and I had to struggle to keep from smiling, but I managed to keep a serious, concerned look.

"I hope you can stay out of trouble in the future and let this be a lesson to you that some of us have ways of knowing what is going on." Later I heard him saying to the sergeant:

"But how could the major have known all that?"

Captain Lloyd G. Porkert was the Assistant Chief of the division, my right-hand man, my mentor and tutor who kept me from making serious mistakes until I knew what I was doing. "Porky" was a slightly reserved individual, prematurely balding, maybe a little overweight but just enough to indicate that his wife, Alice, was a good cook. With a good sense of humor, he looked on life as an interesting experience that he intended to enjoy to the fullest. I relied on him even after I became the "expert" that I wanted to be.

Only a few years after the Porkerts returned to the United States, "Porky" died suddenly and unexpectedly. Pretty sure he never got the Jaguar "saloon" that he talked about so much. Alice was last living just outside Washington, D.C. Regrettably, we have not kept in touch. So many things we wish we had done, or had done differently, but life seems to wrap you in a cocoon of events and "busyness" and you let slide the extras, the "should have dones," and the "could have dones," and the "it would have been nice to have dones."

Colonel Hinckley was a tough little bantam rooster. It took awhile for me to get used to him, and to understand him. Whenever there was some action, some piece of paper, some clarification of a regulation, really anything that had to "go forward," that is, to the Deputy for Personnel, to the Chief of Staff, the Vice-Commander, or the Commander; whenever, it seemed, that I did anything, I had to "prove" it to him, show him the regulation or precedent or ruling and explain each detail and, seemingly, each clause and sentence, and the reasoning behind each line. "Geez," I would wonder, "why doesn't he ever believe me?"

Never did I have to go to the next higher echelon to justify a position. Hinckley had established a reputation for me that I did not know about until later. And that was after Hinckley left; his replacement, another full colonel, George Keene, never questioned anything I wrote. The result: Keene never knew enough about a subject to be able to defend what I had written, or the position I had taken.

Anything controversial or different, I had to go forward on and explain the regulation, the thinking, and the precedents. One day Keene came back to my office and said there was an irate colonel in his office that wanted to see me. I had an inkling as to what it might be so I grabbed a few papers from our files and went to meet the colonel. He looked me over a few moments, it seemed longer, and:

"I've been wanting to meet the major who can say no to the commander of the only nuclear capable unit in the Far East," said he with a half-sneer.

He was referring to his request to put some of his maintenance people on flying status. I showed him the Air Force regulation, pointing out the provisions for doing this for a specific mission or for a specified period of time to accomplish a mission. He nodded. I then showed him how his organization had been granted this dispensation when first requested, and then how the second request for the exact same mission had been requested and had been granted by stretching the regulation to accommodate his unit. His third request for the same mission had been denied.

He had not been aware of the two previous requests that had been granted. His whole attitude changed.

"Thank you, major, for your time and explanation. I was not aware of this history. I see that I will have to have some discussions with my people and my staff. You have opened my eyes to some other possible problems. Thank you."

It was better with Hinckley: his questioning in depth required that I know what I was talking about. Once as I was explaining a paper to the Vice-Commander, Major General McNaughton, he telephoned the Chief of Staff, Brigadier General Arthur Pierce, asked him why he had disagreed with my position, and listened awhile:

"Yeah, I understand what you're saying, Art, but remember, Barbee is the expert in this area. He's never been wrong before and I don't think he is wrong now. Thanks."

Something like that can make you feel good—it can also make you exercise extra care in your work to avoid making a mistake.

Lieutenant Colonel George Geary, lean, laconic New Englander (New Hampshire, I think), was assistant to the Director. Quite a character. Really nitpicked every bit of paper that came his way: grammar, spelling, construction, and subject matter, all of it. Frequently he would walk back into my office with a little note, asking clarification on some small item.

One day he left a small slip of paper written in Russian. I knew that he was taking a course in Russian, but he had never pulled anything like this before. What he did not know was that Alice Porkert was from a Russian family and was fluent in the language. I asked Porky to take the note home, have Alice translate it, telephone me with the translation; I would tell her what to reply and she would write the answer in Russian for me to give Geary the next day. Which I did.

That morning I frequently strolled past his office to see him going through his dictionary to translate the answer to his question. He never did that again, and we never mentioned it. But it seemed to cement a strange sort of friendship — he seldom had anything to do with the other division chiefs, but he would wander back to my office and half-stammer:

"Would you, uh, would you like to, uh, go have a cup of coffee?"

And I would always "like." We would walk out of the offices on the fifth floor, down the hall to the elevator, ride to the basement exchange and lunchroom, order a cup of coffee. Geary gulped his coffee in about two swallows while I was still sipping.

"Ready?" He would say.

"Sure." But I never was.

Back to the elevator, ride up to the fifth floor, return to our offices. Not another word would be spoken. Very strange. We seemed to have a mutual respect that did not require very much verbal communication.

George Geary was a bachelor. At least, he did not have a wife with him. There might have been one at some time or other but never any direct mention was made of one. I mentioned to some of the others that I was going to invite him to dinner.

(Now I am running a little ahead in this narrative: Kay and the girls had arrived about a year earlier, we had lived a year in the little house we had built, and we were now in relatively spacious quarters.) The other division chiefs said he wouldn't come. They had asked him and he never could "make it." But I decided to ask him, anyway. Bear in mind that he had already met Kay.

Geary accepted! We had a coupla drinks, a nice dinner, some relaxed conversation and then George Geary went home. Knowing me, Geary knew that I would not intrude on his privacy in any way or take any advantage of a personal relationship.

There were essentially three places in Tokyo for unaccompanied officers: I have forgotten the name of the place for the young company grade (lieutenants and captains) officers, and the more lavish one for the full colonels and generals, but the field graders (majors and lieutenant colonels) were put up in the University Club.

This was "the place" of action. There was a large dining room, weekends an orchestra played, Sunday morning a delicious brunch was served, replete with champagne and orange juice cocktails and other attractions. Cecil Petty and I were both housed in this former lush hotel. (That's right, I had neglected to point out that Cecil had also been stopped on his way to Korea and he had been assigned to the Far East Command [FEC].)

The night of the Fourth of July, Cecil came to my room and urged me to come up to the roof to watch the fireworks. I was in my undershirts, getting ready for bed, but he insisted that I come right away. I did. And the fireworks were spectacular, but when I heard several of the guys laughing, I turned around to see that the rooftop was filled with couples, men and women, dining and looking, with amusement, at me in my skivvies. I fled.

It was a kind of fun place. After Kay and the girls arrived, we had that Sunday brunch, with French 75's, several times.

As soon as I had word that I would be staying in Japan, I sent word to my girls to get ready to come over. It would mean that we would have a three-year tour there and that sounded interesting. The procedure had been that you put in for quarters and then had to wait about a year for them while you stayed in some sort of off-base housing.

Shortly after we arranged for dependents to come to Japan we, meaning Cecil Petty and I, heard there was to be a drawing for lots that would be made available on the local government housing area: Grant Heights. The area had been laid out and we had the opportunity to select first, second and third choices of the lot we desired, with a drawing to see which choice you did get. Cecil and I ended up with lots almost across the street from each other.

Certain restrictions were imposed: the house to be constructed would be on a concrete base, maximum of 720 square feet in area, cost not to exceed $3200. According to the requirements, the house was to be "portable, trailer-type." Well...

Cecil and I and several others found an architect-builder who finally, after much begging and pleading, decided his son could be more gainfully employed building houses for us than doing nothing, and agreed to design and build a "Japanese-style" house for eleven of us.

It would have frame siding, ceiling rafters of 4 inch poles with the bark stripped off, sliding glass, paper and screen doors. The east side door opened into the laundry, which was an extension of the kitchen. We chose to have a "Pullman" type kitchen, with a pass-through counter to the living-dining room. We ended up eating most of our meals there on the counter.

The design called for three bedrooms — two were connected by a sliding paper door (shoji), and we used one of these as a dressing room. Kit and Lynne shared the third. The bathtub was entirely hand made of small tiles. The heating from the southern exposure glass doors was a satisfactory supplement for the small oil-burning space heater.[52] Japanese workmen scampered all over the house, unerringly on the roof that was too fragile to support their weight between the rafters: the roof consisted of one and one-quarter inch panels of what looked like spray-painted excelsior, tacked to the exposed rafter beams, topped with a layer of asphalt roofing paper, with a final layer of aluminum sheeting. You could hear the sound when a bird landed on the roof. No power tools were ever in evidence — everything done by hand. I asked the architect to have our living room face to the street on the north side.

"No, I will not build it that way. You must have the glass expanse on the south side to provide adequate warming."

So it was built his way. All houses on the north side of the street, like the Petty's, had their living rooms facing the street. All houses on the south side had living rooms facing the backyard on the south. Of course, the architect was right.

From the day that ground was first broken on our house and little men began to carry loads of small stones upon which the concrete base would be poured, from that first day until Kay and the girls arrived and we moved in was exactly thirty days!

A few of the others who had drawn lots decided they wanted an "American" style house, with regular materials, regular shingled-roofing, regular doors which opened into rooms which were too small and had a cramped feeling.

They later regretted their decision, but had been afraid their wives wouldn't like a "different" looking house. Our wives were intrigued and delighted with our "native" structures. We lived in the house almost a year before we came up for regular base housing and, except for wanting more living space, we sorta hated to leave our little Japanese house.

The U.S. Army had, in addition to size and cost specifications, rather definite provisions for the selling of these homes we had been allowed to

---

52 A near catastrophe because of this heater: it did not heat the girls' room adequately so occasionally we had to use a small electric heater there. Once Lynne stepped too close to the little heater and her long nylon housecoat touched the filament and burst into flame. Kit screamed, I rushed in, put my arms around Lynne and brushed down her body to put out the flame. I was wearing a silk smoking jacket, which burned a little and stuck to my arms and I had some slight burns, but Lynne, aside from fright, was all right. We were lucky.

build on the government housing land: any time up to the end of the first year of occupancy, the house could be sold for the original cost, plus whatever had been spent on landscaping and planting. After the first year, the house was to depreciate at the rate of one-sixtieth (1/60) per month, until it reached two-fifths (or was it one-fifth?) of the original cost. It would remain there for the life of the house.

It didn't work out quite that way, but it was certainly a unique way of providing additional housing for those who might otherwise have to live on the Japanese economy. Not that that would have been so terrible — many Japanese did it. And so did quite a few Americans. Our main advantage was that we had base facilities: water, electricity, telephones, and sewers. It was, understandably, difficult to use the Japanese telephone system, and certain precautions had to be taken with water off the "reservation."

After Kay had left me in California expecting to see me a year later, following a tour in Korea, and drove back to Topeka and St. Louis, she didn't have much time on her hands before she received her 27 July 1954 orders: "This is your Standard port call for Water travel, to report to the San Francisco Port of Embarkation at Bldg 209 Ft Mason at San Francisco, Calif on 30 August prior 0830 or 1000 hours. You will not report to the port earlier than the date indicated, or later than the hour and date indicated as facilities will not be available except on the date of the port call."

Now she had to see about arranging furniture shipment and storage (she left our piano with Thelma and Oc), and drive back to California, turn in the car for shipment, and manage to choose enough clothes for herself and two finicky girls to make the trip on the slow-moving USS General Gaffney military transport ship.

Return to George Geary for a moment. I had been Chief of the Officer Actions Division for a little less than a year when Col Geary asked me into his office and posed this query:

"What would you think of taking over the Casualty and Awards Division?"

I knew that Major Mannetti was rotating and that there would be a search for a replacement for him in Casualty and Awards. I also knew, as George Geary reminded me, that this division received a lot of "command attention." Meaning: the front office, commander and vice-commander, were exposed to the division's output daily. It also received a lot of attention from Lt. Col George Geary. We had all observed him frequently, several times a day, strid-

158

ing into that particular area carrying a sheaf of paper and wearing a worried, sometimes exasperated look. So my answer was tempered with caution:

"If you're asking my 'druthers,' I'd druther stay where I am and where I know what I am doing. But if you're really gently telling me that you want me to take over that division, I have one request of you in that connection. Several times a day you go into that office and confer with the NCOIC about some action that has been taken and signed off by Major Mannetti.

"Now a condition: if I am to be the division chief and you have any question whatsoever about any action or piece of paper that comes out of the office, you will come to me and not to the NCOIC.

"You will not have to check, or double check, the facts and figures. They will be correct. If you have any reason to think they might not be, come to me for verification.

"If you feel I have not provided you with sufficient backup, I will be only too happy to satisfy you with complete proofs. Agreed?"

"Perfectly agreed," Col Geary smiled. "That's exactly what I wanted to hear you say. I have been spending almost fifty percent of my time checking on that particular division to the detriment of other things I should be doing. When can you take over?"

"Tomorrow. Captain Porkert is thoroughly capable and can run the Officers Actions Division until you get an assistant for him." So I got the bucket of worms.

In wartime, the casualty reporting function was a big job — keeping track of all deaths and associated notices, and the status of the injured: the extent of the injury, where hospitalized, when their situation and location changed, etc., etc.

Award activity was also greater — the facts for Purple Hearts, the narrative for heroism awards. Criteria for heroism awards were sort of vague. The idea being, I suppose, to have the flexibility to meet varying conditions. But our section was responsible for seeing that all recommendations met the criteria — some of which we established, like for secret missions, with the approval, naturally, of the front office.

We had a number of "canned" recommendations for most of the medals and awards, and these came into frequent use throughout the headquarters, especially when a supervisor wanted to recommend one of his people for service and performance as contrasted to bravery. The supervisor would give us a few facts and figures, real or imaginary, and we would fill in the blanks for him. And sometimes an individual was told to write up a recommendation for himself — some of them hemmed and hawed before admitting that was the situation. Embarrassed with the idea of tooting his own horn.

Regulations required the unit commander to write a letter of condolence to the next of kin, relating the circumstances of death, followed by a laudatory statement and expression of sorrow; Headquarters, USAF, would follow up with another letter to accompany a notification team.

FEAF commanders had decided that they would also send, and sign, a letter of condolence, usually expressed in more general terms. When I took over the division, Maj Mannetti showed me the samples of form letters that the division had been using for years.

"Now the Vice-Commander and Chief of Staff think we need to personalize these letters a little more. I have submitted a number of variations and changes during the past month," he said. "And somewhere along the line of command they have disapproved all of them before they ever reach to Vice-Commander."

"Go ahead and sign out," I told him. "I'll try my hand at the letters."

I took all the original letters, rearranged a sentence here and there, and sent them forward with a note that said: "The enclosed letters now satisfy all the requirements and incorporate the wishes of the Commander and Vice-Commander."

They were approved all along the line and we did not have to redo the letters. After all, none of the intermediate colonels and generals was going to quarrel at all with the "wishes of the Commander." Sometimes,... well, sometimes you have to take positive action. And I could tell that this was to be an interesting assignment.

The division had an assistant chief (Second Lieutenant Randolph Brewster, happened to be black — I'm not sure that we used the term "black" in 1955), TSgt Stephen Jones, A1C (can't remember his name), and three civilian typists, all female.

On the very first morning I got a feeling for the way things were. Sgt Jones handed me a folder of papers for my signature, and I asked what it was.

"The morning report," Jones said.

Now, a morning report is what the lowest unit, like a squadron, fills out to indicate the number present for duty, on sick call, AWOL, etc; it is not a report filed by a major air command headquarters.

This report was not a morning report, as such. It was a status report of all USAF personnel in the Far East who were in the hospital. The sergeant called it the morning report because he prepared it every morning.

Question: "How long does it take to prepare this report?"

"Well, sir, about two hours to assemble the facts and figures and about one and a half hours for a clerk typist to prepare the final report."

"What regulation requires this report?"

"No regulation that I know of, sir."

"What do we do with this report, sergeant?"

"We give it to that office down the hall in room 508."

"What do they do with it?"

"I don't know, sir."

So I take the report in hand and go down the hall to room 508 and ask them what they do with the report.

"Oh, we just file it, sir."

"Do you ever consult it or use it for any purpose?"

"No sir, we just keep it on file for the length of time required for all files and then it goes to permanent storage someplace back on the mainland.

"What would happen if you did not receive this report ever again?" I asked.

"Nothing, sir."

Back down the hall to my office.

"Sergeant, we will no longer prepare this report."

"But, sir, we have been doing this for years."

"We have stopped doing so as of now, sergeant; we will no longer prepare a report that is not required by any regulation, that is not needed by the office to which we send it, that is used for no purpose whatsoever. Understood?"

"Yes, sir," he said, somewhat uncomfortably.

And I turned my attention to:

"Lt. Brewster, there is a whole bank of five-drawer filing cabinets, eight to be exact, on that wall on the opposite end of this room."

"Yes, sir."

"What's in all those filing cabinets, lieutenant?"

"I guess that's where our records of awards and casualties are, sir."

"You guess? If you were looking for a record could you find it there yourself? No? Suppose General Grills (Deputy for Personnel) came down here (and he frequently left his office without his jacket and with his suspenders showing) and wanted a particular file, what would you do?"

"Well, sir, I'd tell the sergeant to get it."

"But, lieutenant, the sergeant is out to lunch. So what do you do?"

"Well, sir, I'd have the airman find the file."

"But, lieutenant, the airman is home sick today, so what do you do?"

"Well, sir, I'd ask one of the clerk typists to get the file."

"But, they don't know how. What happens?"

"Well, sir, I'd tell the general he'd just have to wait until the sergeant got back from lunch."

"Lieutenant, you have the title of Assistant Division Chief. Just what do you do? You don't seem to know very much about the operation of this office."

"Well, sir, Major Mannetti just wanted me to work on recommendations for awards. He never said anything about the rest of the office."

"Lieutenant, regardless of what Major Mannetti may have told you, you have held the position of Assistant Division Chief, yet you never took it upon yourself to learn anything about this office. You never tried to assist Major Mannetti in any way at all. You were content to let him shoulder all the work. He lost leave time because he felt he could not leave the office to his assistant. He got a good start on ulcers because he took all the pressure, and you were happy to let him take all the responsibility.

"Listen close, lieutenant: within a week, probably less, I am going to be an expert on everything in this office, the people, the duties, the files, the regulations governing our functions, actions, and responsibilities. I am going to be here at night and on the weekends (his eyes opened wide) until I can answer any and all questions about this office, and everything connected with it, with complete assurance that I am absolutely correct. I will expect that you will bring yourself to the same level of competence. I will expect that you will accomplish this as soon as, if not before, I do.

"To that end, I have put your name on the list for admission to this headquarters at night and on the weekends. Yes, nights and weekends. You have a week to become familiar with all those files. Until you demonstrate that you

162

are competent to perform the duties of assistant chief, I am withholding your promotion so you may forget about your little nameplate with the title of 1st lieutenant on the reverse side. No questions? Then we go to work."

(Six months later I moved to another job and recommended that Lt. Brewster be promoted to 1st Lieutenant as fully qualified. He told Major Gabriel Cazares, who succeeded me, that he thought I was a fine officer and that he had learned a lot from me.)

Those files that I had asked Brewster about? Most of them contained information about Air Force casualties during the Korean War — police action? Sgt Jones told me that the Army Graves Registration group used the files frequently.

"Do we ever use them?"

"Not that anyone can remember."

So I called the army captain in charge of the Graves Registration Group in Yokohama.

"Captain, this is Major Barbee in FEAF headquarters in Tokyo. I understand we have some files that you sometimes come to see. Yes? Well, how would you like to have those files? Could sure use them in your offices there? You'll send a truck up to Tokyo tomorrow morning and pick them up? Great! We'll be expecting you."

We had just cut our filing cabinet requirement to less than half of what it had been and facilitated the operation of another military office.

One of our three clerk typists — all were young women, wives of enlisted personnel — was trés enceinte, polite French for "with child." I noticed that more and more she would have her typing stand positioned so that her face could not be seen from my desk — she would be dozing off behind her screen. Changes I had made in the office procedures and functions had lessened the workload and there was not really enough work for three clerk typists any longer; but I could not fire this young woman without building a record of poor performance. This would cause a problem for her later on if she wanted to return to the civilian work force.

So, I explained to her about our reduction in workload and suggested that she might want to take a leave of absence until after her child was born; that it would be better for her and better for the child. She agreed without any hesitation, and I was on the way toward my goal of getting this office to what I thought should be peacetime manning.

Shortly after I was moved into the job of Assistant to the Director of Personnel Planning, 13 October 1955. The Casualty & Awards Division, on my recommendation, was reduced to one officer, a major, and one clerk typist — from seven people to two!

I had been in this new job only a few weeks when a war game exercise was laid on. My boss asked me to sit in on the meetings with the Deputy for Personnel in planning for our execution of the war plans. We had a new Deputy for Personnel, a colonel (who had replaced B/Gen Grills) without experience in personnel and unsure of himself. In our meetings were the heads of all the personnel directorates —all full colonels.

As the only major in the group, I tried my best to stay in the background, but I couldn't resist after a lot of discussion about what action we should take when all the colonels agreed that we should wait and see what 5th Air Force did.

5th Air Force was a subordinate command, and I could not understand why FEAF Headquarters, the major Air Command, should govern its action on the basis of what a subordinate command did. 5th Air Force, to my way of thinking, should take its direction from FEAF, not the other way around.

In quite positive terms, I said so, delineating the specific direction that we should be giving to 5th Air Force and the other subordinate commands in Japan, Korea, Okinawa, Guam, Hawaii, and the Philippines. After a stunned silence, Colonel Johnson, the Deputy for Personnel, said:

"Bud's right. We have prepared the plan; it specifies the actions we are to take. We shall follow the plan, and Barbee will act as the Deputy for Personnel in our briefings of General Kuter and the staff. You will all give him the information and assistance he will need in representing personnel. Any questions?"

There were none. It happened I was the only major representing a deputy at the gaming table. I did a good job and made points for personnel.

Coupla months later I was given a different title: Assistant for Special Projects and one of the first projects was preparing a briefing for the visit of Secretary of the Air Force Quarles. Gen Kuter (4 stars) sat in on the dry run rehearsal by all staff sections. At the end he said:

"Excellent briefings. The information is all there, but the accent is all wrong. Now all of you will take that information and turn it 180 degrees. This is not a matter of our saying to the coach that we will take what we have and give it our all and go out and get the job done. No. This is our boss, and we are going to tell him why we can't do the job that we are expected to do

164

with what we have, and what we need to have to continue to operate. That's what we are going to tell him. Any questions?"

I organized my presentation so that one point would lead into the next, and I had prepared the visual aids and slides to accompany each discussion. About half way through my personnel briefing, Secretary Quarles interrupted to ask a question. I flashed the next slide on the screen, turned the page of the visual aid, said: "Yes, sir," and gave him the answer to his question. I had anticipated there would be that question at that point in the briefing. Gen Kuter told me later that I had made money for personnel with my briefing.

Two speakers impressed me: Col B.O. Davis, later the first black to become an Air Force general, who showed the same degree of politeness and attention to a major who asked a question as he did to the stars of generals; the other speaker was a hotshot lt colonel who seemed destined for rapid promotion - but when he stood up to give his short speech he froze, repeated "good morning" three times, stood speechless.

Gen Kuter said kindly, "Let's have the next speaker, please." The young colonel never lived it down. Purely stage fright.

Shortly after Gen Kuter took command of FEAF he was looking to replace his aide and the choice came down to two of us: myself and Major Evans. Kuter called me in and told me he was choosing Evans because I was senior to him and this would speed Evans' promotion.

It certainly did: by the time I was promoted to Lt Colonel, Evans was wearing a star. But there were other considerations — as there usually are.

When the position of chief of the presentations division came open, Gen Scheidecker, the comptroller, requested that I be assigned to him. This put me in charge of overseeing all of the briefings given to the command section, especially the morning briefs by each deputy's representative, a matter of precise timing of each report and preparation of visual aids. We had a staff of artists and technicians available to prepare aids on short notice.

On one occasion, a briefing of Japanese businessmen, I had to begin the session and introduce each speaker. I began by bowing slightly to the guests and said:

"Dozo yorushku." And all the Japanese men rolled forward in their seats as they replied:

"Domo arigato."

Later that day, Gen Kuter called me into his office to inquire:

"Bud, what was that you said to begin the briefing? I have never seen anything have such an electrifying effect upon a group, and I would like to use it at some time myself."

I repeated the phrase, wrote it down for him, and tried to explain that it meant many things, that the speaker is there to help the listeners, will try to assist them in every way possible, that he hopes to enlighten the guests, that he will give them his undivided attention, and that he will expect that they will reciprocate. A phrase with very involved meanings.

Keeping up with flying is difficult when working in a large headquarters. You had to get in at least four hours each month to earn your flying pay, and you had to have at least one hundred hours each year to remain on flying status.

If we had to fly to Korea on business, we received income tax credit for that month; needless to say, most of us managed to find some business in Korea frequently. Most of us flew the venerable C-47, the good ol' Gooney Bird, and occasionally a modified B-25.

The senior staff officers were offered the opportunity to check out in jets by flying the T-33.

At first my young instructor seened bent on trying to make me sick by slapping the plane into sharp turns and pulling several G-s. When that didn't work, we settled down into some good instruction.

On my first solo flight I made three touch-and-go landings, and after the third one I realized that I was doing all the required actions without thinking. I pulled that hot little machine up in a cork-screw climb into "the wld blue yonder." Whee-e! In my exhuberance I forgot to keep my head out of my ass and the cockpit. Two Navy Corsairs scared and awakened me from my reverie, "bouncing" my wings, saying "Gotcha!"

After the fifteen hours of instruction and solo flying I was told I could continue to get in one flight each month in that tricky little jet. Considering some of the horrendous thunderstorms frequently encountered in the Tokyo area, I decided that I would stick with the forgiving C-47 that I felt I knew pretty well. It was about this time that I got "starred," my senior pilot's rating, in January 1956.

So many memories come flooding back about Japan: the friends we made, especially the Pettys whose piano arrived nailed to the shipping crate; Marj heading up and singing in the chapel choir; the game of charades we played frequently with a number of couples; dance lessons and parties at the officers' club with Japanese girls singing "The Terressee Wartz."

166

The dismay of the shopkeeper who said we could have anything in his store if we would trade in our refrigerator and we selected the priceless treasured Imari platter which he had stored away; Keiko sitting on the stairs in our quarters shining my shoes and giggling at the size of them.

Kit skipping a grade and being chosen to commemorate the legendary Nino Mia by planting a tree in his honor and making a little speech; her friend who always answered the phone with "Marcia speaking"; Lynne taking piano lessons, and her favorite teacher "Miss Marshmallow"; both girls taking horseback riding lessons and Kit getting a Blue Ribbon and Lynne falling off and not riding a horse again for many years.

Having to be on my good behavior when I was selected to be Chairman of the Chapel Council; the FEAF carnival when I had to find some small corks to use in our pop-guns and finally got through to the driver when he smiled in understanding and said "Ah so, coroku" and the little manufacturer who gave me a lesson in Japanese economics when he explained that I would have to pay more per cork if I wanted to buy more than two dozen because that would require that he expand his business, get larger machines, move shop to a different neighborhood and not be available to see and visit with his many friends and associates.

The car pool when stodgy Ned Hand was driving and I put my arm out the window and tapped the side of the his car as we maneuvered through cars and bicycles and Stan exclaimed: "My God, Ned, you've hit him," and Ned was apoplectic while we all laughed and Ned would never drive with us again, and he later became a judge on the military court of appeals; the earthquake when I looked out the window of the Meiji Building and saw the building next door move about seven inches in my view; the three wheelers, taxis and old cars jamming into a gridlock at traffic circles until a policeman had to literally walk over the automobiles in an attempt to untangle the tangled mass; bargaining in the Ginza for things that I did not want in the first place; seeing the raggedy, dirty beggar carrying a cat and I remarked to my friends that the cat was probably his only friend and Porky Porkert said "Friend, hell, that's lunch."

Yes, all those things and many, many more, as Kit reminded me how we all enjoyed the delicious sundaes topped with black walnut syrup served in the basement of the Meiji building; how the girls enjoyed shopping even when their total vocabulary consisted of "Ikura desu ka," or "How much does it cost?"

The sale of our 1954 Ford station wagon to this "intermediary," actually a dealer, who made me an offer I couldn't refuse - $100 more than I had paid for the car two years earlier; before the sale was completed, he had to put wire screening behind the front seat, lay the back seat flat, and cover the rear windows with plywood, thus converting the car to a truck on which the duty was significantly lower; then he gave me a grocery bag full of Japanese yen: $3200 at 360 ¥ to $1; could you, today in Japan, sell a two-year old American car for more than it cost?

We had ordered a Volkswagen from Germany, but it had not arrived. Lt Col Charlie Helscher, very nice guy, had his rotation orders and was selling a "pass-down car." This superannuated Plymouth was one of many old, beat up, outdated autos that got passed down from one owner to the next as he sold the auto he had brought to Japan and needed transportation for the remaining week or month.

They were really quite suitable for the Japanese traffic: other drivers could see the multitude of scrapes and dents and would figure you could not be "bluffed out" in a traffic situation. The value of these cars remained fairly constant. Charlie wanted to dispose of it for $75, I was not quite ready for it, so I told him I would give him $50 if he had not sold it by departure time. He agreed. My VW was late arriving, so I had need of the antiquated wheels. When I left, I sold it for $100. Everyone was pleased.

The new VW arrived just three days before our scheduled departure for Hawaii. In order to accept it, take possession, and be able to ship it to Hawaii on my orders, I had to get it through Japanese customs, and drive it for at least one day in Japan to establish ownership as a used car. Normally, the customs procedure took three weeks: many, many offices to go through, each one putting his own little stamp on the papers. I was able to find an "expediter" who could carry me through the various offices, putting just a little change under the table, and emerge after four hours with everything accomplished. Grease a few palms. It was fun to be able to try out that little rascal of a car on the Japanese roads, especially some of those back roads that were impassable with a large car. Had three days with it before putting it on the slow boat to Hawaii.

The military is funny. When I was told that I was going to be transferred to Hawaii, I had only one year to go on my three-year tour. Kay did not want to leave. We had friends, she liked where we lived, the shopping was great, the life was pleasant and interesting, we had a maid who took care of the house and cooked the meals. I was told that in order to be transferred, I would have to extend for at least one year. I told them that I did not want to extend. They said I could not go to Hawaii if I did not extend. I said fine, I'll stay in Japan. They said no, you have to go to Hawaii. I said, fine, but I won't

168

extend. I should not have been so adamant — it probably would have been in my best interest to extend and stay in Hawaii at least two years, but who knows at the time? So they sent me to Hawaii for one year.

No doubt I have omitted some of the more significant experiences of Japan and Tokyo and those two years, but I must get on. I'll come back later if I realize a horrendous omission. Oh, yes: I got the Commendation Medal for doing a number of jobs well but because I had less than a year in each assignment I didn't get an Officer Effectiveness Report (OER) that said what an extraordinarily effective officer I was.

Little Japanese men swarmed over our house packing everything in sight, including coffee grounds in the sink. We said good-bye to Keiko, our maid, and our gathered friends, loaded our baggage in the staff car, drove to Haneda airport. We departed Tokyo on a C-121 (Connie), flew out a short ways over the ocean, had an emergency, dumped fuel, turned back, changed aircraft and took off again. Refueled at Wake Island and on to Honolulu without further difficulty.

Sayonara to Nippon and to an interesting period in our lives. That was early summer of 1954.

CHAPTER XXVI

HAWAII

Yes, there were not good omens about the flight to Hawaii: before we left the ground at Haneda, a crying child promised to make the flight less than wonderful, and losing an engine, dumping fuel, and retrning to Japan aped to our apprehension. Dumping fuel was thought by some to be a dangerous operation, and it was not until a few years later that Lockheed conducted experiments to prove that it was not possible to sustain ignition of dumped fuel.[53]

But things seemed to straighten out after the second take-off. We made the half-way stop at Midway, saw the dumb gooney birds that occasionally caused trouble by gathering on the runway, and flew on in to Honolulu where we received the usual greeting of leis of sweet smelling frangi-pangi flowers.

We felt quite fortunate in having base quarters available at Hickam: 320 C Signer Blvd. That meant that we would not have to buy a house near the base that would cost about $25,000. Later, we realized that those houses became a good investment; the owners more than doubled their money in one year. Within a coupla years they were going for well over 100 thousand. But we were happy with our location and the advantages of living on base.

PACAF Headquarters (Pacific Air Force at the time),[54] was housed in a frame building, dating from the 1930's, that was constructed before air-conditioning but designed to be comfortable in tropic conditions. Newer buildings, built just before the Pearl Harbor attack, bore the scars of strafing by the Japanese attackers. One of these newer buildings would become the headquarters when FEAF moved to Hawaii.

My orders transferring me to Hawaii had a DAFSC[55] of 6831, Statistical Services Officer. I was under the impression that I was to be assigned to the

---

53 A coupla years later (1958-1962) when I flew Connies regularly, and for several thousand hours, I had a number of occasions to dump fuel, which we did with no concern whatsoever about fire.

54 When FEAF left Japan and came to Hawaii, PACAF became Pacific Air Forces.

55 DAFSC: Duty Air Force Specialty Classification.

office of the comptroller and have something to do with visual aids and presentations, but when we arrived in Hawaii, I was immediately assigned as Assistant Director of the Secretariat, duty AFSC 7016, Administrative Staff Officer.

General Kuter liked the idea of a Secretariat directly responsible to the commander, previewing all correspondence to assure correctness and conformity to the desires and policies of the commander.

George Geary had arranged this assignment for me with the approval of Gen Kuter, on the basis that I had more experience with the various staff sections in FEAF than anyone else and that I would be able to assist in bringing about the commander-staff relations desired by General Kuter.

Part of the problem was the 'open door' policy of Gen Smith. His staff directors (colonels) would hand carry their papers to him, bypassing his personal secretary and the Secretariat. It was on one such occasion that the secretary asked me if I had seen a letter to the governor of Hawaii — she had not seen it nor had I.

She had received a call from the governor's secretary that the general had signed a letter to the governor that had the governor's first name wrong and had misspelled his last name. The governor's secretary was sending the letter back.

This was the ammunition that I needed to point out to Gen Smith that the Secretariat could function only if he insisted that all papers for his signature be processed through the Secretariat.

The Deputy for Operations, Colonel Dave Dalziel, really resisted when this procedure was effected. Gen Smith remarked to me:

"I've only known two officers who were more ambitious than Dave Dalziel. Both were named Larry."

He was referring to Generals Norstad, who had commanded NATO, and Kuter. I had never thought of Kuter that way, but I had known that he had jumped from lt colonel to brigadier general. Actually, major to lt. colonel to b.g. in less than a year.

Col John Rushing, Director of the Secretariat, was a nice guy but absolutely worthless in the job. He had been moved around in several jobs in the effort to find something suitable for a non-productive full colonel, and they figured he could do very little damage in a job that had no established description or operational responsibility.

Until I got there Rushing served only as an errand boy, carrying an occasional staff paper in to Major General Sory Smith, PACAF Commander. He had never even attempted to examine any of the content or to do any editing. Rushing would frequently fall asleep at his desk. Once I started to awaken him when Brig Gen 'Zip' Koon, the Vice-Commander, came to the office but Koon signaled not to disturb him and motioned for me to come. He knew that Rushing would not have the answer to his question, anyway. (Digression: Gen Koon had two daughters, about the same age as our girls, but they were hellers. Being daughters of a general, they survived escapades that would have sent others home to the states — now called the mainland.)

When awake, Rushing would gaze out the window by his desk and pat his hands on the arms of his chair. When the question of a regular commission arose, he spent hours talking to me and to himself about whether he should apply for it or not; he held a regular commission as a warrant officer, but was serving on active duty as a reserve colonel; if he took a regular commission, it would be as a major; would he be reduced in grade to major? Would he have to relinquish his warrant? If a RIF (Reduction in Force) came along would he be released from active duty? Would he lose his rank as a colonel?

After spending many hours pointing out the various possibilities, I finally urged him to forget about applying for a regular Air Force commission, which he eventually did. When he got his assignment to head up the Chicago region of the exchange system, he told me that it was the most productive region worldwide. I told him he could change all that. He replied "Yeah," not really understanding what I had said.

Our secretary gave me any paper that came into the office. I would review, make any necessary corrections, additions, deletions, and return it to the originating office, or initial and pass it to Col Rushing — he always liked to carry the routine items in to General Smith. I say 'routine' because if there were any question or controversy he would immediately remember that he had an appointment for the dentist or for a haircut, grab his hat and leave.

Our secretary would give me a knowing wink. Well, it was better than having him embarrass himself. And, if the general did happen to have a question he always came to me. The system worked: we had no egregious errors.

One problem arose when we had a visit from a congressman and his staff. Some of the staff wanted us to set up an airplane to take them to visit some of the neighboring islands, and Rushing told me to make the neccessary arrangements. I pointed out to him that we could not do this because it was contrary to Air Force regulations. He insisted that I do it, that it was an order, we argued, and I asked him to put it in writing. He refused and went to Gen Smith.

"Goddammit, John," the usually calm and quiet Sory Smith said, "are you trying to get us in deep kimshi?[56] Regulations specifically prohibit such use of military aircraft. Not just no, but hell no. Those people know better than to ask, and we don't have to apologize to them for anything. They are just the ones to go back to Washington and spread the word that we do stupid things. Now, go tell them no, n-o!"

As you might expect, I was the one to tell the 'congdel'[57] no.

Early in 1957 Gen Smith laid on a trip to Southeast Asia, specifically Vietnam. Actually, I guess it was Gen Kuter that ordered the trip.

History lesson: The Indochina War of 1946-1954 officially ended July 21, 1954. Dien Bien Phu had fallen on May 8, 1954: the French "had been maneuvered into fighting the decisive battle of the Indochina War on a ground and in a fashion not at all of their choosing."[58]

Our forces in Japan had sent a few supplies in 1950 and more after the truce in Korea,[59] but the French were steadily losing ground and support to

---

56 Kimshi was a particularly vile smelling Korean dish that came to be used in a scatalogical expression (deep kimshi) by troops who had served in Korea.

57 Congdel: Congressional delegation.

58 The Two Viet-Nams, Bernard B. Fall, 1967.

59 By 1953 the U.S. was providing about 80% of France's war effort economy. In January 1954 Eisenhower sent 200 U.S. Air Force technicians to Viet Nam to service French combat planes. Kennedy gradually increased the U.S. advisers to more than 16,000. Frustrated with President Ngo Dinh Diem, who was alienating many Vietnamese, the U.S. supported the military coup that overthrew him in 1963. A series of coups in the next two years brought instability that was exploited by the Communists. President Johnson appointed Gen Westmoreland to head the Military Assistance Command, Vietnam (MACV), increased the advisers to 23,000 and expanded economic aid. Following the Tonkin Gulf Resolution in August 1964, and a Viet Cong attack on a U.S. Army barracks in Pleiku in February 1965, we commenced Operation Rolling Thunder, a restricted but massive bombing campaign against North Vietnam, and sent in 50,000 ground combat forces to protect the air bases. The decision to escalate slowly, to bomb selected military targets while avoiding excessive civilian casualties, and to fight a war of attrition in order to avoid possible confrontations with the USSR and China, seriously midjudged the nature of the enemy and the strategy of a "people's war."
Attrition's only measure of success was a body count of the enemy dead; but Hanoi was prepared to suffer enormous casualties in a prolonged war. The war's statistics were

the Vietnamese communist forces. After Dien Bien Phu, situated about 190 miles west of Hanoi, the French left North Vietnam.

After almost fifty years of French administration and seventy years of "presence, all of Vietnam was free of alien domination, but at the price of division." Now the United States began to pick up where the French had left off. We sent supplies, aircraft, and advisers.

(See Footnote 62 for brief summary of our involvement in South Vietnam.)

"We have forty million reasons for failure, but not a single excuse." (Kipling) We learned nothing from the French failure. We insisted that we were saving democracy in South Vietnam. We could never understand that the peoples of South Vietnam, and especially the Montagnard mountain people, did not really care about the form of government: what they wanted was to be as free of government as possible, to pay the least amount of taxes possible. Whatever and whoever offered the most and required the least was the most acceptable.

As I said, we went to Vietnam in 1957 on a fact finding trip. We wanted to know as much as possible about the forces of the nations in Southeast Asia: how capable and how well trained were the armies and air forces of the Philippinnes, Vietnam, Laos, Cambodia, Thailand, Burma?

How dependent were some of them upon China for equipment and support? How would those nations respond to an attack upon one of their neighbors? Was SEATO, the SouthEast Asia Treaty Organization, a viable pact? Or would the United States be the prime mover?[60]

In a few years, to our dismay, we would learn the answers to those questions — the hard way.

We flew in to Saigon and were met by U.S. Embassy staffers, and Vietnamese officers. My first impression of the country was one of those non-important, non-relevant things that nevertheless stick in the memory: all

---

grim: 2 to 3 million Indochinese killed, 58,000 Americans dead, the expenditure of three times the amount of U.S. bombs dropped on both theaters during World War II. The War cost the United States over $150 billion. (Academic American Encyclopedia)

The greatest lesson for the U.S. was this: the "measured response" strategy foisted on the military was a disaster;. if we go to war, if the civilian leaders decide we must fight, then we must fight to win, and the military must make the decisions as to how to fight the war.

60   Our allies ultimately included 70,000 South Koreans, Thais, Australians, and New Zealanders.

vehicles had white sidewall tires. Not some: all vehicles. Bicycles, motor-cycles, Jeeps, sedans, eight-wheel trucks, fire trucks, even the C-47 aircraft, all had white sidewall tires.

Following briefings by U.S. military and embassy personnel, we had conducted tours of the city: the bustling metropolis seemed little affected by the war which had been mostly in the north. Commerce and cafés, bicycles with impossible cargoes, bicycle-powered cabs or rickshas, automobiles in uncontrolled traffic, street corner vendors of edibles, especially pieces of sugar cane, the palace of Ngo Dinh Diem, the residential neighborhoods of palatial homes.

We were allowed to tour some of the surrounding area. A few miles north of Saigon, near one of the large rubber plantations, a bridge over a small stream was the limit of our excursion. North of there, we were told, there was danger of attack by the revolutionary Viet Cong. We did not venture beyond that point.

From Saigon we flew to Hong Kong for briefings from the British and their contacts in Red China.

In two days, there was time for some personal shopping. Kay had wanted a nice lightweight topcoat (to wear to the grocery store), and the cheapest material I could find was a red cashmere. I had a suit made of fine Italian silk (which I still wear, and can you imagine being measured one evening for a suit and having a fitting the following morning?), a cashmere sport coat (which has always been too heavy), and some shoes, a set of matched leather luggage (we still have), a number of pieces of cloisonné, and a beautiful 10-inch square Chinese ebony box.

Passing by the store window, I studied and admired the box. The proprietor invited me in and showed me the quality of the box - only $25. I told him I had spent all my money and couldn't buy anything more.

He cut the price to $20.

"Oh, that box is worth even more than your asking price of $25, and I really admire it, but I just can't afford it."

He brought the price down to $15.

"I appreciate what a bargain that is for a truly beautiful piece of work-manship, but I just can't handle it." We discussed it a little longer and I bought it for $5! He wanted to make a sale.

All in all, there was about $2,000 of merchandise that I managed to get through customs in Honolulu.[61]

On the way to the tailor shop, the general's pilot, Captain Lanier, and I were beset by a young boy, a mere child, who offered to sell us his sister for $16! We were told later that he had really meant it. Returning to the hotel by ricksha, I had the coolie switch places and I pulled him for a short distance.

After our return to Hawaii, Col Dave Dalziel, our Deputy for Operations, prepared a lengthy report that bore the title "Status of Forces, Southeast Asia," covering in detail the personnel and equipment of the various countries, a document that combined the military capabilities of Viet Nam, Laos, Cambodia, Thailand, Burma.

Destined for CINCPAC,[62] it was comprehensive and generally well-written. In a number of places, however, the language was convoluted, especially with double negative expressions, and conveyed the exact opposite of the intended meaning. Example:

"Under circumstances other than those expected to prevail, the forces of Cambodia would not, regardless of their fine state of training, be unable to meet the challenge of unforeseen incursions that could be anticipated."

There were several statements like that. Hard to understand exactly what was meant.

The report, classified Top Secret, was to be signed by Gen Smith and dispatched to CINCPAC. I made a number of notes on some of the conflicting statements and took the report back to Col Dalziel to suggest changes.

He stormed: "What are you doing with that report? It is already late. You have no business to be holding it. I don't care what you thought about it. That

---

61 Interesting experience in customs: the lines of those waiting for inspection were pretty long, but we were moving. Not moving fast enough for one hotshot, however. When an opening appeared at one inspection table, this guy ducked under the restraining rope and jumped in front of the line. Several of us started to protest but the customs inspector saw, shook his head, smiled,- winked at us, and asked the hotshot to open his bags for inspection. Person after person quickly passed through the customs gate while our hotshot was being checked. He was the last one cleared. The inspector had him open, and empty, each piece of baggage, stopped to check each item for origin and declaration. The hotshot was maddern hell, but the customs official was smiling and polite throughout the entire process. We all got a big kick out of this way to handle someone who gets out of line.

62 CINCPAC: Commander-in-Chief, Pacific, a position always held by an admiral of the U.S. Navy.

is exactly what I intended to say. I have been writing papers long before you came along. I don't have to have to have a major proofreading my reports.

"You should take that report immediately to Gen Smith for signature." I did.

Gen Koon was in Gen Smith's office when I took the report in and explained what the report was. "Bud, you look as if you have some reservations about this."

"Yes, sir," I answered, gave him the report, and listed the various statements, by page and paragraph, that I thought should be changed.

"Bud's right, Sory," Koon said to Gen Smith. "This can't go forward like this. Look at those points."

Gen Smith checked the markings I had made. "Take it back to Dave and have him change those statements the way you suggested."

When I took the report back to Col Dalziel and told him what the general had said, there was no argument or discussion whatsoever. It was now a different ballgame. He made the changes I had suggested to him originally.

It was only a few blocks from our quarters to the office, so I generally rode a bicycle. One day, tootling merrily along, reading some mail, "look, ma, no hands!" and I hit an area of loose sand. Never very much at tumbling, I caught myself with my hands as I fell. Picked myself up and rode on home. Later, some pain and swelling; a sprain or small chip of bone in the wrist according to the X-ray at the hospital.

They put a cast on it and told me to go home: No more free-hand riding.

We no longer have a maid so we bought a dishwasher from the Navy Ship Store, and I declared that I would not learn how to load the thing — if my girls were to be spared the dishwashing drudgery, they could very well load the machine. My resolve did not last forever.

Kay did have an ironing lady come in once a week - she was Hawaiian, the wife of a banker; the chauffeur would drop her off and pick her up. She just liked to get out of the house and see people and do something.

There were lots of good things about Hawaii. The weather. The golf. The beautiful pineapples and other fruit. The visits to the other islands on R & R. The big island of Hawaii and the volcanoes; Kay and the girls walked across the crater of Mauna Loa. Mamomma came to visit us. The Pettys stopped off on their way home from Japan. Stan and Ahden visited during a medical convention.

When it came time to be thinking about leaving Hawaii (I had orders to The Command and Staff College at Montgomery, Alabama), I dickered with a Ford agency in Los Angeles about buying a new station wagon. We arrived at a price just a little over dealer cost, and arranged to pick up the car when we arrived in "the states." Our trusted little Volkswagen was to be shipped to Mobile, Alabama, for pickup at the port.

We had the choice of returning by air or surface. Surface on board the S.S. Lurline, a luxury liner, seemed more appropriate. There were a certain small number of accommodations available for the military, some for officers and some for enlisted.

When I checked with the transportation officer I was told that all spaces had been allocated. I asked to see the list of those scheduled. One of the spaces for officers had been given to a sergeant. I found out he was a friend of the NCOIC of the transportation office.

Explaining to the captain in charge that this was not the way things were supposed to be done, I said that I was claiming that particular stateroom. When we boarded the ship a few weeks later, a sergeant spoke to me and said I had bumped him from a good stateroom to a smaller one on a lower deck. Pity.

"Off will proceed on or abt 17 Jul 57 by Surface from APO 953 to Mainland POD." S.O. 96, reassigned me to Air Command and Staff College, reporting "during the period 0800 27 Aug 57 to 1600 30 Aug 57." But the "Surface" was what was fun. Kay had sailed to Japan, but it was not like the Lurline. This was my first travel on an ocean liner. After the first day, we knew we were going to like the luxury.

The first dinner, I could not make up my mind about the selection of an entrée; the steward said he would bring me one of each. I ate my way across the Pacific: breakfast, mid-morning snack, lunch, mid-afternoon snack, afternoon tea, dinner, late evening snack.

My girls also enjoyed the trip. Kit was the young teenage belle-of-the-ball.

And that ended another phase of our life and travels.

CHAPTER XXVII

Air Command and Staff College

Reluctantly disembarking in San Francisco from the luxury of the Lurline, we are welcomed home by Mamomma and Hamo, who flew on home to St. Louis. First stop is to pick up our new Ford station wagon, which we had ordered from Hawaii, and drive to Los Angeles to see Damma, my brother's family, and Bevvie. Her first born, Stanley, is about one year old and John is due just any day.

We are in no hurry, so we head up toward Las Vegas. The car seems to be running a little warm, so I check it just outside Las Vegas when I stop for gas. No wonder! The outside air temperature is 130° - stifling. Elise and Bob Parsons are in Denver so we make a quick touch there and go to find the Coils who are vacationing in the mountains just west of Colorado Springs. They look like true westerners.

On to Yellowstone, land of the geysers, hot pools, and little mud volcanoes. Next stop is St. Louis. We meet Suzanne Collins soon to marry O.P. Hampton III. Visit with members of the family.

Montgomery, Alabama, home of Maxwell Air Force Base, location of AC&SC, was still pretty "deep south" in the fall of 1957. There were separate toilets for "coloreds" and whites, separate drinking fountains for "coloreds" and whites, separate seats in public transportation, trains and buses, coloreds in rear, whites in front. Schools were "separate but equal." Colored maids did not use the front door of homes. We were not supposed to entertain colored officers in our homes. The United States Air Force was integrated, but United States society was not.[63] I asked a major (colored) of our group if he had his family with him.

---

63 "Until only recently, racial segregation of blacks and whites was the prevailing practice in the United States. In the North, such segregation began well before the Civil War. Although never written into law, segregation was accomplished in informal custom and agreement, sometimes called de facto segregation.
In the South, states began passing laws after the Civil War and Reconstruction era decreeing segregation (which) came to be known as de jure segregation....The dismantling of de jure segregation did not come about smoothly; its enactment required considerable agitation by both blacks and whites.
An incident in Montgomery, Alabama, in 1956, proved to be the start of one of the

"No," he answered gently, but matter-of-factly, "no, they are still back in Detroit. My children have never been exposed to life in the South, and I see no point in forcing them into this now."

Command and Staff School. All services have something akin to this. The program is designed to prepare officers for greater responsibility, for command, and for serving in higher headquarters as staff officers. I had just come from serving three years in staff positions in a major command headquarters. Some of my classmates were from similar assignments. The result was that we had already been learning many of the things that we were to be taught during the year long course. A school year, that is: from August 1957 to June 1958.

Still, there were good experiences in group planning and problem solving, preparing papers and making speeches, assisting and critiquing others. We were tested for reading speed and comprehension, listening, and continually graded on our class participation and preparation.

My background in radio and my experience in the presentation division in Tokyo, plus language studies, made most of these efforts fairly easy for me. Many classmates had very limited experience in writing and speaking — the program was especially helpful to them. I tried to exercise ingenuity in choice of subjects and use of aids for illustration and elucidation, and gave freely of my time in assisting others. I gained from that.

Always a big deal when a speaker was a visiting general — All the school bigwigs (mostly colonels) would gather around back stage after his presentation to chat and make "points."

General Kuter was one of our speakers and after his speech I decided I would go backstage and say hello. It was hard to get past all the colonels trying to get his attention, but I finally was noticed by the school deputy, a colonel, who introduced me:

"General, this is Major Barbee, one of our students," and Kuter responded with outstretched hand:

"Yes, I know Bud quite well. How are things going here?" I answered "quite well, thank you, general." Little thing, but it helped my ego a tad.

---

most important popular movements in U.S. history. Rosa Parks, a black woman, a hardworking woman, refused to give up her seat in a bus and move to the section reserved for blacks. After the driver ordered her off the bus, the black community of Montgomery decided to boycott all public transportation. The boycott continued for months until Montgomery ended segregated seating on its buses." (Academic Amer. Encyclopedia.) The boycott caused some pain in pocketbooks.

180

As big as anything in Alabama was finding Snoopy, our Alabama pound-dog. Both Kit and Lynne were pretty scary about dogs, would go out of their way to avoid them. Not a bad idea, necessarily, but we needed to help them overcome their real fear of all dogs.

So we went to the Humane Society (the pound) and arranged to adopt a furry little white ball of a puppy. Couldn't tell just what it was, but from all indications it was a mixture. We decided later that if she was basically a fox terrier, she had some whippet or greyhound in her background somewhere.

No fancy thoroughbred could have become more a part of our family. We might say she was Kit's dog, or Lynne's dog, or my dog, but we all knew that Snoopy knew that she was Kay's dog. No doubt. She would greet each of us with great joy and tail-wagging, but this show of affection was only because we were part of her "mother's" family. Snoopy was well aware of who fed her and cared for her. Some dog she was.

In February I got my commission in the Regular Air Force as a captain, relinquishing my reserve commission of lieutenant colonel (might not have been a smart thing to do). Special Order Number 255, Air Command and Staff College, 11 April 1958, directed me to report 23 July 1958 to the 960th Airborne Early Warning and Control Sq (ADC) Otis AFB, Mass.

I think I received a certificate as a Distinguished graduate.

Another chapter in my perambulatory, eclectic life.

Flying hours while at Montgomery:

	sep	oct	nov	dec	jan	feb	mar	apr	may	jun
AC	0	0	0	0	18:40	0	15:35	0	0	
IP	0	2:00	10:55	4:15	15:55	25:40	16:55	11:35	9:25	4:00
P	5:25	5:30	2:40	3:45	8:50	14:20	3:30	1:35	1:25	0
CP	5:45	4:00	2:10	0	8:15	13:00	0	0	0	
Tot	11:10	11:30	15:45	8:00	51.40	53:00	36:00	13:05	10:50	4:00

Now that I look back at these times, I am surprised that I was able to get as much flying time as I did while there: over 200 hours. Practically all of the flying was done in the C-45, we affectionately called it the "Bug smasher."

CHAPTER XXVIII

Flying the Connies

Before leaving Montgomery we had to get a tow-bar rigged so that we could tow the VW behind the Ford station wagon. A local blacksmith shop was able to make just what we needed. We hooked up the VW, piled it full of clothes and tootled merrily along. As I remember, it didn't seem to take much more gas to pull the little bug.

(Long time getting around to these later chapters. Right now, 6 April 1992, a few quiet hours while Kit, Felecia, Kim, John, Christopher, and Ryan are at Disney World. They arrived in Florida on Saturday, 4 April, Buddy & Sally arrive tomorrow, Lynne arrives Wednesday from Kent, Swift checks in Saturday from a golf game in West Palm, OPH III and Suzanne come in Saturday, and possibly Hamo on Space A on Sunday.

All for our 50th wedding anniversary, which is really 18 April, but which we will celebrate on 12 April because of difficulty in getting plane reservations for the actual weekend. We are set up at the Officers Club at Patrick for about 90 people from 5-7 in the afternoon.

Ryan is perpetual motion, always going, and must be watched at all times. [Revising on his 13th birthday] Christopher doesn't have a long attention span, is sometimes quite contrary, especially when he is a little tired. He is humored by his parents in his minor tantrums and refuses to obey. We feel they will regret this in later years, but that is not our concern. Anyway, we have a few hours of surcease.)

July 4, 1958, and we crossed the Bourne Bridge to Cape Cod. (Kind of hard to get started on this chapter because so many things affected our lives during the next four years. But on with it.)

When we left Alabama it was warm. We arrived in the northeast along with a cold front and we shivered. Lynne was eleven years old and had been promised lobster for a birthday dinner. We tried several places in Falmouth with no luck, but with a suggestion that a little drive-in stand down the street might have some. They did. And that helped.

When I signed in at Otis I found orders transferring me to the 961st Squadron instead of the 960th. No reason was ever given — nor needed.

We were able to stay in guest quarters for several days while we look for something suitable, at least temporarily. We found a summer rental in a little area called Maravista, and started to look at possible houses to buy. Meanwhile, we had to find where our household goods were stored and get some warm clothes for this New England summer.

In our house hunting, we were referred to a local real estate man, Jim Pafford, who seemed to have a lot of connections in the town of Falmouth. One house in Falmouth Heights was particularly attractive. It faced a ball field and overlooked the ocean. The price was just a little out of our range. Some others in nice locations, but were not what Kay had in mind. Then he showed us 140 Palmer.

There was a *caveat* about this house: the owner had died about five years previously, the son had some sort of guilt complex about her death and had kept flowers in the front window since then. Pafford warned us that the owner, a Mr. Swift, would not sell unless he liked us. He had turned down previous offers.

Kay walked in the front door and said: "I love it!" She fell in love with it at first sight. Maybe because it reminded her of 708 Radcliffe, her home for many growing years. It had a large front porch supported by wooden columns, spacious rooms and high ceilings. It had to be her enthusiasm that caused Mr. Swift to decide right away that he would like for my wife to have this house. He accepted our offer, which was essentially his asking price.

Mr. Swift, according to Pafford, lived frugally, was "property poor." He had wide acreage, a beautiful home, carriage house, overlooking the sea in Waquoit, and other properties, all quite valuable. A few years after we bought our house, Mr. Swift married a younger woman, thought to be his deceased wife's niece. Some years later, after his death, she sold the properties.

Seems to me that we paid something like $21,000 for 140 Palmer. Remember this was 1958. There were a few other expenses:

1.the furnace had to be replaced — it had been an oil burning hot water system, but we were told that it might be more economical to make it a gas burner, inasmuch as there was a gas line to the house.

2.the bath upstairs had a tub, but no shower — not too difficult to build a partition wall between the tub and the toilet and have the shower pipes run up through the wall.

3.the wooden columns in the basement, supporting the floor above, had to be replaced with steel Lally[64] columns in order to be eligible for the FHA loan. The wooden supports had been in position for about 50 years and showed no signs of weakness; on the contrary, when I managed to saw them into smaller pieces and tried to burn them the wood seemed almost indestructible. But, according to the FHA inspector, we had to replace them with tubular steel pipes that began to rust as they were installed.

4.some of the outside wood trim had to be painted, something that had not been done in possibly twenty years.

5.a few incidental plumbing jobs.

It must have been about October when we moved in.

Inside, the house was in good condition. Oh, the wallpaper had aged somewhat, the kitchen and pantry ceilings (especially pantry) needed a little help. But these were minor. Outside, some help was needed. The wood shingles had once been painted, but now showed very little trace of any remaining paint. The trim around the roof and windows was so dry that it sucked up paint like a sponge.

First priority: furnace and plumbing. Mr. Pafford recommended a plumbing company and the Williams, the owner, gave us an estimate of about $1500. I questioned him on the figure, thinking it might be a little low, but he maintained that he could do the furnace and plumbing for that amount or possibly less. So we shook hands on the deal. (I've been through this often enough to know that it should have been in writing, but Pafford was there during the conversation and had recommended this company.)

Before he had finished the plumbing of the shower upstairs, Mr. Williams wanted to go over some of the bills for labor and parts. He then presented me with a bill that was 50% higher than his original estimate.

When I went to see Mr. Pafford the next day to discuss this with him, he called Mr. Williams:

"One of us is going to have to leave town..Major Barbee is upset about the bill you have given him." The plumber wanted to know why I had gone to Pafford with this, that I had not seemed upset when he gave me the bill, and said he couldn't do anything about the bill because his son was out of town. I tried several times in the next weeks to make contact to discuss the matter, without any success. I sent him a check, marked 'Paid in Full,' for the amount of the original agreement, less his estimate for the shower which he

---

64 Lally column is actually a trademark name for the steel structural pipe, generally filled with concrete.

had not done, with a note explaining that since he had not responded to my letter or telephone calls, I had hired another plumber to finish the work.

That got a response. He called to say that he was very disappointed in me, that he had thought I was a good honest Christian man. I wasn't sure that I ever quite understood just exactly what he meant by that.

Kay loved the house and the yard. Spring flowers blossomed along the driveway leading to the unattached garage in the rear: two cars wide and two cars deep. The rear part had been used as a sort of workshop and was not in great shape.

The back yard had blooming cherry trees, purple beech, roses, an arbor, and a deep yard extending maybe two hundred feet back to railroad tracks. (Lynne at one time raised some chickens in the "lower forty" as part of a school project, but someone stole them before they were completely mature.)

An outside cellar door on the southwest side of the house led to the basement, and next to that slanting entrance was an outside door to a porch room off the kitchen.

140 Palmer faced Palmer Avenue on the east. This was the major traffic area leading into town. A full size hedge protected the house from most of the street noise. A walkway through the hedge led to the front of the house.

The columned porch extended the full width of the front. A substantial door with etched glass top gave entry to a small cubicle, which had a deacon's bench that served as a catchall.

The inner door opened into a wide hallway which had a small nook on the right in front, a fireplace on the north wall (right side), a doorway to the left to the living room, a stairway leading to the second floor, a half-bath under the stairs and a storage closet.

Back on the right a large pantry with glass door storage shelves, drawers, lotsa room. Directly at the rear of the entrance hall was a large room. It would have been called a *sala da bagunça*, a junk room, in Brazil.

The spacious kitchen was to the left of that room. To the rear of the kitchen, on each side, was a small porch: the one on the right was used for the laundry, the one on the left for miscellaneous storage and for a rear entry to the house. A door at the front of the kitchen led to the basement: dirt floor, part limited to crawl space, a fruit cellar up front.

The dining room was between the living room and the kitchen. A swinging door led to the hallway and thence to the kitchen. Large sliding doors,

185

built into the wall, separated living room and dining room. Dining room had a nice bay window.

Upstairs all the rooms opened on a hallway. In the front of the house were two bedrooms. Looking toward the front of the house, the bedroom on the left was long and narrow, but had a washbasin: Lynne's room. The room on the right, Kit's, was quite large and more or less square. It also had a wash basin. It had a large double bed, a dresser, chest of drawers, desk, vanity, coupla chairs, and a ping-pong table. Quite large.

Immediately to the rear of Kit's room was a maid's room, also with wash basin, and separate walk-in linen closet with excessive shelving and drawer space. When the plumbing work was going on, we noticed a water stain coming down the wall in the corner of the living room. The plumbers said there must be a leak in the pipes somewhere under the floor near the maid's room. Since we did not need the sink in that room, we told them to leave it shut off rather than tear up the flooring in the hall. Months later I pulled up some floor boards but could not find a leak. We turned the water on. No leak. We could only guess that the plumbers had turned on the water when the pipes were not connected and did not want to confess that they had caused the stain in the living room.

There were two bedrooms at the rear. We used the one directly behind the linen closet. It looked out on the back yard and the driveway side of the house.

As best as I can recall, Mr. Swift asked if we would like some of the furniture and we agreed to pay him $125 for over three bedrooms of furniture, the deacon's bench, some straight chairs and rockers, a large framed mirror,[65] a glass front china cabinet,[66] and a large desk that sat in the living room bay. Ov1er thirty years later we are using the furniture that was in Kit's bedroom, some of the chairs, the mirror is in our entrance hallway, Lynne has much of the furniture that was in our bedroom, the deacon's bench is with Kit, and the

---

65   The large mirror was in the upstairs hallway and was left behind when Kit and Art moved out after we old the house. It was three or four years later that we went to the house, now the Elks Lodge, and asked them for the mirror, and they gave it to us.

66   The china cabinet from 140 Palmer: When Capt Uhl left UNH in 1968 he was leaving a battered cabinet that his daughter had used as a doll house and said I could have it. Refinished and with a new glass in the door it was apparent that the two cabinets were just about a nearly perfect match. Now, we don't know which is which. Felecia has one, Kit has one.

other chairs are around someplace. The large desk and a huge armoire in the rear room on the first floor were left behind when we sold the house.

In the second floor hall a doorway led to a large unfinished, but floored attic. There must have been a leak in the roof at one time because we found a large earthenware bowl directly under what seemed to be a stain. Still have the bowl.

As I said, Kay fell in love with the house. The rooms were large. The ceilings were high. There was more storage space than we would ever need. A beautiful yard: Mr. Swift's mother had been president of the Falmouth Garden Club. A nice home. Many happy memories. A few sad ones.

We had to do some painting, and we learned to wallpaper. The real challenge was the stairway to the second floor: the ceiling was over 20 feet from the first floor.

Well, more on the house later, I'm sure there are things I have omitted.

After headquarters work and tension, it was pleasurable to be in a flying job in a flying squadron. The 551st Airborne Early Warning & Control Wing, Air Defense Command (AEW&C Wing [ADC]), was charged with the mission of frontier control of the North Atlantic to detect and identify aircraft heading for the United States, presumably including any low level attack by hostile (read Russian) aircraft. The mission was carried out by three operational squadrons (960th, 961st, 962nd) with crews to fly the RC-121 aircraft, the 'Connies.'

The plane was essentially the same as the airlines' commercial Lockheed Constellation, the four-engine, triple tailed, tricycle landing gear design. It was a bold, revolutionary advance.[67] The Connie was a very reliable airplane, relatively stable, and could be flown with only two engines functioning if not too heavy. If we lost an engine on station, we would normally call for replacement, knowing it could take as much as 3 or 4 hours for another plane to arrive and assume the station. We could dump fuel if we were early in the

---

67 The original proposal for the Constellation was in June 1939, and the first models were converted to troop transport in January 1942 as the Air Force C-69. In April 1945 the C-69 (or 049) was converted for passenger use and ordered by eight airlines. The next decade saw the installation of more powerful engines, fuel injection, wing tip tanks for increased range, brakes of greater capacity, heavier tires, stronger main landing gear axles and shock strut cylinders, and a lengthened fuselage. One became Douglas MacArthur's "Bataan," another Eisenhower's "Columbine." The U.S. Navy first bought Connies fitted with radar antennas above and below the fuselage, and later models became the Air Force RC-121 and EC-121. The lower radome was 19 by 29 feet, as large as a medium sized swimming pool.

mission and a little too heavy to maintain our position on three engines. The RC-121's, were equipped with the upper and lower radomes. On one flight I made over the North Atlantic in freezing rain the de-icing boot on the lower radome was not functioning and the flight engineer calculated that we were carrying 14,000 pounds of ice.

We normally maintained two, and sometimes three, stations over the Atlantic. We flew a "race track" or oval shaped pattern that kept us in an area where we could control the skies (and the surface, for that matter). Our missions were scheduled for eight hours 'on station.' Considering that time to and from the station was two hours, and that we began our briefing and preflight two hours before takeoff, we were on duty for fourteen hours when we made a flight.

I remember one flight when we were encountering some rather nasty weather, alternately snow and freezing rain, and lost oil pressure on one engine. We feathered[68] that engine, called control and told them we would try to hold until they could send relief. About an hour later we began to lose oil pressure on another engine. I dumped fuel, keeping enough to get home with plenty to spare, called control and told them we had to leave before our relief assumed station. On the way home we feathered that second engine.

A few days later, at the Abort Board[69] meeting, several of the engineering types decided that I could have held station until the relieving aircraft arrived several hours later. I told them how gratifying it was to be sitting in a dry, warm room with them telling me what they thought I could have done differently, rather than freezing my tail off in a life raft in the icy waters of the north Atlantic ocean in case they were wrong about the condition.

We flew in all kinds of weather. I have often said that I learned to fly instruments at Otis. A ceiling of 200 feet and visibility of one-half mile were the established criteria for take-offs and landings. I know for a fact that we occasionally landed below those 'minimums,' and frequently departed in much worse conditions.

I remember one especially snowy night, freezing rain and snow mixed, the snow plows were busy clearing the runways and the parking areas of the

---

68   Feathering an engine consisted of turning the propeller blades to put the thin edge forward, and stopping the engine to eliminate drag.

69   At any time that an aircraft did not meet the requirements of the mission (late take-off, aborted take-off, failure to maintain station or proper altitude, etc.) operations and engineering personnel met to examine and discuss the circumstances and make recommendations.

ramp where the aircraft were parked. Col Ernie White, the Wing Commander, came to us as we were pre-flighting the plane:[70]

"Looks pretty rough out here tonight. How are you doing? Think you'll be able to make it?"

"Should be able to, sir," I replied. "This ceiling tops out at about 2500, so we will be able to get on top soon after takeoff. Besides, Major Hennessey will be making the takeoff," I said jokingly because I was giving Hennessey a check-ride.

"Good luck and take care," Col White said.

The snow plow had to clear the ramp in order for us to get to the airplane. The de-icing truck had to spray the plane so we could check the surfaces. Before we taxied from the ramp to the runway, we had the de-icing truck wash us down again, and then we followed the snow plows out to the end of the runway. The plows went on down the active runway, clearing off the top snow while we did the run-up and checking of the engines. When we were ready to roll, I called for the de-icing truck to wash us down once again. As soon as we were de-iced, and all vehicles were clear, we started our takeoff roll.

We were able to see only about two runway lights ahead of us but the snow was piled up on either side of the runway so it was easy to stay on course. The takeoff was uneventful and we climbed on up until we were in the clear. Such a good feeling to climb out of snow and ice into a clear sky with the eastern horizon beginning to lighten with a promised sun.

---

70   There were a number of preflights: each crew position (pilot, copilot, navigator, flight engineer, radio operator, generally six radar operators) had to inspect and run ground checks on his assigned equipment and position. Pilots and engineers made an exterior inspection of engines (for oil leaks, turbo wheels, wiring, intakes for extraneous materials), gas lines (check drain lines for water in fuel), tank caps, control surfaces, anti-icing surfaces, tires, wheels, wheel wells, landing gear and struts, general overall appearance. In the cockpit the pilots check the controls for freedom of movement and observe the action of the control surfaces (elevators, ailerons, rudders) proceed through the checklist items of brakes, switches, trim tabs, radios and frequencies, instruments, gauges, dials, verify altimeter settings as given by the control tower. The co-pilot would read the check list items and the pilot would answer for the correct condition. Care would be taken not to have a "broken" check list where attention would be diverted from the list for any period of time. Should that happen, it was always recommended to start the entire checklist again from the beginning to prevent skipping or overlooking some critical item.

This deicing procedure is pertinent now in 1992. A commercial airliner has crashed on takeoff because of ice on the control surfaces. The plane had been deiced on the ramp, but was delayed for maybe twenty minutes while waiting for takeoff. Really has to be pilot error: he could have called for de-icing before takeoff, at the end of the runway. The commercial pilot is under pressure to avoid delays and to expedite takeoff after he starts his engines. The military can also experience pressure for on-time takeoffs, but it is not the same.

Well, we made our takeoff and flew our mission without any further excitement, but we had to land in Bermuda, our primary alternate, after completion of the mission. We later learned that we had been the last aircraft, commercial or military, to takeoff from the east coast of the United States. And weather prevented us from returning there about ten hours later.

Our wives never really believed that we did not enjoy having to go into Bermuda after a mission. It meant that we had about twelve hours after landing before we had to takeoff again on another mission. Had we been back home, we would not have been flying the next day. But we did miss the snowstorm back on Cape Cod, and it was always a good booze run.

While I was accumulating enough flying time in the Connie to be an aircraft commander (200 hours), I served as Assistant Squadron Operations Officer and then took over the job of Personnel Training Officer. This required lots of time, charts, and instructional duties. I was assigned a young assistant: Capt Russell E. Mohney, as fine a young officer as I ever encountered in the Air Force. He eventually retired as a major general. Another fine young captain who was an aircraft commander of one of my crews when I was assigned as C Flight Commander in December 1959 was Vane Hugo. Vane and I were rated as Command Pilots on the same order in March of 1959. We have maintained some contact with the Hugos over the years. In August 1960 I was made Operations Officer of the squadron.

Early in 1959 the Air Force was looking for Air Installation Engineers. Criteria for selection included such things as courses in engineering, or practical experience in mathematics, engineering or construction. I met none of the mandatory requirements. In going through my records, someone in personnel decided my "MA degree in Eng" was in engineering instead of English. Once my name had been submitted to Eastern Air Defense Force no one wanted to make changes. EADF said the selection was based on my "managerial potential!" What a crock!

Going out of channels, I wrote to B/G Paul Scheidecker at Air Defense Command (ADC) headquarters. I had worked for him in FEAF. I explained the mix-up, stressed that I had always taken the assignments that the Air Force had given me, but that this was not in the best interest of the Air Force. He passed my letter on to Gen Greene, Deputy for Personnel, who directed his staff to change this assignment. Scheidecker dropped a note to me saying: "Bud, this should take 1 square peg out of a round hole."

EADF did not like this one bit and later tried to "fix" me for it.

The 551st Airborne Early Warning and Control Wing Commander, Colonel Ernest J. White, called me to his office in late October 1960. I had had a few contacts with the wing commander: he frequently flew with our squadron, I would encounter him on the flight line, he had seen me off on that particularly snowy, icy night when the east coast of the United States closed down for air traffic.

Sitting next to him at dinner at a function in the officer's club, he asked my opinion on something, I don't remember what it was, but I gave him a straight, honest answer. It was not, evidently, what he expected to hear. He gave me a hard look:

"Do you really mean that? Do you really believe what you are saying?"

"Yes, sir. It's the truth." And I explained why I felt that way.

"Do you always tell the truth, major?"

"Of course, sir. Don't all your officers give you straight answers?"

He smiled. "You might be surprised."

When I reported to him in his office, he had me sit down, looked at me for a while, it seemed longer than it was, and:

"How would you like to be commander of the electronics Maintenance Squadron?"

"I would like that very much, sir, but before you make up your mind I should tell you that I never really understood electricity in high school physics and I can't solder two wires together."

He laughed. "That's exactly the qualifications I'm looking for. I have a commander there now who thinks he knows more than the technicians, gets in their way, and neglects his main job of commanding the squadron."

On 1 November 1960 I assumed command of the 551st Electronics Maintenance Squadron, replacing Lt Colonel Guy B. Gray. I learned later that neither he nor his wife was pleased that he was replaced by a major.

I enjoyed working for Ernie White. Really all he asked was that you do your job and be honest with him. He detested any officer who "ran scared."

One of those happened to be my immediate boss, Colonel Leonard M. Rohrbaugh. A little pipsqueak of a man.

Once, at a staff meeting, White turned to Rohrbaugh and said, "Leonard, what's this I hear about the commissary over the weekend?" The commissary was one of Rohrbaugh's major responsibilities.

White had not heard a damned thing about the commissary, but Rohrbaugh began to spill his guts about ineptness, thievery, mismanagement, property damage, until White stopped him and suggested they discuss it in his office after the meeting was over.

He could be devious. Well, maybe he wasn't a "nice" guy, but he wanted to have people who would do their job and, when something went wrong, not be afraid to admit it. I liked him, and, as I said, I enjoyed working for and with him.

Once, when White was inspecting my squadron (tailed at a respectable interval by Rohrbaugh), he asked me the nomenclature of a particular piece of radar equipment.

"Damfino, Colonel, but I'll find out for you."

"Don't bother," he snarled, and went on out of the building. Rohrbaugh came back in, all a-flutter.

"When he asks you a question like that, give him some kind of answer."

I replied, "Colonel, when Ernie White asks a question, he expects an honest answer. He knew that I didn't know the technical name and number of each piece of equipment, and he didn't expect me to know. Had I just picked some number, he would have checked personally, found I did not know what I was talking about, and would have lost respect for me. He also knew that I would check that piece of equipment after he left so that I would know should he ever ask me again."

Rohrbaugh never seemed to learn about Ernie White.

Late in 1961 the director of personnel at EADF made an effort to get back at me. A request came to Otis to fill an opening at EADF headquarters. The request was for an officer in the grade of major, with the exact background that I had in operations, personnel, comptroller, and administration, and stated that Major Bud Barbee met all the qualifications.

Col White thought this was a shitty way to run a railroad and said he would get me out of the assignment. He told EADF that I was one of his key people and a squadron commander and that he wanted to keep me. They turned him down. When nothing happened after about two weeks, I applied

192

for attaché duty to assure that I would not be in a distasteful assignment any longer than I had to be.

Shortly, White called me to tell me what had happened. He had called a friend "a BG who sat just outside the office of the Chief of Staff of the Air Force" and explained how EADF was trying to shaft one of his officers.

His friend called EADF and said he was "looking at the record of a Major Barbee for possible assignment to USAF Headquarters, but did not want to take him from his present job unless there were plans to transfer him from Otis."

The SOB's at EADF replied there were no plans to transfer me and quickly called Col White to say that since he wanted to keep me at Otis they would do him "a favor" and cancel my assignment to EADF. I'm sure there are horsesasses in every large organization.

Although we were older than most of the squadron personnel, including those senior in rank, we enjoyed the camaraderie of the flying squadron. We gathered frequently at the O Club for TGIF, after normal working hours, participated in the squadron parties and the entertainment. I enjoyed being Master of Ceremonies at the Christmas parties. We enjoyed the friendship of and association with several couples, like the Bosticks, the O'Connors, the Hugos, the Mohneys, the Tibbles, but Ed and Edie Ann Fredericks became our dear friends.

The Fredericks had arrived at Otis about the same time as we did. We first encountered Edie Ann at a PTA meeting when school started. Lynne and Ritchie were the same age and same grade. Kay and Edie Ann hit it off right away, different as they are, and Ed and I became friends.

The first move was from Edie Ann who wanted to know if we played bridge and we agreed to get together a coupla nights later. This became an almost weekly game, first one house, then the other. And generally, it was the men against the women. It was always a fun game. Nobody 'gave lessons,' there were no quarrels or disagreements, but it was serious bridge. (Sometimes the men would cheat.)

Edie Anne Fredericks is a character study. She plays a good game of golf and tennis. She is an active person, vibrant, intensive, straightforward, direct, and highly competitive. When we arrived at her house to play bridge for the first time, she asked:

"Do you play ping-pong?"

"Oh, I have played some," I replied.

"Let's play a game before we play bridge."

After I won the first game, she wanted one more.

"Do you mind if I switch hands and play right-handed? My left hand is a little sore," I asked.

A third game? I pleaded fatigue, sat down in a chair, and beat her sitting down. Then we went upstairs to play bridge.

Fiercely competitive but a wonderful, likeable gal.

We have kept contact with the Fredericks for over forty years. They bought a small house on Mariners Lane, near the shore, and Ed enlarged the upstairs and created usable basement space. He was a meticulous, precise, dependable navigator, a joy to fly with, and I envied his ability to make structural changes in his house and to do all the maintenance on his autos.

As the incident has been related to me, Ed was helping Ritchie get settled in college and carried a heavy footlocker up several flights of stairs. This aggravated a weakness, caused a heart attack, and brought about his retirement from the Air Force. He was able to control this with medication for a number of years and participated in many activities; he was particularly fond of golf and played a good game. He could hit a seven iron farther than anyone I knew. Good hands and strong wrists.

The Oyster Harbours golf course was exclusively for the residents who owned homes there. John F. Kennedy, President of the United States, was denied membership. When a tournament was held at the course, caddies were sent from Otis Air Force Base. (They were well paid.)

Reciprocating, Oyster Harbours sent a number of passes to the base Special Services office. After a few weeks, the base commander received a phone call. A few friendly pleasantries, then a lot of "hemming" and "hawing," finally:

"You are aware, Colonel, that we do not allow Jews and blacks, and we would appreciate it if you could sort of monitor who gets those passes for the course." (A statement, not a question.) "of course," White replied, "we appreciate your position, but we could not discriminate in issuing the passes. If, however, you could see your way clear to granting a handful of temporary military memberships, we could give you the names of some of our better golfers who will understand the eqiquette involved."

"Splendid!" and Ed and I received memberships.

One occasion I remember: we were playing and let a foursome of regular members go through. The senior of the group, a tall, elderly gentleman, hit a 5-iron right in the center of the green of the par 3 hole. (I was never able to reach that green with a 4-wood.)

"Nice shot, Frank," remarked one of the group. We found out later that the golfer was Francis Ouimet, 1913 U.S. Open Golf Champion. Fifty years later he could "shoot his age."

Playing with Ed was always fun. Walking up to the tenth tee on a sunny autumn day, Ed remarked:

"You know, I'm just one over par on the front nine. I'm playing the best I've done in a long time."

"Yep, you certainly are. I think, uh, no nothing."

"What?" He asked, as he stepped to the 10th tee.

"Well, Ed, I couldn't help but notice that just before you start your backswing you – no,no. couldn't be that."

"Couldn't be what? what? What are you talking about?"

"W-e-l-l. Just before you start your backswing, you are moving your right hand over the left hand on your grip. Not much. Hardly noticeable. Just a tiny bit."

For the last nine holes, Ed was so busy watching his grip and checking the movement of his hands that he couldn't hit doodly squat. I won the backside easily. He finally realized what I had done to him, and wouldn't speak to me on te way home.

We remained the best of good friends.

We last saw Ed during our 1990 Christmas visit to the Cape. He had been growing weaker for some time with congestive heart failure and we knew he was dying. He was gone about two weeks later. We have so many memories of these friends. In the sadness, we can still look back and remember all the fun times.

There is so much to recall and write about the assignment to Otis, that I could keep on for pages. Maybe someday I can come back to this chapter and fill in some of the gaps: like schools, poker games, Kit and her friends and parties, her library work, her elopement (but she should detail some of these things someday from her perspective — different from mine), Macavity the cat and Snoopy, golf and Oyster Harbors. Even difficult to just enumerate.

Special Order A-47, dated 4 May 1962, assigned me to the 1127th USAF Field Activities Gp, Fort Belvoir, reporting 27 June 1962 to begin my training for attaché duty. Prior to this order I had been told that my original assignment to Germany had been cancelled because the man there had to be replaced earlier by someone already in the pipeline. I was given the choice of India, Pakistan, Iran, Finland, or Brazil. Or remove my request for attaché assignment altogether. We chose Brazil.

When I went to Otis in Jul 58, I had 2221 hours of flying time. By March 8 1959 I had the 2500 hours required for my Command Pilot rating, had been checked out as an Aircraft Commander and Instructor Pilot in the RC-121D. When I left in June of 1962 I had 4,305 hours.

"Oh, I should have put this next experience in earlier, just after I talked about the snowstorm:"

There are frequent problems in a community, pitting the military against the civilian population. Most situation are minor and easily settled, others bring a conflict between the two groups, some come about as a result of a local business attempting to take advantage of a 'here now, gone tomorrow' military individual. Case in point:

When I returned home after that big storm the road from the base into town was just one big ice rink. As I started down the the largest hill, going about ten miles an hour, I could see an auto stopped at a crossroad. The driver saw me and made no move to start across the road, until I got close, then he pulled out right in front of me and I could not stop. There was no way I could avoid hitting him.

We called the police to report the accident. When the police took our statements, the other driver and I agreed that I could not stop, that he should have waited, and that it was his fault. He agreed that it was all his fault and that he should be liable for damages, that his insurance would take care of it.

A few days later his insurer called:

"I'm sorry," he started, " We cannot pay your claim. Our client was first into the intersection so it was your fault."

I was surprised. "But your client admitted that he had caused the accident."

"Never the less, we cannot pay your claim."

"Is that your final word?" I asked. He said "yes."

"I just wanted to know your final word because I have a squadron of over 500 men who look to me for advice and guidance when they get insurance for their autos and their homes. I feel responsible to help them sign with reliable companies that will protect them."

196

"Okay," he sighed, "We'll pay your claim, major, what was that total amount?"

(Ed followed me as the Electronic Squadron commander. Maybe he also had to use a little 'muscle' at times.)

CHAPTER XXIX

Spy Training for Attachés

$\mathbf{A}$ttachés, of whatever sort, whether military, economic, agricultural, or scientific, are the collectors of overt intelligence. That means gathering of information about all phases of activity in a country and about the individuals, particularly the leaders, engaged in those activities.

Now if you think the attachés actions are always overt, or open, then I have a good price for you on the Brooklyn Bridge. Attachés are spies! The host country counterparts are well aware of what you are doing; sometimes they volunteer the information you want. But there are facets of military strength, plans and operations, that are highly classified and not for publication.

Certain areas concern a nation's sovereignty, secret plans, secret treaties. These are sensitive areas that do not welcome intrusion, even by the representatives of friendly nations. There are some of those sensitive areas that affect the national security of the United States. Attachés delve into those areas covertly.

The CIA man in each embassy is known by another title. The host country counter-espionage people know the man is not really concerned with the price of exported coffee, but they maintain the fiction in the name of diplomacy. Thus, the military attaché, while gathering needed information covertly, is frequently observed, also covertly, in flagrante delicto, and assisted in a project that will accrue to the benefit of the host country without compromise of any publicly stated position.

As we later learned in our training, if we became aware that we were being observed we were to avoid confrontation and break off the operation in such a way that would indicate we were not aware of the surveillance. Some games that spies play!

Well, I was to learn about these things during the next six months. We had courses and lectures in how to open locks, how to open envelopes without detection, called Locks and Seals, what to look for in microdot[71] tech-

---

71   A microdot, which can contain as much as a full typewritten page of ptinting, can be placed anywhere in a piece of correspondence and looks just like a period at the end of a sentence. A microscope is needed to read the information.

nololgy, coding and decoding, recognition and identification of military aircraft and equipment, with accent on those pertaining to the iron curtain countries. Remember, the cold war was always showing signs of heating up in the 60's.

We were taken to Baltimore, told we would likely be 'tailed,' and that we should attempt to lose the tail. Our ingenuity in this and other exercises, and how we acted, what we did wrong, was critiqued later.

If we could identify our 'tail,' and still evade him, we were praised. This involved such techniques as stopping to look in a store window, but actually using it as a mirror to see if someone stopped when we did, if we could recognize the same clothing several different times, crossing a street and back again, entering a store by one door and leaving by another, riding an elevator to the fifth floor and walking down to the 4th floor, and varying this routine.

It was sort of a fun exercise. Most of us did not succeed in losing our 'tail,' or in identifying him.

Much concentrated time was devoted to photography. At the Technical Applications Center, Wright-Patterson AFB, Ohio, we learned how to use the different types of film, the operation of the latest Leica cameras and mini-cameras that could be hidden in a package of cigarettes. We learned to take pictures from a moving vehicle without being detected, how to compensate for too much or too little light, and how to develop our film.[72]

There were a number of different field exercises, but the most interesting was photographing the Wright Brothers Memorial near Dayton: this monument was an obelisk of mottled grayish marble, on which was a large (maybe 2 by 4 feet) bronze plaque containing the information about their historic flight. Two entirely different substances with different light-reflecting qualities. Object of the exercise was to present the natural appearance of the entire monument. When he critiqued our prints the next day, the instructor pointed out the problem and why each effort had failed. Until he came to my print. With a faint smile, he said:

"There's always a smart-ass in every group."

I had taken separate shots of the monument to get the best definition shot of the marble, and then the best approach to photograph the bronze plaque, cut out the plaque and pasted it on the print of the monument, photographed

---

72   The larger embassies, such as ours in Rio, had an enlisted man assigned to handle film developing.

the composite, made a careful print. An .expert photographer, the instructor had to look closely to see what I had done. It amused him.

The standard procedure was for the students to have their classroom and field photo jaunts in the morning and develop their pictures at the photo lab in the afternoon. Most of the time, I found it convenient, and less crowded, to do the lab work in the evening after dinner. No waiting for enlargers or dryers. This allowed for at least nine holes of golf in the afternoon. Very satisfactory arrangement.

We were flown to Eglin AFB for briefings on aircraft performance and demonstrations of new materials. We were taken to a Thiokol plant to learn about new explosives and solid rocket fuel. We visited installations and intelligence gathering activities. This was preparation for being able to recognize and make intelligence reports on equipment and materials that we might encounter.

All well and good. But much can be learned just listening to conversations. That requires knowing the language of the country. So, back to the Washington DC area for the State Department language school.

Most language courses were six months long: Romance languages, German. Some were at least a full year: Russian, Chinese, Hindi. So those going to Brazil, which included state department and military assistance people, studied Portuguese for six months. Very little attention was given to grammar in the beginning — the accent was on speaking, secondarily reading.

Having studied French in college for three years was in some ways a help, in others an obstacle. After a short while, fortunately, Portuguese began to block out French.

At the beginning of the course we were told that several people had dropped out, so I asked if our wives could attend. Attaché wives, accredited as diplomats, also had courses in protocol and and it was agreed that it would be necessary for the wives to have some language knowledge in order to participate in our mission; so Kay started classes with me and stayed until near the end when we began to concentrate on military items and aircraft terminology.

There was added a short special course on foods and household items for the wives. Not all wives took advantage of the opportunity to learn Portuguese. Later, in Brazil, as they struggled with household problems, they regretted their decision.

Getting ahead of myself again. I drove to Washington from Cape Cod in our VW. Kay stayed in Falmouth. When I was familiar with the time schedule we would have, I found an apartment in Arlington, Virginia, which would be convenient to most of the training locations, and arranged for Kay and Lynne to join me. (Kit had eloped with Art to California in 1960 but they were now back in Falmouth with Felecia and Kim.)

Getting an unexpected ride in a T-33 to Otis, I dropped in on Kay while she was struggling to clean the kitchen stove, getting ready for the move and for people who were going to rent 140 Palmer for a short while.

She was glad to see me. But she had to handle the packers herself and that became another story: The moving company told her when they would arrive in Washington and that we would have to be there to receive our shipment.

There would be some horrendous charge if we were not ready for it.

So we drove down in two days, checked out some bedding from Family Services and were ready in our apartment. But the furniture did not arrive. It did not arrive the next day, or the next day. We tried to check with the moving company, but all they could say was that he was delayed.

After several days of 'camping out' in the apartment we were finally able to contact the president of the van lines to tell him that we were about to move into a motel and charge his company for our rent and meals. That got action. They located our furniture where it had been abandoned in a small town. Seems that the driver had just walked away from the job.

Meanwhile, it had been raining, the roof of the van had leaked and much of our furniture had got wet. Our claim was settled and we were able to refinish the pieces that had white water marks. The joys of military transfers.

Back to language school. We had about six hours of class, five days a week, for almost six months. Much of the instruction consisted of dialogues that we had to repeat over and over until the instructor judged that our pronounciation was satisfactory. (Or decided that some of us were unteachable.) We progressed from bom dia and como vai? to êste é o Aeroporto do Galeâo and por onde vamos agora? to the beauty of them all:

"José, porque você demorou tanto?" *and the reply:*

*"O trafego estava horrivel na Avenida At*lântica."

Seemed like such a silly dialogue to have to learn: 'José, why have you delayed so much (why are you so late?),' and: 'The traffic was terrible (was being horrible) on Atlantic Avenue.'

When could you conceivably use such phrases ? So silly. But one day when Kay had been expecting our maid, Rosa, to return from market, I overheard: 'Rosa, porque você demorou tanto?' Whoever had devised our text knew what they were doing.

We repeated and repeated and repeated these strange sounding words and phrases in class, went home and studied the next days lesson, saying them over and over to each other. We kept a pitcher of martinis in the freezer compartment, and it was absolutely amazing how good our pronunciation sounded to each other after a few 'toonies.'

Our instructors were Brazilians who hoped to get U.S. citizenship. Principal was a young woman from the northern part of Brazil who had grown up in Rio. She could be considered a Carioca — and that was the accent she brought to us and taught us. But, my how she could slur the words together. Often, for our unaccustomed ear we had to have her repeat some phrases several times. Something like 'mesma coisa' would come out 'memuhcoys.'

In 1963 there were several items regarding segregation of the races in the U.S. She said she just could not understand this:

"In my country, the races all live together and there are no problems because of color. Anybody can go anyplace."

We had not been in Rio a week when we realized that Brazil had the most drastic economic segregation imaginable. There were no blacks in the schools. There were no blacks employed in hotels, as waiters, elevator operators; not in even the most menial jobs. In three years we never saw a black person in a theater or restaurant. Public schools did cost some money, and black children did not have it.

Our other instructor was a young man who was trying very hard to perfect his English. A couple of our class members would frequently lead him off the lesson at hand and get him to speak English instead of Portuguese. Once when I protested that we were supposed to be learning Portuguese, not teaching him English, one of our class members, Major Martinelli, said:

"Maybe Portuguese is your whole life now, but it isn't mine."

Later in Brazil, I found that Martinelli never spoke Portuguese with his counterparts in JBUSMC (Joint Brazil-U.S. Military Commission). The Brazilian officers he worked with were surprised when I told them we had experienced the same language training course.

They always had to speak English with him, they said. His wife would frequently call upon Kay to give directions to her maid who spoke no English. Takes all kinds.

In 1962, when I first started training for assignment to Brazil, the attaché aircraft was the venerable 'Gooney' or C-47 so that was what I flew at Andrews AFB to maintain currency in flying. For Jul-Aug-Sep I had 32 hours, 30 minutes; Oct-Nov-Dec: 16 hrs, 30 min; 1963 Jan-Feb-Mar: 28 hrs, 45 min; Apr-May-Jun: 24 hrs, 35 min; all this time in the C-47.

Returning to Andrews from one flight, we experienced such violent turbulence that I recommended a thorough check of the aircraft, especially the wings, before another flight. I heard that the plane crashed on a later flight.

When we learned that the attaché was being assigned a C-131 I was given a concentrated check-out in the twin-engine Convair C-131 at Andrews AFB in July: 45 hours and 40 minutes. The people in Brazil were just then getting their check-out and taking delivery of their C-131 in Panama.

We had finished our training, sold the VW, given the Ford station wagon to Kit and Art, bought a new Chevrolet,[73] turned it in to the port for shipment, received our orders:

Special Order A-53, 1127th USAF Fld Actys Gp, Ft Belvoir, VA., 11 Mar 63 - 1st Ind (AFNIACC) 3 July 1963

TO: MAJOR BUD BARBEE, 41559A

> *You and your dependents will report to Pier 97, West 57th Street, New York City, New York, not later than 1000 hours, 16 Aug 63 for surface transportation aboard the SS ARGENTINA departing at 1200 hour, 16 Aug 63 to Rio de Janeiro, Brazil. Upon arrival thereat report to the Office of the Air Attache, American Embassy for duty.*

Air Force people are supposed to fly to new assignments, but if a member of the family has a fear of flying, you can go surface — which in this case was first class on an ocean liner.

Before cutting orders, the office had asked me if my wife had a fear of flying. I thought about it: if I said she had a fear of flying she might not be able to fly with us in Brazil. So I said:

"No, she doesn't have a fear of flying, but I do. Scares the hell outa me every time I crawl into a cockpit."

---

73   More on automobiles later.

I knew that I had to fly in this job. So they cut orders for the boat, and ON TO RIO!

And enjoy another delightful ocean cruise!!

CHAPTER XXX

Rio de Janeiro

Aboard the SS Argentina, we elected to be seated for dinner with two Brazilian women who were returning home. Using our newly acquired Portuguese, we gained from the association on the trip. One senora had spoken to our group about life in Brazil and had made the interesting observation that when she first came to the U.S. she had to wash her stockings for the first time in her life and didn't know how. The maid had always done that for her: "A empregada faz todo."

We were ten days sailing from New York to Rio. A very relaxing time after the hurly-burly of getting ready to leave. The entertainment was fine, the food outstanding. Lynne made friends with young people, we played bridge, I won the gin rummy and ping-pong tournaments. We were all initiated in the ceremony of crossing the equator. Has some kind of name....

Arriving in Guanabara Bay, Rio de Janeiro (pronounced "hee-o de zhaney'roo"): "chegamos o cidade du Rio de Janeiro," we were met by the officer I was replacing, Hank Lucas, who had just been promoted to full colonel. We were helped through customs — not much problem with a diplomatic passport — escorted to our hotel in downtown Rio, and I went back to the Embassy office with Hank while the women unpacked. An employee of the embassy brought our larger luggage. Some aspects of this job I was going to like.

I'm not sure what my first impression was of my new boss, Col Robert Kalb (kal-bee to the Brazilians). Later I realized that my arrival meant the departure of Hank Lucas who had been the Assistant Air Attaché. Kalb was losing a man who knew more about the business than he did, and was gaining a man who was totally lacking in attaché experience. Gradually, we developed a good working relationship. He was the boss and laid down the rules and I understood that.

There was a misconception of title that was prevalent: the second man was the Assistant Air Attaché, not the assistant to the Air Attaché. A fine point, perhaps, but an important one: an assistant to someone is just that. He helps the main officeholder. And assistant (whatever) not only helps the main officeholder, but acts in his stead in his absence.

Hank Lucas introduced me to all the people in all the attaché offices (Army and Navy as well): the officers, the secretaries, the civilian employees, the flight engineers and radio man on our aircraft; gradually I got to know many of the State Department employees and formed friendships with a few of them.

The Miramar Hotel, on Avenida Atlantica in Copacabana was a good hotel — not the tops by any means, but certainly not just an economy tourist hotel. We had nice rooms with all the facilities except, occasionally, water. This encouraged us to accelerate looking for a permanent place to live.

Water was short for the downtown hotels, so they had large holding tanks on the roof. These tanks were filled by bringing in tank trucks from the surrounding mountains. It was certainly inconvenient to run out of water just as you were all soaped up in the shower. Of course, we drank only bottled water. Meals we had there were good. And we were comfortable. Cannot remember how long we stayed before we found Rua General Venancio Flores 35.

While at the hotel I made friends with a little street urchin who would shine my shoes for whatever I would give him. It was always more than he expected, but he never let on. A mixture, not entirely black, not entirely Indian, not quite white. But definitely poor. He did not go to school. No money. I thought he had a pretty sharp mind. I could not understand everything that he said in his 'street' Portuguese, and I could not get across the idea that I wanted him to speak more slowly. He had a few choice English words, some not used in genteel society.

A good kid. But no future.

(Break here for timely news: 13 July 1992 - Marj Petty called to ask Kay if it would be possible to get an appointment with Dr. Tollinche. The Pettys are in Nashville for the funeral of a friend and could come on down to Florida. She has had a lump in her breast for some time. Marj met Tollinche at our anniversary party, liked him, and had heard Kay praise him highly. Kay spoke to Tollinche and he agreed to see Marj on Thursday 16 July. Upshot: Marj had lumpectomy on Wednesday, 22 July, some lymph nodes were also removed and the report came back that the lump was malignant but lymph nodes were clear. She came home from Patrick hospital on Tuesday, 28 July, is scheduled for further checks on Monday, 3 August. She will start radiation treatments back home In Illinois. Kay And Doctor Tollinche chastised Marj for delaying and for not having had a mammogram for over eight years. Marj is now emphasizing to her daughters the importance of regular checkups.)

206

Back to Rio, "Cidade Maravilhosa," the city of the fabled Copacabana Palace Hotel, Pâo de Açucar, Ipanéma, the Corcovado: Christ looming far above the city, the Dois Irmâos (Two Sisters)hills overlooking Leblon where we lived, hand-laid mosaic sidewalks, the Maracanâ stadium holding 200,000 screaming futebol fans, the excesses of Carnaval, the Jardim Botânico, the favelas of the poor up the hillsides and having the best views of all, the luxurious apartementos along the beaches where rent controls kept some penthouse suites at less than $50 a month while other less grand places skyrocketed in price, the fun at Gavea Country Club.

Also non-potable water: to be filtered and boiled. Poor telephone service, when you could get a telephone. Horrendous traffic. Expensive gasoline. Polluted ocean at all the beaches. Dog droppings on the fancy sidewalks.

Someone had aptly characterized Rio as a beautiful woman with dirty underpants.

Really don't remember how we found 'Venancio Flores' but it turned out to be a nice apartment for us: second floor (really the third storey), private elevator into an entry way (about 8x8), which led into a nice sized living room (24x28), dining room (12x24), three bedrooms (each @ 12x18), a similarly sized dressing room between two of the bedrooms, large kitchen, a laundry area separating the kitchen from two maids' rooms and bath, and storage room. A service elevator and stairway led from the ground floor to the laundry and maids' quarters. All in all, about 2500 square feet.

The apartment was owned by a Djalma Ferreira, one of the leading "pop" musicians of Brazil. Djalma was preparing to visit the U.S. for a lengthy period to determine if he and his family would like to emigrate. There were some apartments that we could have had for a lower price, although $350 a month was not too bad, but none had the possibilities for entertaining that were required in our position. And there were many facets about its location and its security that made it quite attractive. Our military housing allowance at the time was not sufficient to cover the cost, but because of the diplomatic nature of our assignment, the cost was within the additional amount allowed. We were quite comfortable there during the three years.

Robert Kalb and Margo made a good team to represent the Air Force. He spoke the language pretty well, had good contacts with the Brazilians, knew how to entertain to gain the most benefit from the money spent. He did most of the entertaining, but we (Kay and I) were generally included. When I had a need to entertain some of my counterparts, Kalb usually agreed to using representation funds. I was able to retain many of the contacts that Hank Lucas had, and I developed my own sources. This is what Kalb expected.

207

Margo: she was friendly with Kay, but they never achieved a "close" relationship. Once Kay asked Margo for the recipe for some dish Margo had prepared. Margo refused, saying she never gave away a recipe. Takes all kinds. Margo developed a serious illness shortly before the end of their tour and had to be airlifted out on a stretcher. The Pettys knew the Kalbs from class reunions and reported she was in a wheelchair and that Bob Kalb had died a few years after the Brazil assignment.

George Call was an entirely different person from Bob Kalb. George never really learned Portuguese. When he tried it came out with such a Texas accent that it was almost comical to attempt to correct the error. When we left the officer we had been visiting, George would ask me what we had been talking about. For this reason, when Call entertained at home he would invite only those officers who could speak English.

Doris Call was smarter than George, but she never learned the language either. She particularly enjoyed having people do things for her. She always wanted something when someone took a trip away from the city. Especially Panama.

That brought a request for several cases of Diet Cola. She drank Diet Cola and ate chocolates and could carry on a conversation and play a bridge hand brilliantly at the same time. Many of the other Americans thought she was sorta dumb. Not Doris. That dumb act enabled her to ask sometimes outrageous favors. And she had a pet. Many years later a woman who visited Rio while we were there remembered Doris as "the woman with the monkey."

Shortly after Call took over as attaché, we took a tour of the other South American countries for orientation and to get acquainted with the other attachés. As we ended the trip, he remarked that these other attachés "acted like God," and said: "remind me if I ever start acting like at."

It didn't take long for him to get infected with the bug of power, but I knew I could not remind him of his earlier statement.

He was soon taking two hours for lunch, gambling with Ray Kahl, returning to the office to take a nap and/or study Barron's financial reports for the rest of the afternoon. Captain Kahl had been assigned to Brasilia for close contact with headquarters of da Força Aérea Brasileira. When George learned that I was not overjoyed to spend two hours gambling at noon, he wrote a convincing justification for bringing Kahl to Rio, at first for a few days of "coordination," and later permanently. Ray also served as "procurer" for visitors who wanted female company.

George designated Ray as our flight operations officer, responsible for filing our flight reports when I refused to falsify the records regarding illegal passengers carried, and flights to unauthorized areas (e.g. a fishing expedition with a local dentist to an offshore island where we had no business whatsoever). George broke all the rules and regulations regarding customs and exchange purchases.

He was a liar, a cheat, a disgrace to the Air Force. Needless to say, we did not part amicably. It eventually caught up with him, but he retired and avoided any penalty for his abuse of position.[74] He died some years ago and the world suffered no loss.

When I left after my three-year tour, the flight crew (radio operator and two flight engineers) came to me to say they hated to see me go because they were afraid to fly with George and Ray who made the enlisted members gamble with them, stayed up drinking until two in the morning, showed up drunk for a six a.m. takeoff. Neither one, George or Ray, was worth a "pitcher of warm spit," as Vice-President Garner once evaluated his high office.

Ray Kahl had fooled around with a lot of Brazilian girls, and started the same with the daughter of the Air Minister, the highest ranking general in the Brazilian Air Force. When it appeared that he did not have "honorable" intentions, it was made clear to him that he had gone too far to back out, and that his future career would hinge on his marrying the girl. They were married, but she did not get any kind of bargain with a guy like him.

I haven't covered all the bad parts, but that would be a volume. There were a lot of good times in Rio.

We averaged about five cocktail parties a week - sometimes two in one night. Most were official, as at the Residency (the Ambassador's home), but some were purely fun with friends. Gavea Golf and Country Club was the scene of many good times. We both played golf. Either or both of us would drive in the front gate, change clothes in the locker room, walk to the first tee, and the caddie would be waiting with our clubs, because the caddie master had seen us as we drove in.

When we finished, we tipped the caddie, he took our clubs to the caddie shack, cleaned them and stored them. We would shower, join some friends, have a drink or two, enjoy a delightful dinner served on the porch of the second floor of the club. Lynne would occasionally join us at the club, have a swim, and eat with the other teenagers.

---

74 The USAF Office of Special Investigations (OSI) interrogated me at my next assignment at the University of New Hampshire regarding some of Call's activities in Rio.

Ambassador Gordon, at one of the staff meetings, announced that we were to be "favored" with a visit by a U.S. Senate committee chaired by Senator Fulbright. It was a question of having a designated escort for each senator (and wife), preferably someone from his home state. I was the only one from Missouri, so we (including Kay) were selected to escort Senator Stuart Symington, who had been the first Secretary of the Air Force, and his wife.

The agenda of the committee included a boat ride around Guanabara Bay and a visit to a Kennedy housing development some distance out from the city. The housing was to replace the shacks that had been built by squatters on the hills around Rio. These people were poor, had no regular jobs, had to really scrounge to stay alive. Now they were to be moved to an area without transportation and without any opportunity to make a few cruzeiros.

I spoke to Senator Symington: "That agenda sounds deadly. How would you like, instead, for me to arrange a golf game with a local business man?"

"Good suggestion. But first I had better check with the committee chairman, Jack Fulbright."

They decided that the golf game sounded more interesting. I offered to have a local businessman round out the foursome of Symington, Fulbright, and Jack Valenti, but they insisted that I play with them. Valenti was sort of a special assistant to President Johnson who had assumed office only a short while before, following the assassination of Kennedy.

I challenged Valenti about his statement, played up in the press: "I sleep better at night knowing Lyndon Johnson is my president."

"I don't know what those press bastards wanted me to say. That I hated the sonovabitch?"   (Recently, 2004-5, Valenti retired as long-time 'czar' of the motion picture industry.)

We had a good game: Symington and I beat Fulbright and Valenti. They were impressed with lush Gavea, the golf and polo country club. Kay and I entertained Symington and his wife and they reciprocated by taking us to dinner. We presented them with a figa, the Brazilian symbol of fertility, and Symington later wrote us a nice letter, saying it had a place of honor on the mantel of their home in Washington.

Symington remarked to me: "Aren't you a little old to still be a major?" I explained about having been in the reserve for almost seven years after WW II.

210

Shortly after Senator Symington returned to Washington, I was promoted to permanent Lieutenant Colonel.

At the end of the committee visit to Rio, I flew them down to São Paulo, the 'Chicago' of South America. Sen Fulbright came to the cockpit after we landed and said:

"Nice landing, Bud. I think I owe you some money on our game of golf.

"That's right, Senator. A dollar seventy-five." And he paid me from counterpart funds.

Another interesting visitor: B.O. Davis, then a Lt General. He was the black colonel in Japan that impressed me so much with his innate courtesy. Kay and I sponsored him and his wife on their short visit to Rio. Took them to the horse races, as I remember.

General Curtis LeMay, U.S. Air Force Chief of Staff, came to Rio in 1965 for the Chiefs Conference: a gathering of all the Air Force chiefs of North, South and Central America.

LeMay was to give an address at the first meeting. I got to his hotel suite early, and was watching Mrs. LeMay folding and hanging her 'unmentionables' when Gen LeMay came into the room.

He 'harrumphed' me and we went to the other room. He mentioned that he would give the address in Spanish. Aside from Canada, the U.S. and Brazil, all the countries spoke Spanish, but Portuguese was the language of Brazil, the host country.

As tactfully as I could, I pointed out to the general that the Brazilians were quite sensitive about the language and recommended that he give his talk in English and let us translate into Portuguese for him.

He recognized the persuasiveness of our argument and agreed. I took a copy of his speech and we made up a Portuguese version. It was well received. We avoided the protocol error that the White House had committed when they sent out invitations to a reception for the Brazilian ambassador in Spanish.

Rio de Janeiro was a nice assignment for Kay. Rosa, our live-in maid, would prepare breakfast and lunch, clean the house, serve the meal when we entertained. The cook took care of shopping at the markets for the food and prepared dinner.

Soon after Lynne returned to the U.S. for college in the fall of 1965, we discovered that Rosa could cook, so we no longer needed the cook and Rosa took over that job, too.[75]

Kay had a woman who came in to do the laundry and ironing, a man who cleaned the windows, and our porteiro would bring our car from the basement garage when Kay needed it, and would wash it and park it when she came home. Doesn't take long to learn to like a lifestyle like that.

Another "perk" was travel. Whenever we were going to call on a headquarters away from Rio, there would be entertainment and the wife would be encouraged to go along. Kay was always ready to travel, especially after Lynne went back for college.

Frequently the ambassador's wife would accompany the ambassador on one of our flights. She enjoyed having Kay along for company. We had several flights to Panama for aircraft maintenance, and the return flight would take us down the west coast of South America where we could visit other countries.

Among the interesting persons we came to know was Vernon A. Walters, "Dick" to his friends. He was a colonel, the U.S. Army attaché, when we arrived. He took over as Defense Attaché when he was promoted to brigadier general, a promotion he never expected because he had never "been with the troops."

Dick subsequently became the Defense Attaché in Paris where he coordinated secret meetings between Secretary of State Kissinger and North Vietnamese representatives leading to the end of hostilities in Vietnam.[76]

---

75   I never got to know the cook too well, but the maid, Rosa, was a story in herself. When we were getting ready to leave Brazil, we had a call from another American, who was going back to Yale University and wanted to take along a maid to care for their small children. They took Rosa, she became active in a foreign student group, met a Dutch scientist, was married, went to live in Italy, later returned to the U.S. and a home in Connecticut. This for a little half-Indian girl who grew up in the poverty area of northern Brazil. She was in her early twenties; we asked her what she wanted for Christmas the first year, gave her a Sears catalog and she picked out a doll. She had never had a doll. She seemed to take such great pleasure in making clothes for her little doll.

76   These and other experiences are related in detail in the book Silent Missions, by Vernon A. Walters, Doubleday & Company, New York 1978. From the dust jacket: "For thirty-five years, General Vernon Walters lived at the center of world history, moving in the highest echelons of military and government circles. He entered Rome with Clark. He witnessed Truman's historic Wake Island meeting with Mac Arthur. He was in Paris at the aborted U-2 conference. He served as top-level interpreter, negotiator, and trouble-

Kay and I were in Paris in November 1970 when Gen de Gaulle died and we saw Dick in the funeral cortege. After promotions to lieutenant general, Dick became assistant director of CIA where he figured in the Watergate scandal.

The 'White House people' directed him to lie to the FBI about CIA interest in the Watergate scandal. A man of great integrity, he refused.

Dick had a number of important intelligence and diplomatic assignments after retiring from the army. Most prestigious, I suppose, was Ambassador to Germany and U.S. Ambassador to the United Nations. He's worth more than one paragraph.

Walters joined the army in early 1941 (he was 24), was assigned as a truck driver, switched to intelligence when the army recognized his knowledge of and flair for languages, went through OCS and was commissioned in May 1942. Shipped to North Africa, he had varied staff assignments, including interrogating German and Italian prisoners of war. Returned to the U.S. in 1943 for more POW work, accompanied a Brazilian general on a tour of the U.S. military installations and went to Brazil with him.

While there he acted as an aid and interpreter for Mrs. Roosevelt when she visited Natal. In 1944 he was ordered back to Europe as an aide to Gen Mark Clark in Italy. (This assignment provided a number of exciting insights into the personality of one of our leading WW II generals.) Dick was requested by the commanding general of the Brazilian Expeditionary Force to be liaison between the Brazilians and the Americans, and Clark let him go, along with a promotion to major.

For a year Walters was a roommate and close associate of the Brazilian operations officer, a Colonel Castelo Branco. In 1964, this man, Castelo Branco, was the ranking army general, and became the president of Brazil when João Goulart was overthrown in the revolution.

---

shooter for five Presidents. From Cold War policy to détente, to the Paris peace talks and Watergate, General Walters was directly involved with the leaders who made history - de Gaulle, Khrushchev, and Tito; Kennedy, Eisenhower, Nixon, and Ford; Harriman and Kissinger."

Lt. General Vernon A. Walters
American diplomat and military officer (b. Jan. 3, 1917, New York, N.Y.—d. Feb. 10, 2002, West Palm Beach, Fla.), served as U.S. ambassador to the UN from 1985 to 1988 and as U.S. ambassador to West Germany from 1989 to 1991; fluent in numerous languages, he also served as an interpreter to five U.S. presidents. Walters began a 35-year military career when he joined the U.S. Army in 1941.

I was in Brasilia (having flown Ambassador Lincoln Gordon there) for Castelo Branco's inauguration, along with Dick Walters. Quite late, the night before the inauguration, President Branco telephoned Walters to have breakfast with him. Walters asked:

"Why me, Mr. President?"

"Because, Walters, you are the only one I know in Brazil who does not want something from me."

Castelo Branco and Dick Walters were more than just 'military' friends, they were personal friends. In spite of that, Walters never asked Castelo Branco anything about the impending revolution in 1964, nor did Branco divulge the plans the military had to overthrow President Joâo Goulart. But, it was impossible to avoid minor slips.

Since taking office, Joâo Goulart had been 'courting' Fidel Castro who had sent agents into north-east Brazil offering help to impoverished areas. Goulart, in attempting to hold office beyond his elected term in violation of the constitution, had also encouraged navy and army enlisted men to revolt against their officers.

With intelligence (mainly from Dick Walters) predicting the imminent action to overthrow Goulart, Ambassador Gordon did not want to be absent from Rio, but did not want to cancel a scheduled trip to the northern city of Recife. He told me to fly the number two man, Minister Mien, in his stead. That way there would be no suggestion that the U.S. was aware of or part of the revolution plan.

I flew Mien to Recife the next day. We spent the night, he had some brief conversations with local government people, and we flew back to Rio during the height of the revolution.

Downtown there were barricades of office chairs and tables, but the pedestrians paid no attention as they pushed them aside and went on their way. The crowd was so great that the soldiers had no room to bring down their guns to shoot someone, so no one was hurt.

The beaches of Copacabana, Ipanéma, and Leblon were filled with young people playing volleyball and futebol, no soldiers to be seen.

TIME magazine reported a war that never happened. The article reported clashes between opposing forces. What really happened? The large army heading south met the larger army heading north. Instead of fighting, they joined forces with no shots fired. Reports of aerial activity? I was flying the only aircraft in the skies of Brazil during the revolution.

214

Deposed President 'Jango' Goulart, escaping to sanctuary in the south, flew to Brasilia to loot the treasury but couldn't get out with the gold and monies loaded on his personal plane because they could not get the engines started. He had to take a smaller aircraft to leave the country, leaving the treasures behind.

The pilots later found(?) a defective solenoid.

Military aircraft were grounded when the hydraulic fluid tubing was missing. Some planes had flat tires. Some of my Brasilian friends in aircraft maintenance were not able to explain (?) these discrepancies.

General Castelo Branco was chosen president and the military remained in power until legitimate elections could be held.

Well, I could tell many stories about Walters. A most exceptional man. No knowing when and where he might turn up. Kay and I were walking up the steps of the Châo Pyah officers' hotel in Bangkok, Thailand, in late summer of 1970, when we met Dick coming out of the hotel. He had been in Vietnam, "canvassing the joint," prior to going to Paris as Defense Attaché. He wanted to have experience in Vietnam when he had encounters with some of the French generals who had been defeated at Dien Bien Phu, and wanted to be able to discuss Vietnam from a view of experience.

I feel honored that I had the opportunity to serve along with this man of magnificent talent and consummate integrity. I had observed him at diplomatic functions conversing with the French attaché in French, with the German in German, with the Italian in Italian, in Spanish with the Spanish speaking South American attachés, and responding to the Russian ambassador who was once, in English, caustically belittling Americans for not speaking the language of the country:

"You are so right, Mr. Ambassador," he said in fluent Russian, "let us continue our conversation in Portuguese."

And the flustered ambassador could not keep up with Walters in Portuguese.

Once when Dick and I were traveling in the south of Brazil, he wanted to stop for a haircut. While chatting, the barber asked him his occupation and he replied that he was an army officer. The barber said that was not possible, because his Portuguese was too classical for a Brazilian army officer!

No matter how hard I might have tried I could not begin to speak perfectly grammatical Portuguese. Oh, I had sufficient fluency to carry on conversations, to understand and be understood.

215

It was about a year after we arrived in Brazil, while enjoying myself at the home of the Scientific Attaché, André Simonpietri, that I suddenly realized that I "had arrived." I was no longer "translating" each sentence and thought, I was thinking in Portuguese; I was following, and participating, in two discussions in Portuguese while listening to someone else speaking in English - and understanding all that was going on!

I attended many of the ambassador's staff meetings. George Call found he could not answer questions about the Brazilian air force, so usually sent me to attend in his place. Ambassador Lincoln Gordon was new to Brazil and was anxious to learn. Sorry to say, he found many of his state department key people were not as knowledgeable as he expected.

Once, when he asked me a question about the Brazilians' use of the North American Apache aircraft (what we called the AT-6, or advanced flying trainer), I explained how they had adapted it for counter-insurgency use by installing machine guns in the wings and equipping the man in the back seat with a supply of hand grenades to use as small bombs. Adding information about the size of the aircraft, engine horsepower, its speed (take-off, cruise, landing), and altitude limitations, how many there were in country and where they were located, I asked if he wanted more information. He smiled in appreciation and said that was all he needed. He already knew what an exceptional man Dick Walters was, and now he was convinced that his other military advisors knew their business.

Ambassador Gordon was an exceptional man. Not career diplomat, but knew his job and did it well. Whenever we landed at some airfield away from Rio, he was ready to answer questions from the local press and dignitaries in Portuguese. This endeared him to people throughout the country and improved the image of the United States.

Our aircraft, a Convair C-131, was assigned to the attaché for the purpose of collecting intelligence. We could report on the topography, locations and sizes of airfields, and it enabled us to move around the country visiting different military installations. According to regulations, we were to bill the State Department if we flew the ambassador, or any of his staff, anyplace. Exception: if we were planning a trip to "some place" and the ambassador wanted to go along "space available," then we would not charge the State Department. Our "guidance" from the Deputy Chief of Staff for Intelligence was to find some business to go wherever the ambassador might want to go. And we did. Never, during my three years in Brazil, did we bill the State Department for travel on our aircraft. The Ambassador was aware of the procedure, and he always phrased his request diplomatically:

"If you are planning a trip to Brasilia next Thursday, I would like to be able to ride along."

He always had business to conduct in Brasilia the morning of our scheduled return to Rio, so we could never leave before afternoon. Thunderstorms always formed a line between Rio and Brasilia in the afternoon, and we inevitably had a bumpy trip home. One afternoon there was just no way around or over the line of heavy thunderstorm activity.

We had to land at a small town about two-thirds of the way from Brasilia to Rio. After we landed the ambassador came into the cockpit:

"Bud, if we had radar, could we have found our way through these storms?"

"It is possible, Mr. Ambassador, that with radar we could have located some of the weaker cells and made our way through safely."

Not too long after this incident, we had the word from the Air Force Chief of Staff that we should go through the regular military channels when we wanted something. We were "not to use the state department to procure equipment".

Well, we had been asking for radar but this time we got it. Seems the ambassador had gone to the Secretary of State, who spoke to the Secretary of Defense, who passed the word to the Secretary of the Air Force, who told the Chief of Staff, who directed the Deputy Chief of Staff for Intelligence to get radar for our plane. On our next trip to Panama, radar was installed.

Kay could handle the language pretty well. Some of the other newcomers would ask Kay to translate for them to their maids. Of course, Kay had to have an entire vocabulary of food names that I never learned. Lynne had to take an hour a day of Portuguese at the Escola Americana and picked up a lot of street or colloquial vocabulary.

The greater part of intelligence gathering is overt, in the open, reporting on events, personnel promotions and assignments. Reports of conversations, troop movements, strengths, personal and family activities were usually classified.

After a social evening, Dick Walters would be able to dictate pages of information, sometimes critical, sometimes rather ordinary, but always with some meaning to the intelligence analyst.

George Call never seemed to have even the slightest idea of what went on around him. I remember when the Air Force DCSI (Deputy Chief of Staff, Intelligence) sent a message to Call, remarking that the Army attaché,

Walters, was sending "volumes" while the Air Force was doing practically nothing. Call would sign my reports, but seldom initiated any. After this chastisement, he began clipping news items from the English newspaper, and once wrote a complete classified report on the issue of a new stamp.

Kay and I made friends with the young assistant naval attaché, Pat Dillon, and his wife (not knowing the purpose of a bidet, they used it for a goldfish bowl), played bridge with them and other groups, did entertain with cocktails and dinners at our apartment, and usually spent our weekends at Gavea.

We have kept Christmas greetings with Pat Dillon over the years. He got out of the navy, he and his lovely wife were divorced after two children, he has remarried (Vicki appears to be a delightful woman) and they have a full, and active life. They lived in California many years before moving to Arizona. We will have to visit them someday.

My life at the office was pretty miserable for the last year, but all in all the good times were aplenty and many good memories. I must now move on to New Hampshire and our experience in the "nawth country."

Again, we had a marvelous 12 day cruise on a Moore McCormack luxury liner - this time from Rio to New York. A number of friends brought along booze for our bon voyage party aboard ship. We had so much left over that I anticipated a problem with customs in New York. Naah! I started to tell the customs man about extra load of liquor, but he wanted to tell me about his son who had just graduated from the Air Force Academy. Our luggage passed without question.

Now our diplomatic assignment was over. We were just another Air Force officer and wife. But that ain't all bad.

218

CHAPTER XXXI

AFROTC - University of New Hampshire.

Special Order 25, 13 April 1966, ordered us to report to Pier Maua, Rio de Janeiro, on 15 May 66, for departure on SS Brazil, and to report for duty at Detachment 475, University of New Hampshire as Professor of Aerospace Studies.

I know that we had ordered a new VW Van, or station wagon, before we left Rio, but we cannot remember how we took delivery of that machine. Was it waiting in New York when we arrived on the SS Brazil? Did I have to go to some other port? Was it at some dealer's? Geez, that was almost 30 years ago. Maybe it will come back. Anyway.....

Arriving in Durham, NH, I found that I was to report to "charm school" in Montgomery, Alabama. I had been at Maxwell AFB in 1957-58 for Command & Staff College, but this was a course for those assigned to AFROTC units; we had to be taught how to teach.

(Break here on 2 March 1993: the Pettys arrived last Saturday for Marj to have her check-up on the lumpectomy. Cecil was not feeling very good. Thought he had pulled a muscle using the snow blower at home. He got worse, was admitted to Patrick hospital where they are conducting tests. Could be gall bladder, but nothing definite has been diagnosed so far. - Much later: 18 March: Dr Tollinche operated late on 3 March. Said it was the worst gall bladder he had ever seen - completely gangrenous. Another day and Cecil could have been in grave danger. Pettys left on Tuesday 16 March by Air Evac. They should be back home at this date.)

Surveying the housing situation in Durham, we were directed to a developer who was underway at the edge of town. Was it Charlie White? Anyway, we chose the New Englander style, a garrison. Original design was for five (5) bedrooms - all on the second floor - but we combined two of them for the master bedroom . Good master bath, and second bath serving the other bedrooms. A total of 2358 square feet of living area, not including basement, including two-car garage, of 1144 square feet. A nice livable house. Front door to an entry hallway with stairs to second floor, living room to the right, and dining room in L-shape. Straight back in the entry hall to half bath and laundry closet, to the right the kitchen, to the left of the family room. Not counting the basement, the house was about 100 square feet smaller than our house in Florida. The family room had about 4 square feet more than family room of house in Florida. The basement/garage gave us the extra space that we sorely need in Florida for storage.

Kay spent some time in Falmouth with Kit, just recently divorced from Art, while I was in Montgomery. Making extemporaneous and planned talks, along with visual aids, was easy for me and I had a good time doing unusual subjects. I was able to get in some good hours on the golf course.

Wish I could remember just when the house was completed and we moved in, but it must not have been that significant a date. I can recall that we had to buy a washing machine and a dryer - wasn't it Sears? And they delivered? From where? (Both still in use in 1993.) And the breakfast set that we are still using almost thirty years later. We have had the vinyl on the seats and backs replaced. Done by the same man who reupholstered our family room couch. He does do good work...

The house. A rock ledge caused a problem on the location of the foundation, causing us to put it a little too close to the lot line on the right (as you face the house from the street), which then brought our driveway slightly over the line. We were able to "buy" a small sliver of land from the adjoining lot and that problem was solved. .

(Another long break here. Kit arrived on March 27, 1993, and Buddy and Sally came the next day. So we have had "company" for about the last two weeks. After picking up Swift in Boynton Beach, Kit and he spent one night here on the way home. Buddy and Sally visited friends on the west coast (of Florida) for two days, returned here, and left on Saturday, 10 April. Twenty-eight days of house guests in the last thirty-eight days. We are not really rested yet, and it is now Monday night. Well, off to bed.)

Back to the house in Durham: an acre of ground, neighbors not readily visible, good stand of trees in the backyard, nice slope to the front yard for sledding when there was snow — and there was adequate snow now during the long winter months. Kit and the grandchildren visited occasionally — she went skiing and I had to learn that "white mustard" meant mayonnaise for Buddy's sandwiches.

Adequate snow. On good advice from a "nawth country" native, I bought a self-propelled snow blower. When there was any threat of snow, I stationed the machine just inside the garage door, ready to assault the three-foot wall of white stuff accumulated during the night.

220

Kind of enjoyed running that machine up and down the driveway, building six-foot walls on either side. By noon the sun had completely cleared our blacktop driveway of all traces of snow and ice.

In contrast, many people, especially the natives, merely drove over the snow until they had made tracks, and continued to do this all winter. Result: buildup of one to two feet of packed snow by the end of winter, sometimes an impossible situation.

We always hated to visit someone who did not clear their drive. Mowing grass all year long can be a pain, but I have never got "stuck" in deep grass.

The university had some fine handball courts that my officers and I put to good use, for recreation and exercise. Once, at the end of the school day, some good games going, we were oblivious to time and weather.

Snow was accumulating rapidly when we finally emerged from the gym. I was able to reach our edge-of-town development, but when I made the turn at the top of the hill into Denbow Road, my little "sports car," an antiquated VW Bug, came to rest atop the deep snow, wheels no longer touching ground, and was powerless to move in any direction.

Fortunately, I was only about a long city block from home. I abandoned the marvelous little machine and made it home on foot. Kay had been worried. The other wives had also called, wondering what had happened to the four of us. In a few hours the wheels of the VW touched ground and I was able to bring it safely home.

That VW bug was some car. About twelve years old, probably a 1954, the bottom pan on the driver's side was pretty well rusted through. A rubber floor mat cut off the view of the ground underneath. The ignition key had been broken off in the keyhole so we just used a screwdriver to start the car.

The vehicle was battered and bruised but it was transportation for the short distance from our house to my office at the university, and I never worried about someone stealing it. No gas gauge, it had the little lever on the floor for switching to the reserve tank, which allowed around forty plus miles before coughing dry. Windshield wiper had one speed, when it worked at all. Reverse gear required patience, skill, and determination. I can't recall that the car ever got beyond thirty-five miles an hour. But, it didn't need to for my use.

The personalities. Major Don Thompson, Major Jerry Driscoll, Captain Don Uhl, Mrs. Jeannette Carignan, Tech Sergeant (blank), and Airman (blank). Someday my memory may return and I can fill in the blanks.

Maj Thompson: tall, nice looking guy, attractive wife (also tall), taught some classes, responsible for the flying program. Quiet, pleasant, not exactly forceful, lacking in initiative, but agreeable to suggestions. Cadets who were destined for pilot training were allowed, required is a better word, to take flying lessons at a local airfield and obtain a private pilot license.

This served as a screening program to eliminate those who just could not manage to fly an airplane — either lacking in depth perception, coordination, or subject to air sickness. I made the mistake of allowing Major Thompson to operate without any real, direct supervision. I accepted his reports, verbal and written, without question — the mistake of assumption: he had been running the program before I was assigned and I assumed he must have been doing a proper job.

His problem was that he did not supervise the program as he should have. But, maybe my predecessor or myself never gave him sufficient guidance. In any event, an inspection from Headquarters AFROTC revealed some glaring discrepancies in training, reports, and procedures. I was given the choice of reflecting his below average performance on his OER (Officer Effectiveness Report) or having the area supervisor give him an even lower rating than I proposed.

Thompson never accepted his shortcoming and never forgave me for recording it. He is an insurance agent in Durham now; don't know if he was ever promoted to lieutenant colonel.

Major Jerry Driscoll: short, sort of chubby, vital, energetic, Catholic: he and Marge eventually had eight children. His classes were lively, interesting, and the students participated freely. Jerry was in charge of all cadet programs other than flying training. He arranged orientation visits to Air Force bases (on military aircraft), field exercises, and prepared them for summer encampments. When the Air Force came out with the V-neck T-shirts that did not show when wearing the open neck summer shirt, Jerry just refused to conform. I needled him, heckled him, and came just short of ordering him to observe the regulation, but I finally gave up and let him be. He retired shortly after promotion to Lt Col and took a job as Commandant of Cadets at a military academy. It was hard not to like the Driscolls.

Mrs. Carignan, Jeannette, the secretary, brought continuity to our program. Oh, we could change things, but if we wanted to know what had gone before, either at the university or from Headquarters in Montgomery, she could furnish the information. It was she who kept up our regular reports, reminding us when we were delaying action on a required subject.

Jeannette was a quiet, competent, conscientious person. She was like a mother confessor to many of the cadets who were away from home for the first time. One morning, about 3:00 am our phone rang. Mr. Carignan had died during the night and she wanted to let me know that she would not be coming to work that day. Yes, conscientious.

We made friends with the Army PMS (Professor of Military Studies) and his wife. Pierre Boy was a ranking Army colonel who was delighted to have the ROTC assignment to his alma mater at the end of his career. He wanted to retire right where he was. And he did. Built a nice home on several acres of ground not far from town and maintained all the connections he had made at the university.

Anne Boy was from a prominent Long Island family that owned most of an island offshore from New York (Fishers Island?). She had been a Red Cross worker in Europe during World War II and one of her friends and co-workers was Mary Pitcairn.

Mary had been one of our young peoples' group at Second Presbyterian Church. He father was president of Missouri Pacific Railroad. I say she was one of our group. Well, she came to our evening church meetings and occasionally went out with our group (see Chapter IX)) after our Tuxis meeting. I dated her a coupla times, escorted her to the Veiled Prophet Ball, but I'm sure her father felt that my family's Dunn & Bradstreet rating was not what he was looking for. Neither Anne Boy nor I knew what had happened to Mary after the war. But, an interesting coincidence.

New Hampshire is an interesting state. You would think that the summers would be very nice, but it did get warm. We had to use fans for cooling. I guess it was the summer of '67 that Pierre Boy and I played golf frequently at Pease AFB. And the mosquitoes!!

Once, coming from a tee in a shaded glen, I looked down at my golf bag and it was black with mosquitoes. It seems the natives were very conservation minded, especially since Rachel Carson's Silent Spring had recently been on the best seller list, and would not allow any spraying of insecticide for fear that poisoned mosquitoes and other insects would be eaten by the birds who would die.

Kay lost whatever taste she had for the winters when she fell on some "black" ice and fractured her knee-cap. Wearing that long cast for six months (was it only three?) was certainly not pleasant.

Small town life can grow on you though, 'cause we had enjoyed Falmouth, too. (Part of the reason we settled in Satellite Beach in 1972.)

And we were close enough to see more of Lynne who was a student at Mount Holyoke in South Hadley, Massachusetts.

In the summer of 1968 I was designated Commandant of Cadets for the summer encampment of AFROTC seniors at Plattsburg, New York. Kay would have our VW van, I had to have some transportation and the "sports car" would not hack it. We contacted dealers to find a car with air conditioning and bucket seats. Bucket seats rather than the prevailing bench seat in most sedans.

They laughed about the air conditioning bit in the "nawth" country, even after I explained about the advantage of quieter driving on the highway with the windows closed. Then we found an ad in the Pease AFB paper about a young man who had a "Texas" car for sale. "Texas" meant that it had not been exposed to the salted wintry roads of the north and was not rusted.

A sporty little 1964 Buick Skylark. Seems that his fiancé's parents had given them a car for a wedding present and they could not afford two cars. I had my transportation to and from Plattsburg. And it was some car. More on that later.

Plattsburg is really northern New York - I mean northern. The morning of the Fourth of July there was frost and ice-crusted little puddles. I had several young "Training Officers" under me, several majors and captains. Their job was to lead the cadets through athletic and academic exercises. At the time, I was fifty years old, and I could outrun almost all of them.

One young man had brought with him his Jaguar coupe. Quite a machine, but he could never get it started without a long push or jump-starting by someone else. Have never thought much about the Jaguar since then. It was an interesting summer.

HQ AFROTC had to find a place for a full colonel in the fall of 1968, so I was relieved of the job and became just another Assistant Professor when Carl Yeaton arrived. After a somewhat "rocky" start with him, we arrived at an understanding and got along fine. We have maintained Christmas greetings with Carl and Maggie, who have retired in Maine, through the years.

Our last year in Durham was relatively uneventful. Rosa Maria, our maid in Rio, came to visit one Thanksgiving dinner, and helped Kay in the kitchen. We maintained our relationship with our duplicate bridge group, learned more about ice hockey rules, and waited for our orders.

The orders were dated 21 Apr 69: Survival Training Class 70-7 at Fairchild AFB, Washington, 28 Jul 69 to 6 Aug 69; Combat Crew Training

224

in EC121R (the Connie), Class 69-10, at Otis AFB, 11 Aug 69 to 31 Oct 69; then Jungle Survival training in the Philippines for 5 days enroute to Thailand.

My promotion to the permanent grade of Lieutenant Colonel was dated 21 May 1969.

We sold our house to Marvin Seperson, Asst Prof of Education, and we learned from his ex-wife (when we visited the house in January 1993) that they were separated or divorced. Somehow it didn't seem quite as big or attractive as when we lived there. Kay said it was because there was so much furniture in the family room, but the living room, dining room, and kitchen seemed so much smaller than memory had it.

Our home in Florida is so open and free-seeming that other places feel closed in.[77]

So we packed it up in the "nawth country" of New Hampshire, rented an apartment in Falmouth where Kay would stay during my year in Southeast Asia.

---

77   According to my income tax records: we bought a two-story frame house on 5 October 1966, for $33,000 plus closing costs of $312.90, plus $307 for carpeting for a total of $33,619.90. Sold on 15 July 1969 for $35,000 minus 6% real estate fee of $2,130 for a total of $33,370. A net loss of $249.90. Three years of real estate taxes were $3,443.91. Figures out to a monthly rental of $102.61. Not too bad.

CHAPTER XXXII

Thailand

Survival Training Class 70-7, at Fairchild AFB, Washington, was a one-week plus of instruction and orientation about what could happen if we were taken prisoner by the North Vietnamese. This included an effort at escape and evasion in which we were inevitably "captured" as would be the case if we were downed in enemy territory. Simulating capture and incarceration under the conditions to be expected in North Vietnam was a difficult, if not impossible scenario.

During the night "escape," one of our trainees was almost killed by a "patrolling" Jeep. Careless action on the part of the staff. The use of enlisted personnel to "mistreat" the "captured" officers and to administer confinement and harassment procedures led to attitudes that eventually affected the relationship of officers and enlisted personnel.

I was unwilling to undergo some of the "training" that was provided[78] and, as the senior officer in the group, when the program had been carried beyond the point of learning, led the rest of the "captured prisoners" back to the home base, ending that phase of training one day earlier than scheduled.

As might be expected, this was not looked upon kindly by the commandant of the school. He intimated that I would have this insubordination put on my record. When I replied that it would be a good idea if we carried the problem to Air Force headquarters, he retreated from his position, as I thought he would. I could document too many examples of dangerous practices as well as insubordinate personnel. He was not eager to have inspectors look into his training program.

But it was interesting to be back in the north-western part of the country for a few days.

The next two months of refresher flying the C-121 at Otis were fun. It was good to return to the cockpit after three years. And I did not realize how rusty I had become. It still is like a bicycle, and other pursuits: it all comes back with practice.

---

78   Such as being forced to hold unusual positions for extended periods of time. I told them I did not have to "practice diarrhea" to know its discomforts.

At this time (1969), Buddy, our grandson, only six years old, would spend some time at the apartment with Kay before or after his ice-hockey skating practice. He would see me in my orange colored (to enhance visibility and improve chances of rescue and survival in case of ditching in the ocean) flying coveralls and had been told I was going "flying." It was only several years later that he revealed that he thought that I would just flap my arms and go moving around in the air when I put on that flying suit.

We are never totally explicit with small children and never appreciate their thought processes, whether based on some sort of reasoning or exposure to TV heroes who "fly through the air with the greatest of ease."

Next stop: the Philippines for Jungle Survival Training. This was to be very similar to the Panama survival training I had been through enroute to Brazil. Difference here was the accent on escape and evasion. We were to try to avoid detection by Philippine natives who received a "chit" worth money for each person found.

After spending the night in deep grass all the while worrying about the foot and a half long rats that abounded in the brush, I was delighted to give myself up in the morning when a helicopter appeared looking for some of us stragglers. My first ride in a chopper, and being hoisted up in a sling.

Yes, quite a difference from Panama where we had spent several days existing on hearts of palm and roasted snake. Really.

Military transport from Clark AFB[79] to Saigon, then to Bangkok, where I flew in a small Army plane to Korat AFB, Thailand, my "home" for the next year.

A lot of familiar faces: Ted Ostendorf, who had been a squadron commander at Otis and was just finishing his tour as wing commander at Korat, Paul Downey, a captain, who had been a young lieutenant at Otis, and others, from Otis and from McClellan, that I had not known very well.

We had several Lt Colonels who outranked me so I was assigned as Aircraft Commander, primary duty, with a number of additional duties. Lt. Col Frank Moore was the squadron commander. A really dumb guy, but there were a lot of us to help him out. I was housed in a "hooch," a building with two bedrooms on each side of a lounge that was in front of the shower and toilet room. The bedrooms had originally been intended as singles but we

---

79 A volcano eruption (1990?) effectively closed Clark AFB at just about the time that the U.S. and the Philippines were negotiating a new agreement.

had so many majors and lieutenant colonels we had to double-up. Company grade officers lived in large barracks-style buildings.

My first roommate was Mac McCreary, a sort of dull tool, who snored so loud and so hard that the building seemed to shake. I moved to another hooch where the other occupant spent all his nights in Korat with his little Thai girlfriend.

After only a few short weeks I was named Executive Officer of the Wing, a senior staff position that entitled me to a private room. My old roommate, McCreary, was having a difficult time of checking-out in the Connie — mainly because he just could not get around to reading the manual — so he volunteered for an assignment in the Philippines, and I moved back into my old room. Much better to be alone.

At the end of the year (1969) a dealer in Korat, concerned with the slow sale of motorcycles and motor scooters because of a crack down threatened by the base commander, before he shipped his supply of mopeds back to Bangkok, offered them for sale at cost, $100. I couldn't resist that price, and besides, riding my bicycle was slow when the rains came.

Later, when I was authorized a Jeep, I continued to use the moped for going to work and to the movies at the Army base, Friendship, located adjacent to and connected with our air base. Good little machine: I kept it for almost thirteen years before moving up to motor scooters that would go a little faster.[80]

The base commander had threatened to ban all motorcycles from the base if there was one more report of an accident with one. I was returning from the adjacent Army base, Friendship, going about 20 mph down the middle of a crowned asphalt road, right along the oil slick, and the rear end of the moped started sliding to my right from under me and I started sliding down the street right after the thing. Military Police stopped by in a Jeep:

"You all right, Colonel?"

"Yeah, I'll just straighten out this thing and be on my way."

My khaki uniform was pretty well messed up, but I had only a few scratches on my arms. The oil slick that caused my problem had also greased

---

80 The moped was limited to 25 mph, but the main feature was that it could be pedaled if you ran out of gas. My first motor scooter, a Honda Aero 80, could get me to about 40 mph on level ground. Later with the 250 Elite I had a top speed of something over 65 mph, and still got 70 miles per gallon. Really beat having a second car.

my sliding down the road. I went immediately to the Flight Surgeon for some first aid for the scratches.

"How did this happen?"

"Well, my motor scooter slipped from under me and I started...."

"You say you had just stepped out of the shower.."

"No, my motor scooter..."

He persisted: "You slipped as you stepped on the slick floor just outside your shower?"

It dawned on me that the Flight surgeon rode a motorcycle and did not want to have to report another accident that would outlaw motorcycles from the base.

"Must have happened something like that, doctor."

The following morning, little men appeared all over the base laying down non-slip material outside every shower. Things really do happen that way, not always, but sometimes.

Our living quarters, the hooches. There was a maid assigned to each hooch. She kept the rooms clean, did all the laundry, bed linens and personal clothing. We just threw out dirty clothes on the floor and she would know to launder them. If we put our dirty clothes in a laundry bag she wouldn't touch them.

I can't remember the name of our girl, but she did her job well. She was busy all day long until the Armed Forces television network began showing the pro wrestling. Then all stopped. She was hooked on our wrestling "exhibitions."

In the center of each hooch, the lounge room had a refrigerator and a bar. Each man had his own bottle and soda, and any food for snacks. The only man who ever violated our honor system of personal refreshments was the squadron commander. A real nerd.

Our missions were essentially 12 hours of flying, but a total of 15 hours. We reported to the briefing room two hours prior to scheduled takeoff for weather and intelligence briefing. The intelligence officer told us where the North Vietnam anti-aircraft batteries were located, what weapons they had, either 30 or 50 mm anti-aircraft guns, their range, our optimum altitude and flight pattern to avoid ground fire. Our normal patrols, along the border between North and South Vietnam, focused on the Ho Chi Minh trail, the infiltration routes of the Viet Cong into South Vietnam. (For a period of a few months we also flew missions over the Plain of Jars in northern Laos, but we came under heavy ground fire there and our collection of information was not effective).

After the briefing, each person on the crew did his preflight of his equipment. The flight engineers and the pilots overlapped on many items in checking the aircraft general — fuel leaks and water in tanks, engines, controls. Aircraft commander and pilot began the Before Starting Engines check list at ten minutes before scheduled take-off time, followed by Starting Engines check list — several hundred items to be checked.

All four engines ticking off, all pressures and temperatures "in the green," the copilot called the tower for taxi and takeoff instructions, and we began to move from the parking ramp to the takeoff runway. At the end of the runway, set the brakes, run the engines up to atmospheric pressure, check the magnetos of each engine, begin our takeoff roll as the second hand reached our scheduled takeoff time. Pilot calls for "METO" power: Military Emergency Take Off power. The Flight Engineer eases the throttles forward to the desired power. Copilot calls:

"V1," the calculated point down the runway where we should reach a certain speed or abort the take-off.

"V2" the calculated takeoff speed. Rotate the nose wheel off the ground, ease back on the control column, and fly the airplane off the ground.

"Gear up!," and "Climb power!" Trim the controls for climbing, turn on course, engage autopilot and re-trim. Reach assigned altitude, level the aircraft, call for "Cruise power." When we reached the proper altitude, with the power set for the desired speed and aircraft attitude, I would have one of the navigators come to the cockpit and take my seat while I lay down for a nap.

The Flight Engineer handles all the power settings after the pilot starts the takeoff roll, unless there is an emergency. The Flight Engineer adjusts the throttles for the proper manifold pressure, controls the propellers for optimum RPM, and monitors all power, temperature and pressure readings and pressurization to maintain between cabin pressures between 5,000 and 8,000 feet.

After about two hours, when we reach our assigned area of patrol, we begin flying a "race track" pattern, making 180o turns every half-hour. And we do this for eight hours.

Normal flight crew: two pilots, two navigators, two flight engineers, two radio operators, six to eight electronic technicians who continuously monitor the signals from devices which have been planted in the ground by aircraft overflying the area.

230

These were sophisticated devices which recorded activity in the area, infantry, bicycles, trucks. The operators on our planes could tell what the activity was, how many units, and they could also tell what had taken place in earlier hours.

We relayed all information to an orbiting C-124 control ship which could direct fighter aircraft to the area, or pass it on to the headquarters in Saigon.

If all systems are working, our relief takes over from us 1,000 feet below, we depart for home, and he climbs to the orbiting altitude. We reach home in about two hours, shut down, debrief, turn in our equipment, go eat.

Should we lose an engine because of low oil pressure or fire, we advise Korat and stay on station until our relief can be expedited to assume station. If we should lose another engine, we advise that we are departing station and heading home, but maintaining surveillance as long as possible.

Once, when this happened to me, I began to lose oil pressure on the third engine when I got back "over the fence," (crossing Vietnam and Laos into Thailand), dumped excess fuel, and was able to stretch out my descent until I was able to land in an eastern field in Thailand. got a little hairy. New, young copilot got a little excited about landing with only one good engine and one-half of another. He was worried about being too high on the approach as I aimed for the near end of the runway, but I reminded him that you can't use altitude above you or runway behind you. He learned about handling emergencies calmly. I had several thousand hours in the Connie, with similar emergencies, so I did not get excited easily. A Connie flying transition training was dispatched with a maintenance crew and took me and my crew back to Korat.

By the end of my tour I had flown 71 combat missions, a total of 763.3 combat hours. On only a very few of those missions did we have problems that affected our safety. A few times the anti-aircraft fire was close enough, but below us, to rock our wings slightly. Once, a B-52 bombing mission that we did not know about dropped bombs right through our flying pattern. We did not know this was happening until we saw the concussion circles and bomb craters forming on the ground. All we could do or say at the time was "Whew!"

Backtracking: According to my Flight Records I flew about 80 hours in August and September at Otis, regaining my currency, and my last flight was on September 22, 1969. I left Otis on 2 November, Travis AFB on 3 November, Honolulu on 4 November, Wake Island on 5 November to Clark AFB,

Philippines. Left Clark, after Jungle Survival, on 15 November, to Saigon, South Vietnam, and Bangkok, Thailand. To Korat on 16 November.[81]

In Bangkok on Thursday, December 24, I was trying to figure what I could send back home as Christmas presents. I had not seen anything in the exchanges on the base that I liked. I found some interesting little boxes covered in Thai silk and some very nice ties. Got 'em wrapped up and in the mail. Didn't know when they might arrive in Massachusetts. This was on 24 December, mind you.

Within a few days I learned that everything had arrived in Massachusetts on 24 December! The same day that I mailed them from Thailand!! Now that's fast mail.

We had Christmas presents and decorations, and festivities, but Christmas and New Year's are not the same without your loved ones.

When I was offered the chance to take home leave in April, I wasted no time. Got a ride to Saigon, then to Guam, to San Francisco, to Boston. It was a refreshing break, and I had been worried about Kay because she had had health problems. My homecoming helped. I flew back via Seattle, Alaska, Tokyo, the Philippines, and Korat.

When I returned in May, I learned I would replace the Wing Executive Officer who was ending his tour. We overlapped on the job for a few days while he was clearing the base.

Standard procedure when a senior staff officer rotated was a "roast" party at the Officers' Club. Several of the "roasters" made jokes about his never having spent a night on the base because he had maintained a house and little girlfriend in Korat; other pretty snide remarks were an indication that he was not very popular with the other officers.

I found myself watching the expression on John Mitchell's face: Col Mitchell, the Wing Commander, had replaced Ted Ostendorf a few weeks after I arrived in Thailand. Mitchell was my boss now that I was Wing Executive Officer, and still the boss of the rotating ex-Executive Officer. Wing Exec was what we were called. Mitchell's face evidenced surprise — whether it indicated he did not know what the situation had been, or whether he was surprised that it was such common knowledge, I could not

---

81   My first flight in Thailand was 23 November 1969, and my total for November was 33.5 hours. For the rest of my tour, the hours were like this:
Dec: 102.7 - 1970 Jan: 86.2 - Feb: 99.0 - Mar: 104.7 - Apr: 28.4 (Got a break to fly home on leave) - May: 62.9 - Jun: 52.0 - Jul: 34.7 - Aug: 106.6 - Sep: 48.9 - Oct: 25.5.
Made a total of 785.1 flying hours, 763.3 combat hours, 71 combat missions.

tell. In any event, it was clear that he was not pleased. The Wing Exec is the commander's right-hand man; in the absence of the commander, he answers all questions and passes "the word" to the troops.

Mitchell took this examination of the foibles of his Exec as a reflection upon himself. And this he could not overlook. The next morning he had me call the next higher command to see if the general had indorsed the Officer Effectiveness Report that Mitchell had submitted on his ex-Exec; the general had not signed the report so they returned it to us.

Having worked with Mitchell on the writing of this particular OER, I knew that it had highly praised the departing exec's effectiveness. I tried to persuade Mitchell not to make changes that would forever affect the promotion opportunity of the ex-Exec, but he would have none of it. I am certain that the changed report assured that the ex-Exec was never promoted.

When you look at it another way, he was guilty of adultery, which is punishable by dismissal from the service and one year at hard labor under Article 134 of the Uniform Code of Military Justice. Very seldom is anyone actually charged with adultery as an action that is prejudicial to "good order and discipline in the armed forces." Should officers be like Caesar's wife? I think so.

Jack Mitchell was a feisty little guy who wanted a star so bad he insisted on perfection from everyone; there could be no criticism of his ability to command his 553rd Recon Wing. He flew more missions than the commander should, but that made my job a little easier. It was apparent that he tried too hard and he was never promoted to BG. Shortly after his Vietnam tour he retired and devoted his time to developing John's Island, an expensive development of homes, condos, and golf courses on the east coast of Florida near Vero Beach.

I said that his frequent flying made my job as Wing Exec easier. Well, when he was on a mission I did not have to get up at 0500 in order to pick up and have all the mail and messages ready for him at 0700. I could sleep in until 0600, take a longer lunch hour to squeeze in a few sets of tennis, and leave the office fairly close to 1700. I could eat a bite, take a short nap, maybe take in a picture show, and be ready to play poker for a few hours. If Mitchell flew a late afternoon flight he was as strict with himself as with everyone else in having eight hours of rest before flying. I averaged about 7 flights a month. Pilots who had no other duties had about 10. Mitchell came close to ten a month.

For some years, off and on, I had been trying to get used to smoking a pipe, thinking it would be better for me than cigarettes. Figuring I had to stay with it, I just about gave up cigarettes. On a flight I would light up my pipe after we reached altitude and keep it going except when taking a nap. A regular furnace. After a month or so, during routine dental check, the dentist told me I was burning up the inside of my mouth with that pipe going constantly. So back to cigarettes — better take a chance on lung cancer than cancer of the mouth. A few years later, after retirement, I quit altogether. More on that later.

Korat was a Royal Thai Air Force Base. It was split in the middle, with U.S. aircraft on one side and Thai planes on the other. The Thais did very little flying of their training aircraft. We had F4 fighters and EC121 recon planes. Facilities were excellent: all sorts of hobby shops. Lapidary, or gem stone shop, music recording, other crafts. Good officers club, with game rooms and a fine dining room. Swimming pool. Well-stocked BX. Movie theater was on the adjacent Friendship Army Base.

The town of Korat had a good tailor and excellent boot and shoe maker. We led a life a far cry from the grunts, the infantrymen in the jungles of Vietnam. During the year I was there we did not lose a single aircraft as a result of enemy action or accident.

I mentioned Paul Downey. Hadn't really known him at Otis because he was a young lieutenant in one of the other squadrons, but we became friends in Korat. I remember he used to come into the game room and watch the poker games. Can't recall that he ever played, but he got to be a pretty good player after we retired and were both living in Satellite Beach.

Kay and I corresponded mainly by tape recorder. As soon as I received a cassette from her I sat down, listened to it, and right away dictated one back to her. That way we were talking to each other almost daily. One tape that I sent to her was a recording I made in flight of an attempted rescue of a downed pilot. North Vietnamese troops were quite near him and it was going to be difficult for a helicopter to locate his position in the jungle. The pilot's transmissions to the aircraft attempting to rescue him stopped and we were never able to find out if he had been rescued. It was devastating to be powerless to do anything in situations like that.

We decided it would be good if she would come to Thailand for a coupla weeks at the end of my tour. Our memories of exactly when she came were not so good, but I found one of the tapes that we used to correspond. Listening to that tape made twenty-three years ago was interesting. There were events and names that we just could not identify. There are several

234

other tapes and I will have to try to organize them in some fashion. But, on the tape, dated 10 September 1970, Kay says she is excited about leaving in one week exactly. That would be Thursday, September 17, arriving in Bangkok on Friday, September 18. There was something about not having a dependent in the area for more than six weeks if you wanted credit for an overseas tour. Well, I wasn't overly concerned about an overseas tour at this time in my life and career. It was much more exciting to anticipate seeing my lovely wife and being with her. The way it worked out, as I remember, we were just under the wire for that six-week caution.

When she came through the gate at the terminal in Bangkok, tired and slightly disheveled, she was the prettiest thing in the whole world. We spent the night in Bangkok, then to the beach at Pattya (?), a recreation center, took a small boat to an offshore island where a Thai company was filming a movie. Got a ride on a small Army twin-engine courier to Chiang Mai, up in the northern part of the country. Only a few years later, we learned that Chiang Mai was the main entry point from Laos for drugs that eventually made their way to the United States. At the time, though, it seemed to be only a small village with mainly craftsmen (and women).

Humorous sidelight on my occasional (!) poker playing in Thailand: Kay and I were walking down this little street, in this little town hidden away in Asia, when we heard some American yell at me: "Deal!"

A few days before Kay arrived in Thailand, I was playing tennis with the base commander, John Grow, and mentioned that she was coming to visit. He asked where she was going to stay and I said I would arrange a hotel room in Korat. He said:

"You have your own private hooch, why don't you have her just stay there with you?"

I agreed that would be a good idea.

As you can see from footnote 81, my flying in October 1970 was curtailed. I think the word must have gotten around that my wife was present and it wouldn't be good if something should happen to me during my last weeks while she was right on the base.

I mentioned about playing tennis. A few hours a day on the tennis courts combined with reduced food intake, brought my weight down to 168 pounds from about 180. I had bought a small Sanyo refrigerator (sold with our house in 2001), which I used to hold milk, soda, cheese, etc. Normally, I had breakfast in my room, generally skipped lunch to play tennis, had a late supper of scrambled eggs and toast at the club after a little poker.

235

Lt Col John Susko and I became good friends. We were both homebodies, stayed on the base, and did not party at the club in the evenings. He didn't play poker, but we played tennis regularly, doubles mostly, but singles against each other when we couldn't find some younger players to beat.

John and I enjoyed flying together because neither of us was chatty in the cockpit. Some pilots seemed to talk incessantly while flying, but John and I talked only on business or when we really had something to say. Most of the time we sat quietly, keeping a lookout for other aircraft, monitoring the instruments. I'm sure that the younger pilots regarded us as crotchety old men.

People arrgh!: We had a navigator, a major, that several pilots refused to have on their crew. He just couldn't seem to hack the program. All he had to do was to get us to our orbiting location (pilots could do it without a navigator), maintain our position as we orbited on our racetrack pattern (hard to screw that up), and give us a heading back to Korat.

He was about to be taken off flying status and grounded. He claimed his pilots rode him too much and made him nervous. I volunteered to have him fly with me on a coupla flights. I worked with him in the air on his procedures and calculations, tried to keep him relaxed, and found him to be satisfactory. Just barely, but satisfactory. I recommended he stay on flight status and work with an instructor navigator for a few missions. Saved him money.

And was he grateful? Listen: Registering for circuitous routing to come home by way of Europe: The Transportation Office in Bangkok required that those desiring space available travel had to sign in in person. This major I had helped registered a complaint, stating he should be ahead of me on the roster, that I had not signed the register in person, that he knew I was in Korat the day my name was put on the register. I had been granted an exemption from the requirement because I was a key staff officer and could not get away to go to Bangkok, but he complained and objected until the day of departure. He did happen to get on the same flight, but all I could say to him was:

"You sonuvabitch."

And you wonder why I sometimes say "People are no damn good"?

So Kay and I said good-bye to Thailand, flew to New Delhi, India, spent the night there. We had time for a short sightseeing tour of the city, cows in the streets, people sleeping on the steps of public buildings. Did not lose a thing there. Would not want to be assigned there. Next stop was Saudi Arabia at an airport stuck out in the middle of the desert. Had just enough time to buy a small rug at the gift shop. On to Madrid, Spain, where we stayed a few days doing the tourist things.

The prospect of getting a space-available flight to Germany seemed dim, so we went commercial air to Paris enroute to Frankfort.

Paris - 10 November 1970 - Saturday - weather cold. Bought a beret, Kay bought some little boots. Learn that Gen De Gaulle died 9 November, day before we arrived. 11 November was Armistice Day - the day celebrating the end of World War I. All stores closed early Saturday. Not much chance for Kay to do any serious shopping. Too bad!

While sightseeing we saw the funeral procession for the dead hero, and caught a glimpse of Gen Vernon Walters in one of the cars in the procession. That man sure does get around: Kay and I had encountered him in Bangkok about two months earlier. (Chap XXX.)

There was a memorial ceremony at the Arc de Triomphe, honoring de Gaulle, with spectacular crowds. Before joining in, we observed the people filling the Champs d'Elysée leading to the Arc. The street is either six or eight traffic lanes wide and it was jam-packed as far as we could see. It was quite a sight. The soldier, le grand Charles, acclaimed as the hero of France, was suitably mourned.

We enjoyed Paris, but I occasionally got in trouble when I would say (with my beret on my head):

"Pardonnez-moi, s'il vous plaît. Je suis Americain. Je ne parle pas Française." Then ask a question in English.

They would smile as if I were joking with them and answer rapidly in French. The problem was that I said the French words too swiftly and too well. But we managed to get things straightened out. We did the things and saw the places that were explored more fully in later years.

Then we went to Germany, where we stayed in the von Steuben Hotel for American officers. We rented a car, drove along the Rhine, visited Heidelberg and took a while to figure out what was meant by all the signs pointing to the "Schloss." All we were looking for was the castle. It took a while to realize that "schloss" was the castle.

In a light, misting rain, we walked the parapets of the 13th century castle as darkness was settling over the Neckar River valley. It seemed almost ghostlike as we imagined we could see the lords and ladies listening to the sound of students singing below.

We enjoyed Germany then, as we have several times since.

Too soon it was time to come home.

CHAPTER XXXIII

Mc Clellan Air Force Base
Last Stop on Active Duty

Strange how the memory can sometimes present a blank page regarding an occurrence that seemed quite significant at the time: Leaving Germany, from Frankfort, there was no space available on military air so Kay had a reservation on Lufthansa. I had to take her to the commercial side of the Rhein Main air base, and I was to leave shortly after she left.

My reservation (from my Korat orders) was on a contract carrier, departing on 20 November at 0900 hours, scheduled into McGuire AFB. Kay's flight was to land at LaGuardia (?). Exactly when and where we got to our destinations, and how we managed to get together from two different airports, neither of us can remember. Someday it may come back to us. We eventually got together and made it to Falmouth and our apartment.

The orders allowed 30 day of leave and travel time to get to Sacramento, California, where I was assigned to the 963rd AEW&ConSq (ADC). So we had ample time to visit with Kit and the kids, pack up our apartment and arrange for shipment of all our household goods to California. One exception: we decided to leave the piano with Kit, and it was an exciting time to watch the movers, using a "cherry-picker" extension, dangle that instrument from the second floor porch to the ground.

Although our Volkswagen bug was the newer car, we thought best to sell it and drive the Buick Skylark to California. It was a heavier car and a little more comfortable. A young woman who came with her mother was delighted to have the VW.

Our trip across the country was relatively uneventful, except for the puzzlement of the car. It seemed to get better gas mileage as we increased our driving speed. Better mileage at 65 than 55. Better at 75 than 65. Never could figure it out.

At McClellan AFB we rented a temporary apartment (#204 at

5244 Hackberry Lane) and were soon assigned nice quarters in the base housing down the road from the air base. Address: 7829 Seneca Way, North Highlands, CA. Our quarters were very roomy, in good condition, and just across the street from the golf course. We could play a few holes in the afternoon if we wanted to, and we occasionally did.

They couldn't find a suitable job for me in the operations squadrons so I took over the Organizational Maintenance Squadron. The OM Squadron was responsible for all maintenance on the aircraft except the larger overhaul jobs.

The normal workday was 0730 to 1630, but I had to get information and papers from my office before attending a maintenance meeting held by the Chief of Maintenance at 0730.

A young black airman who had no training beyond basic was assigned to the squadron so I told him that he should open our office at 0700 each workday and be there to run any errand or carry any message I might have when I arrived a few minutes past 0700. The First Sergeant would find additional duties for him until 1600.

The young airman made it on time for about three days, then he was late. I asked him what happened and he "forgot to wind his alarm clock." I told him to get an electric clock.

He made it OK the next day, but missed again. I advised him to get a second alarm. He made it OK the next day, then missed again. He even went back to sleep after the CQ[82] awakened him.

Then I let into him: I cussed him up and down, using language that would be unthinkable today, reflecting on his parentage, and his utter worthlessness, interspersed with all four-letter words I could think of. His eyes got real wide, he looked a little faint, and said:

"Yes SIR, I didn't know you really meant it until now."

What can you do?

Shortly after this I gained some insight into the problem that plagued many employers of young, poorly educated black people. A black Air Force major wrote an article for the base newspaper pointing out that most young blacks from poor families had never been exposed to a society that regarded timeliness as important. As long as you were within a couple of hours of the appointed time, you were all right. Some households did not even own a clock.

---

82   The CQ was the "Charge of Quarters," a person designated to contact individuals after duty hours in the event of emergency.

It was going to take some time to change this attitude among young, relatively uneducated blacks. After reading this article I had a much better understanding of, and patience with, young black people.

Some years earlier the Air Force had adopted the maintenance procedures and organization that had originated with the Strategic Air Command. The chain of command for an operations squadron commander was like this: Wing Commander > Deputy for Operations > Squadron Commander. The chain of command for a maintenance squadron was like this: Wing Commander > Deputy for Materiel > Chief of Maintenance > Squadron Commander. In many cases the operations commander was a lieutenant colonel, the maintenance commander a major, sort of second class citizen.

So my boss was the chief of maintenance, a colonel whose management principles were: criticize, blame, and condemn in public, praise and laud in private. He made a lot of people terribly unhappy, especially when he would never acknowledge when he had wrongly accused someone of not doing his job. He seemed to particularly dislike me; the feeling was mutual.

Early January, 1971, I was told that I had to take the parasail course in Florida in order to become current in the aircraft again. This was the procedure of equipping you with a type of parachute, pulling you behind a power boat until you were about 25-30 in the air, then cutting you loose to glide to the water.

If the parachute should fail, as it sometimes did, I could injure my back, as sometimes happened, so I didn't want to take that chance. I was close to retirement and being an invalid was not on my agenda for my later years.

Flight pay insurance, which I had carried for several years, would compensate a little for the loss of income. So I went to the Flight Surgeon and told him the truth about my back problem. His examination concluded that I was not only unqualified for flight status, but that I did not meet the profile for active duty. The doctor's writeup makes it sound as if I were in pretty bad shape.[83] So I was taken off flying status and I began to draw my flight pay from the insurance company for the next six months.

---

83   The record of 6 Jan 71: "26 Jan 71 - ORTHOPEDIC CLINIC: This 52 year old male has had back trouble dating to sometime around 1960 (*actually 1954*)when he was carrying his daughter who had a cast on her leg and felt a snap in his back. He has had some degree of back trouble ever since. He has also noted occasional locking and giving way of his left knee, With respect to the back, currently and for the last few years he has had pain in his low back, muscle stiffness, and difficulty in moving quickly, pain on prolonged sitting or standing, occasional numbness on the dorsum of the right foot. He was hospitalized once in 1963 for low back pain. He has difficulty with prolonged flying

After I had about six months of that chief of maintenance I was ready to put in my papers for retirement. It seems that many thought his wife was responsible for his unsociable, uncivil, disagreeable manner. She was supposed to be an invalid in a wheel chair, unable to walk, bathe, get in or out of bed alone. I say supposed because she was seen walking in her house several times. It has always been my belief that a person should leave his personal problems at home, not bring them to the office.

---

missions with considerable back discomfort after a short while in the cockpit. The knee is a small problem to him. It gives way, on continued questioning it does not actually lock, it does not swell, it is not normally painful; however, after it gives way it is painful for awhile. The locking episodes are relatively infrequent.

"On physical examination this is a well nourished, well developed 52 year old male. He stands straight. There is no lift or tilt to the pelvis; however, there is a slight scoliosis of the lumbar spine. The lower lumbar spine is tender to palpation in the midline. He is unable to bend more than 15 degrees on forward bending with the legs straight and does not reverse his lumbosacral lordosis. Right and left lateral bending is painful and hyperextension is even more painful. Straight leg raising is painful in the low back with some radiation down the posterior thigh at about 50 degrees on the right, it is negative on the left. Neurological evaluation indicates a slight hypalgesia over the dorsum of the foot. There is no weakness of the toe flexors or extensors. The ankle jerk and knee jerk reflexes are brisk and symmetrical. With respect to the left knee the range of motion of the left knee is normal from full extension to 135 degrees of flexion. There is no effusion. The collateral ligaments and cruciate ligaments are stable. There is a tenderness over the joint line in the anteromedial part of the knee. There is no patellofemoral crepitus. McMurray's testing is positive for medial meniscus.

"X-RAYS: X-rays of the left knee is normal. Examination of the lumbosacral spine demonstrates anterolateral spurring of L3-4 with a scoliosis and narrowing of the L3-4 disc space. There is some narrowing of the L5-S21 disc space with overriding of the facets and a considerable amount of facet arthritis on the right at L5-S12, and L4-5. There is also some narrowing of l2-3.

"IMPRESSION: 1. Degenerative disc disease, multiple levels, more advanced than expected for age, manifest by low back pain and occasional numbness in the toes, characterized by x-ray findings and positive straight leg raising on the right.

2.Ruptured medial meniscus, mild, manifest by giving way in the knee, characterized by positive medial McMurray's sign and positive medial joint line tenderness.

"RECOMMENDATIONS: I believe that this man's condition will slowly become worse over a period of time unless his activities are markedly limited. No surgery is foreseeable for the back. It is possible that his knee might require surgery for the future. I believe this man is not qualified for worldwide duty, not qualified for flying, and recommend a permanent L-4 Profile for him."

HARTLEY L. FALBAUM, MAJOR, USAF, MC

Anyway, one day I knew I couldn't put up with him any longer. I found Kay doing Red Cross volunteer work at the hospital and told her I was putting in my papers. Kay was surprised. She said she was not ready to retire, but was willing to go along with my decision. Throughout her life my wonderful wife was willing to accept my decisions. (Some of them pretty bad.)

By the time the Air Force had reviewed and reviewed my physical exam, and lost the correspondence at least twice, I was retired effective 1 February 1972.

Meanwhile, because of my pending retirement, I was moved to a job with no special responsibilities or duties: Special Assistant to the Deputy for Materiel. I did whatever came along that did not need to have the attention of the Deputy. Taking my job was an old friend from Otis days, Lt Col Frank Logwin. I kinda felt sorry for him, but Frank was an entirely different personality from me. I think eventually he could learn to live with the chief of maintenance — I never could.

As retirement neared, we began to think about our travel back to Cape Cod. We thought we would settle on Cape Cod where Kit and the grandchildren were, so our plans centered on that idea. We considered the idea of a travel trailer, especially an Airstream. That would require a little heavier car and one in good condition. Our little Buick Skylark was going to need extensive work. Looking at various dealers, even the Mercedes, which we dismissed as too expensive to maintain, we found that Mercury offered a 4-door sedan with bucket (or split) seats in front, cruise control, air-conditioning, large trunk, lots of other features, and a good, comfortable ride. It had the most comfortable seats we had ever had in a car. The local dealer did not have what we wanted but he found just the car at a dealer north of Sacramento. The car was delivered to us on 1 July 1971. And it helped me to stop smoking — more later

Touring through the wine country of Napa, Sonoma, and Mendocino, we put a little over 7,000 miles on the car by the end of the year. We also managed to locate Frank Morgan who had been best man at our wedding almost thirty years earlier, and I at his. He and Jane were part of the producers of Lindsay Olives and the Sun Sweet consortium of prune growers, with their farm (or was it called a ranch?) just outside Chico, California, where Frank had grown up. He also had some peaches. Peaches that set a standard that we have never found again. We might say about some peaches we buy: "Good peach, but not a Morgan."

Kay and I have never been much for camping out — we never had done any, but the Morgans prevailed on us to bring bedrolls and go camping in

242

Lassen National Park, about 150 miles north of Sacramento. After exploring the park for several hours, we located a spot to spread our bedrolls and went to sleep under the stars.

Apprehensive about bears, some of those sounds of the wild were a little unsettling, but we did sleep finally in spite of the rock right in the middle of my back. In the morning we packed up and the Morgans led us a little distance downstream and told us to set up for breakfast while they went fishing. Before long they were back with a string of mountain trout that we cooked over a small campfire. That fish and a coupla slices of burned toast were a delicious breakfast. We enjoyed the trip tremendously, but we haven't done any camping since then.

Several years later we were saddened to hear that the Morgans had decided "to go their separate ways." They had sold the ranch for a substantial sum. Split the money, I guess? The last contact we had was to the effect that their daughter was working in Disney World in Orlando. If we learned her married name, I don't know.

So the movers came, packed our household goods that were to go in storage until we had a house to put them in, and thereby hangs another tale.

With the new car we decided against trying one of the travel trailers, like the AirStream. They were nice, but there was the problem of finding a trailer park, and the expense, when we could probably stay in military guest housing along the way. It worked out. Most nights we were able to find space available in guest housing on a military base.

We agreed that we would travel leisurely across the country, stopping wherever and whenever we wanted to, making 5 miles or 500 miles in a day as we felt like it. There are a number of attractions that seem to be just enough out of the way that there is never enough time to make the little side trips to see them.

This time we did it. Carlsbad Caverns, Fort Huachuca, Tombstone, the whole schmeer.

CHAPTER XXXIV

Begin Retirement & Self-Analysis

Leaving California was not entirely easy. We never would have liked the Los Angeles area, but many parts of California were quite appealing. At the time we felt that we were too far away from our children and grandchildren. We knew that we wanted to retire on Cape Cod. If we couldn't find what we wanted, we would build a new house.

> *"The best laid schemes o' mice an' men*
> *Gang aft agley."*   *(Robert Burns)*

As I mentioned, we did take a leisurely drive back to the East. We visited briefly in the Los Angeles area with my mother and brother, decided we were not ready for Sun City, a retirement community in Phoenix, did our sight-seeing-travel across the great United States to Florida.

Over the years, we had maintained communication with Don and Bettye Calland with Christmas cards and they had encouraged us to visit their little town of Satellite Beach. It was now early April 1972.

After we checked into the guest house at Patrick AFB, we located the Callands and found they were helping Bud (Howard) and Janet Harbaugh celebrate their new home. And who was also visiting there but Paul Downey who had retired in Falmouth after he had returned from Thailand.

Don showed us a few houses that were for sale but recommended that, if we wanted to live in the area, we buy a lot and build exactly what we wanted for about what we would pay for a house already built. He showed us the development that Jimmy Caudle planned with canal waterfront homes, and recommended specific lots, not too close to the Grand Canal nor too far from it, on the south side of the street so the pool and patio would have southern exposure: Lot #19 on the layout sketch met the criteria.

We couldn't get much excited about an area that had nothing but sand, no houses, no roads, nothing. Things seemed expensive - $12,500 for "a little mound of sand" — and we knew we were going to go on to Cape Cod so we did not make any commitments.

A few weeks after we arrived in Falmouth, and after having looked at a number of houses, we realized that inflation had hit the Cape: little houses that had cost about $12,000 when we had lived there ten years earlier were now over $39,000! We could not find any house that really satisfied all our criteria: near, on, or within view of the water, and within what we considered our price range.

One day when we were considering all these imponderables Kay said:

"You know, we can live now wherever we want, and I don't really like cold weather."

So I called Jimmy Caudle and told him we were sending a 10% down payment of $1250 for Lot #19 in The Fountains. Part of the agreement of buying in The Fountains (from either Caudle or Joe di Prima who would build your house) was that you agreed to begin construction within six months. Their idea in having this clause was to prevent someone from speculation buying of a lot and holding it until prices went up. This had caused the continuing upset of construction in other developments for years after most of the houses had been built.

We had a delightful summer on Cape Cod living with Kit and Sam and the grandchildren. They had expanded their Maravista house, adding another garage and rooms over the garage, an indoor swimming pool, a large family room off the pool, a sauna and two additional baths.

Sam was having his people, primarily his 'second in command,' conduct an inventory of Wright Oil Company. I volunteered my help. There were interesting developments. First, there was no precise count of items, large or small. Men who were working on heating systems would take whatever items were needed from the storage bins and load up their trucks. I asked Sam's right-hand-man about inventory control:

"How do you know when to order replacement items?"

"Oh, whenever we run out we order more."

"You don't have any usage history, no way to tell how many of a particular item are used during a set period of time? No idea of the consumption of large, expensive parts and fixtures?"

"No. Whenever a driver needs something for his truck he just comes in to supply and takes what he needs. It'd be too expensive to try to keep track of all the stuff that comes in and goes out. I guess we do lose some stuff now and then."

Not particularly surprising, then, to find that a complete oil delivery truck was missing!

"Have you told Sam about this?"

"Naw. You know how it is. People don't like to hear bad news."

After a summer of revelations about how a business is run, in early September we drove to Maine just to see where we had lived in Durham, New Hampshire, and some of the quaint coastal cities of Maine. Then it was September and time to head for Florida to get definite with our house plans.

It would be an understatement to say that we were surprised to find that there were still no streets and no houses in The Fountains when we arrived in Satellite Beach. We knew some lots had been sold shortly after the project had been announced in January or February; two houses were soon started and we began working with Jimmy Caudle on our house plans.

We did work with his standard plans, making changes here and there, in the size of the kitchen and the arrangement of appliances, the location and size of the master bedroom, the shape of the master bath, entrances and exits, especially from the house to the patio and swimming pool. In the end, our house was essentially Kay's plan: the family room, kitchen, dining room, west hallway, and master bedroom opened onto the patio and swimming pool.

The basic design is fairly common in Florida: Master bedroom and bath on one end of the house, guest bedrooms and bath on the other, separated by the family room, kitchen and living/dining rooms. Our arrangement is good: in our daily living area where we generate the laundry that goes from bedroom through the bath to the laundry room that opens into the garage. And we have no need to cross the living/dining room area regularly. Anyway...

After the plans were finalized we had time on our hands. We drove to Washington D.C. to join Kit and Sam at his daughter's (Ginny) house for Thanksgiving dinner, then went on to Falmouth, returning to Florida in December. On icy, snowy roads we trailered Sam's boat, Ducky, to Florida.

Kit and Sam joined us at the apartment for Christmas. We decorated a small Norfolk pine for our tree, and later we planted the tree in our front yard. It grew to a nice height before a couple of freezing days one winter killed off many of its branches. Some pines in the area were left standing but they looked pretty scraggly. We cut ours down.

The first work on the foundation began in December, after what seemed interminable delays:[84] workmen misread the house plans, put the lintel for

---

84 A supplier delivered the boxed air conditioning unit and left it (still in the box) in the garage which did not yet have a door. The next morning, the unit and the box were gone. Naturally, the builder had some discussion with the supplier, but we got another unit. Who had to pay for it? It was probably the supplier. The builder said the unit should never have been left in the garage without some kind of connection.

the front door in the wrong place, had not built in a closet, someone stole the air conditioning unit from the garage, etc, etc, we were able to move in our new home in May 1973.

The military will hold your household goods (furniture, etc.) for one year from the date of your retirement. After one year you must begin to pay for storage — unless you are hospitalized or in a training program. Rather than have a reason to go into the hospital, I signed up for VA sponsored training in welding. Never know when some -thing like that will come in handy. With a few months extension the program lasted just long enough.

While the building progressed we lived in the Shoreview Apartments on Highway A1A and had very little to do. So we arranged with Caudle to give us credit for doing the interior painting. It worked, but it was more work than we had originally thought and it was a learning experience.

Paul Downey and Bud Harbaugh had paid only $5000 for their inland lots and thought we were crazy to pay $12,500 for ours. That was the original price. By the time we had returned to Florida in September 1972, before any construction had begun, the price of the lots had gone up twice. When the second phase of The Fountains was opened for sale the canal lots were at $39,000. In the third phase the price had reached $55,000. One of the last canal lots, sold in just a few years, went for $180,000.

When we sold our home in December 2001 for $330,000 our friends' homes were bringing in less than $100,000. We never thought of the home as an investment, but it turned out to be a good one.

"I don't want a nice little house, on a nice little street, in a nice little town, in Florida," I had said, "I want to be on the water, where I can watch the fish jump, dolphins splash, cormorants dive, the pelicans land on our pilings, the manatees surface their nostrils for a breath of air and the blue herons strut imperiously in the yard.

"Just looking at the same fence separating our backyard from someone else's backyard, nothing ever changing, would be tiresome." We knew our neighbors across the canal and they recognized us as friends.

So began our retirement, mine actually 'cause Kay pointed out that she was still doing the same amount of work plus having me home for lunch. We both were busier than ever before.

Somewhere in these notes I seem to have completely omitted mention of "Sea Wings," a 28" foot Morgan Out Island sailboat. We bought the boat in January 1975, had many enjoyable and interesting years of sailing it, and

Kay was an excellent sailor. But in the end it was just too much for me to maintain and too much sun, so we sold it in the summer of 1994.

(Writing this chapter was delayed several months while we traveled to St. Louis for Kay's 55th reunion at Washington U., in May 1993, a visit to Lynne in Cincinnati, and on to Westport to surprise Kit for the celebration of her 50th birthday arranged by her children. Kit was dumfounded when she saw her mother come in the door of the party where her friends and children, and grandchildren, were gathered... We were supposed to be on our way to home to Florida. Further delay while we visited Lynne in Seattle (her temporary assignment until summer of 1994) from 7/22 to 8/2/93. Back home for laundry and then off to Michigan, St. Louis, Cincinnati and home 9/3 to 9/19/93. Writing in September 1993, we were scheduled to leave 1 October (1993) for the wedding of Swift's son, Jim, and Anne Borow. Probably more later on the wedding that was held on a boat in Boston harbor.)

Forgot about the new car and smoking: I decided that I would not smoke in the new (1971) Mercury. Many times I had jumped around in an automobile to brush off burning cigarette ashes. No more. I would wait to have a smoke until we made a stop. Result: we stopped more often. But that was probably good, too. Anyway...It wasn't long into retirement, and being home a lot more, that Kay began to remark about how often I seemed to be lighting a cigarette. I wasn't smoking more than I ever had, about a pack a day, but she was now seeing more of me, and therefore more of me smoking.

Well, I got upset, but said to myself: "I will wait a little while before I have the 'next' cigarette." I held off for hours, days, years.

It has now been many years (over thirty?) since I had my last cigarette, and am I glad! Kay had stopped when she was ill in 1969. Problem is that neither one of us can stand even a little smoke from tobacco. Former smokers are the worst about tobacco smoke, and we must be among the worst of the worst. It is hard to understand why we ever had anything to do with cigarettes.

My beard aggravated the situation by "locking onto" any smoke anywhere near and retaining it until I washed my face. This holding on to odors also applied to people with bad breath who came too close, ace to face.

The beard was the result of treatment for actinic keratoses — the precursor of skin cancer. In 1975, Dr. Hornell, dermatologist and skin cancer specialist in Melbourne, started me on treatments that removed affected skin and left my face raw. I couldn't shave for a number of days. At my next appointment Dr. Hornell said he thought the beard was a good idea: it would help protect my face from the sun.

Our activities from 1972 until we went to England for the first time in September 1981, will be detailed later in some of our trips and travels. While mother had been ill we had not felt free to travel extensively. 1981 was a busy year, all in all.

Mother (Rose Ammerman) died at the end of January and we took her to Dickson, Tennessee, to bury her between her first husband, Early Hooper, and my stepfather, Walter Ammerman. In April 1981 we went to St. Louis when Thelma Hampton (The Duchess), Kay's sister-in-law, died, and went back again in June for the wedding of Sheri Hampton, daughter of nephew O.P. III and Suzanne Hampton.

My life didn't end with my retirement from the United States Air Force, but significant changes in the direction of it did. The greatest change: when my dear wife had a stroke in 1998.

Self - Analysis

But who am I? What am I like? Have I made any sense about the people, the things, the events that have shaped my life and my being? And, importantly, can anyone be objective about the subject of himself?

You be the judge, I'll make the attempt. My daughters and grandchildren will retain some memories of physical attributes, possibly remember what I looked like with a beard, and perhaps personality traits; but for the great-grandchildren I likely shall be remembered as a sort of large and old and gray-haired man who touched their lives maybe a couple of times a year for a few days.

When I asked the doctor what the prognosis was for degenerative disc disease, he replied: "It will begin to slow down and the rest of the population will start to catch up with you." As for the skin cancer, I try to avoid the sun as much as possible. My knee cartilages don't seem to be much worse now that I have had arthroscopic surgery on my left knee and avoid doing deep knee bends.

All in all, in my late eighties, I remain in fairly good health, with limitations. Cancer of the colon surgery, followed by radiation and chemotherapy (which I should never have volunteered to go through), in the spring of 2003, left me in a weakened and unstable condition and I fell flat on my back, throwing things out of 'whack.' When I retired from the Air Force, the Veterans' Administration awarded me 40% disability in consideration of degenerative disc disease, skin cancer, and weakened knee cartilages.

Driver's license stuff: almost 6 feet tall at one time (about 5'9" now but I have shrunk with age), weight down from 185 pounds to about 175, hazel eyes (my dear wife says they are sometimes almost blue, large legs (perhaps a little too large for my upper body), shoe size 12 (had to wear scoutmaster shoes when I was a scout), nicely shaped head, nose perhaps a bit too long, ears normal except for the inevitable lengthening with age, eyes sort of squinty, "stingy" smile with very little teeth showing, slightly receding hairline. Not an unattractive person overall, especially before I grew a beard and mustache. Some years ago in Rio de Janeiro, at a diplomatic function when I was all "gussied up" in my white uniform with ribbons and braids, Major General John Bell looked me up and down and said:

"My God, Bud, you really look like the Hollywood version of the handsome Air Force attaché."

I'm left-handed. According to granddaughter Kim, who is similarly afflicted, only southpaws are in their right mind. Ordinarily a pleasant, quiet, receptive, understanding individual, not particularly argumentative, except perhaps on questions of grammar and spelling. I do object when people make "statements of fact," when they do not know the facts, and later admit their error saying, "Well, you know what I meant." I'm not any good at 'small talk.' Think women talk too much on the telephone. My mother talked too much all the time. Wish I had listened more.

I am impatient with fools. Had a neighbor, three doors down the street, who had to be told something several times, over a period of days, before it soaked in — then it would be regurgitated later as his original idea. Leads to a definite shortcoming: I find it difficult to ask the advice of, or seek information from, someone whom I regard as less informed, less knowledgeable. On rare occasions when I have done so, I have been pleasantly surprised to find I learn something I had not expected.

Generally calm, not easily excited, I can react (some say over-react) violently when pushed too far. Do I hold a grudge? I guess so. When I have been disappointed or let down, in a serious matter, by someone I have trusted, I never place trust or confidence in that person again. It was said: "We read that we ought to forgive our enemies; but we do not read that we ought to forgive our friends."

Have never regarded myself as a strongly ambitious person, certainly not to the point of hurting someone else, like Macbeth's *Vaulting ambition, which o'erleaps itself.* Have always tried to give 100% in whatever job I had, teaching, flying, staffing, commanding. Making a lot of money has not been a goal, not a driving force as with some men.

250

Do not misunderstand: I enjoy having enough money to do the things I want to do, but my desires are modest. Francis Bacon, in *Of Marriage and Single Life*, wrote *"He that hath wife and children hath given hostages to fortune,"* but I console myself with the line from *Othello: "Poor and content is rich, and rich enough."*

A procrastinator? Oh, yes. Worse and worse now. I take on too many different small tasks and leave a trail of unfinished projects. Small bits of writing, several books waiting to be completed, ideas only partially developed, sewing (!) items of clothing never brought to conclusion, that ten-minute walk that I plan to do every day, that program I promised to do but haven't "worked up" yet. Oh, well......

Competitive? Sure. I like to win. I was a "low level" champion at table tennis (ping-pong) for small sums of money. What may be classified as a "C" tennis player well into my eighties, but Kay was better, certainly at golf.

I have always enjoyed playing cards: poker, gin rummy, bridge. We had a "poker group" in Florida for 27 years; every year I was a winner, sometimes only a few dollars, but at the end of the year I was always ahead. As mentioned in Chapter IX, I was initiated into the game of bridge when I was about seventeen or eighteen. In college we played for small amounts (tenth of a cent a point), but it provided a little spending money. Once, in a short session in Buenos Aires, we played for 10 cents a point. As a couple, Kay and I enjoyed a social game with other couples. Now, in my dotage, I find mental stimulation in playing highly competitive duplicate club and tournament bridge for master points.

As I promised Kay when we married: we'll never be rich, but it will never be dull.

She agrees that it has never been dull.

CHAPTER XXXV

Settle Down and Travel

Hard to say about where to begin the recounting of our travels after retirement. A lot of happenings in the period of 1972 to 1981 that must be remembered.[85] 1981 was the first of our trips overseas after retirement.

---

85   Brief review of early trips:
For most years, between 1973 and 2001, after we moved into our new home in Florida in May 1973, we traveled to Cape Cod at least once, and many years we went to Macatawa over Labor Day.
Other trips within U.S.:
1980: Kit's wedding, and to California after mother's apartment caught fire.
1981: to Dickson for mother's burial, and to St. Louis for Thelma' death andShei's wedding.
1982: America's Cup races and Mary Ellen and Vaughn Ball
1984: Cape Cod for Felecia's wedding 8/11/84
1985: McKinley HS reunion.
1987: Cape Cod for Buddy/Sally wedding 6/23
1989: Meet Wolters in Lucerne, Stan died 8/24, Chicago for Sue Parson wedding 10/6, Clarksville cemetery 10/13, to Ft Myers for Helen Fraser wedding, 10/21
1990: 50th reunion at Washington U.
1991: Ed Fredericks dies in January
1991: Lynne buys her first car! 3/1, Ft Myers wedding Marj Vallowe to Jay Phipps, visit w/ Roemer & Billie Ruth.
1992: 4/12 50th wedding anniversary 4/18, NH see old house
1993: Lunch w/ Comptons, Kirkpatricks at Hilton Head 1/6, Kay's WU 50th, Kit surprise at 50, Seattle to visit Lynne, Jim/Anne wed 10/3
1994: Kay cataract out,
1995: Marj Petty dies 3/3, 55th Wash U 5/19, left knee surgery
1996: to Cape for Kay's 80th, in hospital for pneumonia 12/28
1997: Kim/Peter wed, Lynne's 50th, Kay has colon cancer
1998: Kay stroke 5/13- a little of me dies.

The following pages will give some details of our travels during the years 1981-1995.
1981: England and Scotland
1982: Yugoslavia
1983: Germany and Alpine Capitals
1984: Iceland, Italy, Switzerland, London, Wales, Stratford, Mildenhall
1986: Hawaii, New Zealand, Australia
1987: Germany, Belkgium, Holland, Netherlands

During the years of retirement we traveled about twice each year to Cape Cod and Westport; many years we went to Macatawa, Michigan, over Labor Day to spend a few days with Suzanne and Bud Hampton at their cottage *Inverlochy*.

Memorable was our trip up the Intracoastal Waterway to deliver Sam Wright's Morgan 33 Out-Island to Virginia from Florida.

Once, when Kit and Sam were visiting, I asked him to take a look at a Morgan Out-Island 28 sailboat I was interested in. At the marina he spotted the 33 footer, decided he would go home and talk to Kit about it. They came back the next morning to find the 33 footer had been sold. That made them more interested. The boat broker checked his book and found there was one available across Florida in St. Petersburg. In the morning, they asked the broker to take them over to see it. No longer available, it had been sold overnight. Now they were really interested.

"There is a used one, a demonstrator, in Tampa," suggested the broker.

Without hesitation, Sam said "Here's a deposit, hold it until we can get over there tomorrow." Just can't let this one get away!

(Meanwhile Kay and I concluded the deal for our 28 footer that someone else wanted. Act fast!)

We all drove to Tampa, took possession of the OI 33, provisioned it (food, drinks, ice), sailed across Lake Okeechobee, made it to Satellite Beach four days later.

May 18, 1975: for the next seventeen days – 920 miloes – we sail north on the Intracoastal Waterway, Satelite Beach Fl. To Norfolk Virginia. Kay has done an excellent job of provisioning — food amd utensils – expecting we will eat most meals aboard the boat. We have taken on as our 'anchorman' Jim Cheal, son of friends down our street. Jim provides the 'muscle' to set and haul the anchor; as 'Captain Zodiac' he would occasionally have to use the inflatable to row the anchor to the desired spot and retrieve.

Jim proved his worth fifteen minutes after we got underway and immediately ran aground on a small sandbar. Those who cruise the waterway tell their stories about multiple groundings; it is almost routine, even for experienced sailors.

1988: London
1989: France, Swirzerland, Venice
1994: Denmark, Sweden, Norway, Finland, Russia
1995: Alaska

Swinging just a little too wide to avoid a dredging operation at the Shalotte Inlet – Mile 344 – we go aground three times. The incoming tide and wake of passing power boasts (stinkpots) rocked boat enough to create a channel in the sand enabling us to motor clear. Extreme effort to shift engine into reverse required us to do a little 'juryrig' with a two-by-four and angle iron to stiffen the shift cable. Result: a short day underway.

Captain Charles' restaurant in Swansboro was a delightful place to pauase and celebrate Kay's birthday,May 29. Was fun to walk through the small country town – dim lights, old frame houses, cats, kids, little road and the 'quiet' sounds.

Thunderstorms, high winds, rough seas, made for a few days of ucomfortable motoring and sailing across the Pamlicio and Albemarle Sounds, and we were through the Dismal Swamp of George Washington's day. Made it to Norfolk on schedule.!

An interesting, exciting, educational trip for neophyte sailors.

Many of the miles along the Intracoastal Waterway the channel is quite narrow and requires attention, fore and aft, to stay between the red and green markers. The channel is maintained to a depth of 12 feet in the center, fixed bridges allow clearance of 65 feet. Opening bridges come in all types: bascule bridges which open upward from the center (either one or both parts), single leaf (opening from one side only), (some with control towers, some with only a small shack for the operator), swing bridges opening sidewise.

Some bridges open on demand, often limited during certain periods of heavy vehicle travel, others limit the hours of operation, some require an advance notice (maybe an hour).

1979: we traded in '71 Mercury for '79 Mercury demo with 7717 miles.

My brother, Presley (Pres') Freeman Hooper died in California on February 15, 1979, in his seventy-first year.

1980: Late January: to Pawtucket for Kit's marriage to E. Swift Lawrence on 2 February.

June: to Arnold AFS, St. Louis, Tinker AFB, Kirtland AFB, Kingman, Arizona, Monrovia, Luke AFB, Van Horn, Kelly AFB, Mobile, Alabama, home: 6079 miles.

I promised I would get started on the 1981 trip. It was a busy year, all in all. Mother (Rose Ammerman aka Damma) died at the end of January and we took her to Dickson, Tennessee, to bury her between her first husband

Early Hooper and my stepfather Walter Ammerman. While mother had been ill we had not felt free to travel extensively. In April we went to St. Louis when Thelma Hampton, Kay's sister-in-law died, and went back again in June for wedding of Sheri Hampton, daughter of nephew O.P. Hampton III and Suzanne.

Travels

1981 - England and Scotland

September 4, 1981, to London, and on to timeshare at Elmers Court in Lymington, in the heart of the former kingdom of the West Saxons; the Solent, a world renowned yachting center; the Isle of Wight; ancient battle grounds. Kit & Swift arrived the following day, Sunday; we had drinks with Jean de Burgh who filled in as a sort of receptionist/concierge, and we dined at the Club. Our large two bedroom apartment was very new and all the furnishings were tasteful. Kay took a liking for the teapot, a Kutani Crane design by Wedgwood. I asked the manager what the replacement cost would be if we should "accidentally break" the teapot.

"You mean, broken into irretrievable smithereens, I suppose. Well, I shall inquire as to the cost of that particular item and shall advise you."

Kay decided not to "break" the teapot, but later we bought one in London.

We took in some of the tourist sights in London on Monday, visited Salisbury on Tuesday, and then to New Forest and Beaulieu (pronounced BUE-LEE) to see an excellent collection of old automo-biles and auto history. Toured through the gray stone homes of the Cotswolds on Wednesday. Thursday: London Tower and the theatre. Took boat ride and toured the Isle of Wight (so many Hampton families settled in the Isle of Wight, Virginia, in the seventeen and eighteen hundreds.).

Saturday (12 Sept) rode the rails to Edinburgh and our share in the ski country at Aviemore, Scotland, a Coylumbridge Highland Lodge: 'A' frame construction, ideally suited for the climate, architecturally designed to create an atmosphere of relaxation. Sunday we drove to the ski mountain, walked almost to the top - and I went so far I was nearly left behind when the wind came up and everything began to close. Visited Inverness and Cawdor Castle (of Macbeth fame) on Monday, Loch Ness on Tuesday, Golspie (in northern peninsula of Scotland) on Wednesday, took a ride on the ski lift on Thursday when Kit and Swift left to return to London.

For the next few days we toured a bit: Edinburgh, York and Cambridge. We saw the Changing of the Guard at Buckingham Palace, Westminster

Abbey, Brighton, Canterbury, Dover, Hampton Court Palace, the British Museum, St. Paul's, Windsor Palace, and a performance of "Hamlet." A very busy week in London-town!

Left London 29 September 1981, at 1250, arrived home at 2300!!

1982 Yugoslavia

Early in 1982, Marj Petty started talking about a trip to Yugoslavia, and then we heard that Howard and Molly Peckham (Travelcrafters Travel Agency then) had a special tour to Yugoslavia. The price for both of us was $2158!; this included all airfare, two weeks of hotels, two meals a day. We could hardly eat at home for that price. We called the Pettys that night and they said "Let's go!" So we signed up the next day for the May 3 to May 18 tour.

The Pettys met us in New York; the next leg, New York to Belgrade, was via Jugoslovenski Aerotransport, JAT, or Yugoslav Airlines, Long, tiring flight. After customs in Beograd (Belgrade) and finally left on a short flight to Split, the hometown of tennis player Goran Ivanisevich; we had a few hours to explore some of the old Roman ruins in the town. We then boarded a hydrofoil for a 35 mph run over blue, blue water to the little island town of Hvar, population 5,000. Our hotel sure looked good, right on the harbor, overlooking the old boat house that had sheltered the war boats of the Venetians hundreds of years ago.

"Hvar, with exceptionally mild winters, offers a setting of vineyards, olive groves, and pine forests.. The island is so ancient the Greeks were here in 400 BC and the Venetians made a little Venice in the harbor. Rosemary and lavender and laurel grow against pale stone houses down to the waterfront, and the Adriatic is so clear and blue you can see a coin 30 feet down."

(Wednesday, May 5) Our guide, Cvite (pronounced tsu-veetah), took us to the armory, the gallery, the theatre, the museum, the cathedral with seven altars, each made with a different marble, a bus ride to the old castle above Hvar, lunch at "Rabbit" (soup, cheese, wine). I sat in the confessional of the Franciscan monastery Church of the Holy Cross, built in 1565. In the afternoon I assisted a boat from Sweden in docking - the boat was owned by 10 young men. Later we took a swim (in the Adriatic - TEMP 54°!!, even Kay went in).

(Thursday 6 May) Rain shower during breakfast, air cool. Leave at 1400 for bus tour of island: to the old town of Stari Grad, picked rosemary and

257

lavender. Hobbled donkey in road. Visited fortress-like home of poet Petar Hektrovic. Raining, streets slick. Long bay and harbor. Visit little church of St. Lawrence: paintings by Titian and Venetian Bassano. No guards, no security. Marj and Kay ring bells of St. Mary's after " just a few stone steps." On to Jelsa, bought apples and "lozo," a grape brandy, picked up Sonia, another guide, and returned. Dinner at eight & ready! To room at 2140, long day and Kay doing laundry.

(Friday 7 May) No hot water. Fish-fry cancelled: too much wind. Walk up hill, observe old man shoveling gravel into plastic sacks held by old woman. Donkey carrying two sacks, each weighing about 100 pounds. Kay and Marj take off to find new store. We visit leather shop, book store. Sent postcards, game, saw sailboats. Relaxing day.

(Saturday 8 May) Skipped tour of palace in Split and went walking, coupla miles. Found department and hardware store. Lather shop open. Marj bought two purses. Kay ordered one to be made by Monday 1900. Bought three belts. Looked in on "nite club" - not much. To bed at 2320.

(Sunday 9 May) Long bus ride to small restaurant for Roast lamb - anchovy, fish, bread, wine, figs, lozo. Guide told us of Yugoslavia monthly salaries: low of $170, average $452, highest $1016. Hard to get ahead in a socialist country — unless you are already ahead.

(Monday 10 May) Walked to store and cemetery. Stopped at home of Racic for wine. To church service at 1900. Impressive with two bishops. To leather shop for Kay's purse. She pleased.

(Tuesday 11 May) Hydofoil to mainland. Hotel Excelsior nearer the old city. To concert at Benedictine church — impressive.

(WednesdayThursday 12-13 May) sightseeing tour of walled city. Visited Franciscan pharmacy dating back to 1317. Boat trip to Lokrum, an island discovered by Richard the Lionhearted in twelfth century. Old monastery, nudist beaches, quiet coves, botanical gardens. Tired - to bed at 2130.

(Friday 14 May) to Cavtat. Gypsies - stalls of wares. Bought whistle, priced 600 dinar, paid 50 dinar. English couple just arrived gave us the first news of "the world." To folklore concert, fascinating costumes, impossible dance steps. Two pretty young girls as MC's: one in English and German, one in French. Both cute as bugs.

(Saturday, Sunday, Monday 15-17 May) cable car ride up mountain. Panoramic view. (Sunday) Bus to Cilipi at 0850. Visit church - again "the Hand" above the edge of the pulpit, holding a cross. Took seats early on church steps for folk dance and show. (Monday) Graduation groups similar to our junior college, parade in old Dubrovnik - no obese, no skinny, all healthy looking. They sing and dance: Folk songs and "Red River Valley," "Old MacDonald Had a Farm," "Jingle Bells." All perfectly fluent in English and colorful: black for law, yellow for economics, white with blue for medicine, pink for languages, red skirt with white tops for computers. Bought books and purse for Lynne.

(Tuesday 18 May) Homeward Bound! Leave Belgrade at 1115 (scheduled at 1030), 0515 EDT. Arrive New York about 1530 EDT, through customs easily. Home in Melbourne early at 2345. HOME SWEET HOME! Wheee!

1983 Germany

Alpine Capitals, Ste. Mère Eglise, Monaco, Switzerland

18 May 83-Wednesday. Arrive Frankfort. Drive rental car to Heidelberg, Mercedes factory in Sindelfinger, ChiemSee, original Budweiser (Budvar), Berchtesgarden, Berchtesgaden, Zell am See - Krem and interesting hotel: Hotel Alte Poste; Young girl at desk could not see our wives, so could not understand why Cecil and I needed " zwei Zimmer, zwei Betten." two rooms with two beds

21 May-Saturday. Finally to Vienna, meet with tour group and to lush hotel. Sunday: tour of city and Hapsburg Castle, accent on Maria Theresia and Franz Joseph and Marie Antoinette, betrothed at 2. At age of 6 or 7 Franz Schubert fell in love with her. Visited Vienna Staats Opera, Then to Museum of Fine Arts - lots of Van Dykes and Rubens. Monday: Salzburg. Started tour at 1400 in Mozart Platz. Tour guide 33 yr old look-alike for Billie Jean King -Barbara- delightful sense of humor: Bishop built 4 churches and could not be buried in all 4. Cut him up: brain in University church, stomach in hospital church, heart in church he attended, unmentionable parts in convent church. On to Munich. Swim pool and sauna: man with no clothes. women with some. Tuesday: Nymphenburg Palace and grounds . Pictures of pretty girls on walls-done by order of the Emperor. Walked Marienplatz, visited churches, with old skeletons and bones and lots of gold leaf. Hofbrau Haus for dinner. Food so-so. Entertainment was loud but good. Woman singing and yodeling. Boys and girls dancing - blowing on long Alpine horns. Music sounded like Taps, with variations. Then whip-cracking, bell ringing and trumpet solos. Wednesday: first stop to take pictures of Neuschwanstein and then coffee stop and tourist trap where we bought Hummel and "shticker." Then on to Oberammergau (much too commercial). Ornate Linderhof

Castle . On to Innsbruck (Bridge over the Inn River), House with gold roof. Dinner and evening show: Tyrolean dances & music- cute little girl (16-18) with harp. Songs of all countries. Thursday. From Innsbruck to coffee shop in Arlsberg (mt) Pass Snow on both sides and falling fast, wet and heavy. To Liechtenstein for lunch. Another hour & half to Zurich and Nova Park Hotel. Some hotel! With closed circuit TV offering erotic movies, swim pool and fitness center. Friday: Lucerne, lunch at Wallischer Spycher, good fondue, old church with high steps, old wooden bridges with scenes painted on each rafter. Saturday: Long day started from Zurich, visited Rhine falls, Wiesbaden @ 1700. NassauerHof Hotel- very plush rooms, telephone in bath, bidet, infra red, hair dryer, Pierre Cardin soap, two bath mats, etc., etc. To pharmacy for cough medicine - medicine $3, cab $6.

29 May-Sunday. Happy Birthday! American Arms Hotel, a comedown from NassauerHof Gave Kay embroidered pin cushion.

Monday. Late start. Located Bleyle knits and Willy Geck porcelains. Coughed all night and Kay had bad gas pains. Les miserables! Tuesday. 0755 special to Paris, Marne River,Épernay (Champagne country), Hotel Altona, Champs Elysees. Wednesday: Paris, Sacre Coeur cathedral -painting of Christ and God (?).Stad Roland Garros: McEnroe falls to pieces after winning first set 6-2, and leading second 4-1. Wilander faultless and dull. 2 June-Thursday. Paris to Carentan to join up with Cecil's WW II group.

Friday. To Bayeux to see tapestry of William the Conqueror, Mont St. Michel, to St. Mère Eglise for reception and dinner. Met Mme. Simone Renaud, age 84, widow of 1944 mayor, amazing resemblance to Damma. Same blue eyes, mouth, nose. Handwriting almost identical. Very eery feeling to look at this woman so much like my mother. Saturday. Visit to Utah Beach, Isigny for lunch, Omaha Beach, To 1st cemetery, beautiful spot, but the Crosses! Row on row. To reception and buffet. Presentation of flags of states. Sunday. Dedication of C-47 and plaque to Bob Murphy and to Yves Tariez who was moving force in securing and reconditioning the C-47, flying it to a nearby airfield, dismantling it to truck it to Ste Mère Eglise where it was re-assembled and became the centerpiece of the museum. Yves and Murphy jump, followed by 60 parachutists.

6 June-Monday. Leave Carentan, to Chateau Lonrai. To Chateaudun. Tuesday: Reception, Cecil honored. Our hosts, the Chauchats (warm cats), have us to dinner. Andrée (who teaches English), her two sons, her husband, Yves, (2004: nineteen years later and we still have occasional correspondence with the Chauchats. Wednesday: Leave Chateaudun for Bordeaux, Tours cathedral. Thursday: Aracachon By Sea. Highest dune on coast of

France. Took overnight bedroom to Nice. Friday: Arrive Hotel Suisse. Dinner at Negresco Hotel, fancy, Viennese waltz music. Saturday: to Cannes, Isla Marguerite, learned about peanut oil for popcorn and deep-fat frying. Found fort of Napoleon's time. Back to Nice. (Change clothes unnecessarily for Monte Carlo.) Pettys decide no on Monte Carlo. Arrive Monaco. Walk harbor. Large boat from Panama with three (3!) large boats in compartment on stern. Restaurant with wine, beer, Perrier, avocado, onion soup. Walked long way to casinos: Loew's at first level: new and bustling. Then the old casino - fabulous. 20 francs to enter interior room of higher limit betting. Roulette, chemin de fer, baccarat. Saw man win 40,000 francs and he was not the bank. Didn't even blink an eye.

12 June-Sunday. Up early to gare.- Taxi 55f. Breakfast at gare cafeteria, good. Good orange juice. First class train is fine, made up in Nice. Changed trains at Valence. All on first section at Chambéry and Cecil left briefcase on train. Many arrangements and 1 day later- thru Mr. Ming's secretary - recovered at Vevey. At Geneva we decided to go on to Vevey, 15 minutes past Lauzanne. Nice town. Got Hotel Papillon directly across from gare. 50Sf (Swiss francs) a person per night. OK. Good beds and shower and toilet - room with balcony. Beer (served by tough black gal). Kids carried bags upstairs. Walked old town. Delightful hostess and excellent food at Au Port restaurant. Bill 85Sf.

13 June-Monday. Pouco afeiçao. To Chillon, just past Montreux. Castle of Byron's "Prisoner of Chillon." Most delightful of all castles visited. 12-13 century to 15th century construction on rock. All in rain - castle sticks out into Lake Leman. To Montreux and finally, with directions from a meat market shop, found restaurant to serve "raclette": melted cheese and small potatoes. Bill $95. $18 each for raclette. To Vevey and out for walk in old town and shops. Sopping wet. Dry out and take 2030 funicular. Walk up farther and Cecil pets cows. Home for coffee.

14 June-Tuesday. Morning train to Pleìades. Beautiful vista, but cloudy, and turned around to come down. Walked town and river to sea. Pettys on boat ride. Bought knives. Checked out. Train to Lauzanne, changed at Basel, switched to Frankfort. Dinner on train before Frankfort. Excelsior Hotel across the street from Hauptbahnhof. Checked schedules to Wiesbaden. Cecil decided to go in morning.

15 June-Wednesday. Packed and ready to go - train to airport. Good flight. Good seats. (L1011 had 2 by window.) OK thru customs in NY. Agent really pulled apart luggage of character in blue jeans. Moral: travel, but don't go thru customs in blue jeans. TWA Agent (Carole Gale) changed NY-MIA

ticket to NY-Orlando. 4 hour wait instead of 5, and 1 hour drive home instead of four. Talked with young girl from Switzerland. Offered to help and she (Nicole Wolters) and her friend (Christina Meyer) came to our house on Thursday. We went on boat (Friday and Saturday) to see Cape Canaveral launch - rafted with Kendall and Barrett. Girls went waterskiing on Sunday with young boys who had brought us a new refrigerator. Girls left on Monday morning.

(This 1983 trip was essentially in four parts: driving a rental car through Germany to Vienna, joining with the TWA Alpine Capitals Tour in Vienna, the reunion and reception at St. Mére Eglise, Monaco and Monte Carlo and Switzerland.)

1984 Iceland

Luxembourg, Italy, Roquebrune,Lugano, Thun, London, Devon, Wales, Stratford, Mildenhall.

27 April-Friday. Left Lynne's about 1730, arrived BWI about 1900. First to check in. Stewardess spilled O Juice on me. (Gave us champagne later.) Saturday: Keflavik. Sunday: To Luxembourg - 3 hour flight. Passed U.S. cemetery. Monday: Train at 1454 to Basel. St Gotthard hotel across from gare. Walked to Rhine River and around town. Tuesday: Train to Florence. Changed trains in 10 minutes in Zurich. Milano to Florence a rougher ride than usual. Arrived Florence and taken in tow by proprietor of Pensione Edelweiss. Kay and I checked it out. OK for $28. Proprietor put board under my side of double bed. Wednesday: Had a cold and noisy night. Asked proprietor's wife for quieter room - "Only 1!!" with thumb sticking up imperiously. Made the rounds. San Marco Church, Duomo and Museum, Del'Opera del Duomo, Michaelangelo La Pieta, Donatelo's Magdalen. To Palazzo Vecchio and Palazzo Uffizi. Across Ponte Vecchio to Palazzo Pitti. Back to Galleria Degli Uffizi. We to Battisterio and Medici Chapel of San Lorenzo. Changed money: again, as in Switzerland, traveller's checks better than dollars. Thursday. Breakfast with "Happy face!" the proprietor's grumpy wife. Settled room charges: I started to tell her the exchange rate her husband had quoted, but she cut me off with: "I dunt care fwat he sade, dis is de rate!" and she quoted me a better rate. Oh, well. Mixup on 1st class cars. Shared compartment with young lawyer from California. I slept most of way to Rome. Long line at exchange, man started to push into line ahead of me, I pushed him out, he said "Donta you poosha me!" I said "I'll not only poosha you, I'll knock hell out of you, now get to the end of the line."

He said "Okay," and shrugged his shoulders. Signed on for tours for Friday. ($11 each) USO nice place. Gave us directions to Spanish Steps, palace and museum. Long walk to Spanish Steps. Very colorful. Friday. Full day! Tour AM and PM from USO. High spot of AM was St. Peters, PM was St. Pauls. Many other places, like catacombs, Scala Santa, St. Johns, Fountains. Make reservations for train for Saturday AM. Cecil feeling punk. I'm improving. Running short on Lira - I owe Cecil 16,500 lira. Saturday: Early start. Used porter to carry bags. 10,000 lira! Shared cabin with man who had been Italian prisoner of war in U.S. in 1942-43. He taking trip to Barcelona on boat from Genoa. Cecil getting worse and unable to do very much - barely walking on arrival in Genoa. Got wheelchair (how do you say that in Italian?) to wheel him across tracks from waiting room where he could not seem to move. Called for ambulance in Monaco and Cecil went to hospital from gare. Marj went with him. We took luggage and cab to Roquebrune (100f-$14). Looks great! Marj gets ride with nurse and we go eat. Restaurant high-class. Soup $6.60 a bowl (plain package soup). Sunday: Train to Monaco to market. Stash food in station, take bus to Princess Grace hospital. Cecil doing better, but at least one more night. Walked to Rainier's palace. Saw family leave in Mercedes limousines. Visited church and grave of Princess Grace (Kelly). Monday. Cecil still in hospital, doing better. Timeshare advertised all the amenities and necessities, but: the fine laundry facilities had no electricity connected to the building. So, we had some laundry done for us - and done quite expensively! Train to Menton. Got separated from Marj but she joined at station. We walked to casinos. Saw Hotel de Paris, gardens.

Tuesday: Cecil will be in til Wednesday. Rode bus around Monaco and to *plages* (beaches), after marketing. Back to Roquebrune. Walked old town (vielle ville). Wednesday:To Nice. Walked main street. Visited posh Hotel Negresco. Found Marc Chagall museum. interesting place. To Monaco. News: attempted coup against Khadafy. Russia to boycott olympics.

10 May-Thursday. Cecil sprung today. Hospital bill ridiculously low and they told Cecil he could send them payment when he got home! Try that in U.S.! Three minute ride to Carnoles. Big supermarket. Air Force control station. Big hospital and clinic - interesting town. Friday: To Eze. Old Roman town. Walk up to Eagles Nest and back. Girls go to perfume factory. Cecil and I have beer and coffee. Saturday: Moving day. Roquebrune to Monte Carlo, to Milan to Lugano. Long wait in Ventimiglia. Much conversation with Italian woman who lives in Central Africa. Husband died there. She visits brother and sister in Italy. Has apartment in Monte Carlo. Knows California. Marj did not know about reservations Milan to Lugano but lucked out as usual and we ended up not paying! Funicular from station to city.

Walked coupla blocks to San Carlo Hotel. Sunday. Walk to Gandria, Bus to funicular up Mt. Bré. Pettys to museum. Walk on mountain top. Great view. May-Monday. Train to Luzerne and Interlachen and Thun. Beautiful route - up into hills on narrow gauge railroad. Spectacular scenery. To Luzerne - shared with Swiss couple, very nice. Hotel Bio Pic in Thun. Pretty young owner/hostess, reservation for Paris, Wednesday, not Thursday as desired, no two-twos together. Tuesday. Early on train to Berne. Walked. Saw old tower with moving figures and state house. 10 o'clock tour of city. Rose garden, bear pits, cathedral with *danse macabre* windows. Tour parliament. Much like our two houses: two senators from each canton, representatives at large and Back to Thun. Then on to Interlachen. Pettys stayed put. Walked Interlachen East to Interlachen West. Train back.

16 May-Wednesday. To Bern and Lucerne after calling Nicole Wolters who gave us tour of city, old wall and tower. Then to her home for lunch. Mother (Henie) and grandparents from Holland. Father (Theo) was first Dutch pilot to train in U.S. Thursday: Up early on train in Paris - mixup on trains but made it to Boulogne where hydrofoil was waiting. Good trip across English Channel Wait for train in Dover. Arrive Victoria station. Get reservation at Clavenger Hotel - good but no one happy. One bright spot: when I called regarding the rental Ford, the man knew who I was and said the car was ready. Friday: Good reception at Ford Import-Export car pickup (Heather King). Too low idle speed, dies in traffic and Cecil misses his navigation. Off to Lymington. Arrive about 1700. Jean de Burgh was standing in middle of the road at her home. Michael comes home. We drink and go to "Chamber Pot" Inn. Good time. Saturday. Jean and Michael de Burgh serve us breakfast. We visit Beaulieu (byu-lee) auto museum. Kingsbridge for groceries. Arrive Court Barton at 1800. Greeted by "Rosemary" and boss Michael. Sunday: Sheep out the window, roosters crowing at 0630. Drive to Malborough and Salcombe. To Kingsbridge and home. Monday: Fairly early (0900) start to Dartmouth and along beach where invasion was practiced (Slapton Beach). All English were cleared from the area — homes, farms , all. Visited castle - old 1300-1500! Tuesday: Drove to Plymouth where Round-World Single Hand race will start and where Nelson sailed from to defeat Spanish Armada. 24 May-Thursday. Marj Birthday: 61! To St. Mellion time share. To Exeter and cathedral. Friday: To Penzance, Land's End. Sorry to leave Court Barton. Saturday: On to St. David's. Small, but guess OK. Saw cathedral and ruins. Sunday: St. David's cathedral for 1030 bell ringing. Monday: Visited ruins of bishop's palace. Artists galleries. 29May-Tuesday:Kay birthday. Drove to Pembroke, Haverfordwest, Pembroke Castle. Extensive. Long history. Wednesday: Drove to Shitesand and walked to St. David's Head. Thursday.

To Cardigan. Return to Nevern and Celtic cross and then to ancient stones nearby: 2,000 to 5,000 BC: "Cromlechs."

1 June-Friday. To Whitesand and climb hill of WWII outpost. To Aberriddy: abandoned slate mining town. To Porthgain: slate and rock quarry stopped in 1931. Had railway, chutes, etc. Nice little port on rocky coast. Saturday: England: VOQ at Fairford RAF. KC-135 base. Stop at Carmarthen. Sunday: Cotswolds. Burton on Water, Stow on Wold, Broadway, Cirencester, Bibury, and Burford. Ate in Mermaid. Monday: Stratford. Walked to "i" for information and Shakespeare. Tickets for *Henry V.* Walked river to Holy Trinity Church, Shakespeare's tomb. Saw *Henry V.* Tuesday:. Spectacular wax model of Countess Sutherland. St. Mary's church - tombs. Warwick Castle. Peacocks and hens strutting. Anne Hathaway's cottage: William Shakespeare's birthplace. Excellent *Merchant of Venice,* Pettys enjoyed as much as we did - 2nd row!

6 June-Wednesday. To Mildenhall. Stopped in Oxford. Saw English court in session. Christ Church Cathedral. Alice in Wonderland. Thomas A'Becket slaying window - face taken out and later replaced. Thursday: Looks possible for Space A. Kay and I drove to London to turn in car. Take tube and rail from Liverpool station back to Ely. Flights cancelled. Nothing til Monday - except Germany. Train to London. Taxi to Knightsbridge Hotel. Thinking of staying over for Queen's birthday on Saturday. Friday. London. First no room at Claverly. Got room at Columbia Hotel. Pettys to Victory Club. Walk across Green Park to Lancaster Lane to Columbia Hotel. Looks OK. Called Claverly. Got room for Fri/Sat/Sun. Now need for Monday also. Rode buses and tube to St. Paul's. Walk around. Decide to stay for 1700 Evensong. Beautiful young voices. 15 minutes into program everyone was cleared out of the church. Thought to be bomb threat. Talked to King's College group. They are going to Reading as warm-up for Henley's. 9 June-Saturday. First to Horse Guard Barracks. Cut across St. James Park to see Prince Philip in ceremony down Mall. Final rehearsal for Queen's Birthday. Then to Greenwich. 0° latitude - was originally 9 feet off. Rode boat down Thames. Must see more of the boats in the museum. Walked under the Thames. Elevators 60 feet down each side. Then to St. Katherine's Docks and Dickens Restaurant. Sat by window - cool. Kay saw City of London Town Crier who had been in Veiled Prophet Ball in St. Louis. Knew Florida and all over U.S. Saw boats in marina locked in from Thames. London Bridge. Ice cream cone in Picadilly Square. Home.

10 June-Sunday. To Westminster Abbey for 1030 service. Beautiful boy voices. Walked through church. Saw police gathering for control of Sikh

protests against Mrs. Gandhi. Cecil had forgotten to take his medicine. They went to Victory, we agreed to meet at Green Park at 1800. We went to WW II control center: underground bunkers and facilities. Then to 10 Downing Street. Blocked off. Changing guard at Horse Barracks. Walk across mall. Talk to retired guardsman we encounter in the street. To Clarence House, St. James Palace. To Horse Guards for 1600 inspection. To the Ritz - tea is £7.50. Met with Pettys. To dinner at Wolfe's: hamburgers great! To Piccadilly for ice cream. Home for coffee and tea. Cecil lost watch in restaurant. Then lost glasses! No definite plans for Monday.

11 June-Monday. Look for Bull prints. Petty saw us at Harrod's. China place across street for Kutani Crane teapot (£26.80 - about $37). To Windsor Castle. St. George's Chapel, beautiful. Henry VIII, Jane Seymour, Queen's seat. Prince Albert memorial: etched and enameled marble. Doll house. State apartments closed. Home. Pack. Last night.

12 June-Tuesday. Up and away! Taxi to Victoria for train to Gatwick. People, from Santa Fe, on train getting car at Gatwick to begin drive tour. Lotsa time at airport. Choice of seats — all tourist. 1st row. Good. Good flight. Guy on left drank too much. Lynne met us at Baltimore (Flt 1400 GT to 1650 EDT). Lynne went to meeting. Lowered shower head. Slept in basement. Cooler. Pretty hot here.

13 June-Wednesday. Exchanged MCO for tickets on PanAm. Lunch with Lynne. Visited Washington Cathedral. Installed air conditioner. Dinner at Irish place. So-o-o noisy. Watched Lynne's slide show.

14 June-Thursday. Up at 0630, rarin' to go home!

Biggest event of 1984: 11 August:Felecia married to Jon Blake in Falmouth.

Hawaii, New Zealand, Australia, Fiji, Hawaii

8 April-Tuesday. Several days in Hawaii, then on to New Zealand as we lose April 11. See Capitol and palaces.

And now we have begun to lose April 11.

12 April -Saturday. Auckland! Changed hotel to Barrycourt Motor Inn on Gladstone. 2 block walk. NZ $115 for 4. About US $65. Drove into city. Tried to find View St. for publishers. Must go farther across bridge. Sunday: Off to Paihia, north of Whangerei. Interesting drive. Some bad roads. Many cows and sheep. All horses seem to have blankets. New Best Western gave directions to our motel. Jon Van Veen a very good host. Long day. Monday: Tooth

acting up. Got 1500 dental appointment. OK. Good job, tooth better (held till we got back home). $20 NZ. Tuesday: Long drive to and through Kauri Forest. Saw big tree - I mean big. Visited excellent museum at Matahoke. On to Glenview, to Stoddard & Houghton to buy Bull Pen (4 for us, 3 for Petty.), through Auckland and Hamilton to Cambridge. Riverside Best Western. Wednesday. To glowworm caves and small museum. Arrived Rotarua at @ 1700. Went to 1800 Hangi at Sheraton. Thursday. Went to see animals. Buck hot to trot after doe. Kiwi hiding in darkness. Khawarewarewa and geysers. Interesting, but not Yellowstone. Friday. Sheep shearing is great show! All different kinds of sheep. Trained dogs sat on back of sheep. Outside: whistle commands to dogs herding 3 sheep. I tried it, and it worked, to the amazement of the sheep herder and amusement of spectators. Pettys surprised us with wine and Pavlova dessert for 43rd anniversary. Saturday. From Turangi to Tongariro National Park to Wanganui, climbed tower- view of city, ocean, and men in whites bowling, and on to Wellington.

20 April-Sunday. Old St. Paul's church - musty smell. New church with bell ringers and choir practicing for evensong. Mount Victoria and stunning view of city, harbor, sea. North Island mileage - 1817 km. = 1129 miles.

21 April-Monday. Turned in north island rental at ferry. Large ship to Picton. Ferry carried train and trucks, cars, and people. Three hour 30 minute trip. Drive to Havelock. Some mountain roads and down to wide, wide flats. On to Nelson: Courtesy Court motel (NZ $35.55). Tuesday. Drive thru forest and mountains. Buller Gorge, Westport, Weymouth, passing Pancake Rocks and Blowholes. Then to Hokitika, to Glowworm Dell: fascinating. Wednesday. To Greenstone, jade shop, saw cutting and grinding, bought about $200. About 1030 toward Franz Joseph Glacier. Took ski plane and landed on Fox glacier. Flew over Franz Joseph glacier and up to Mt. Tasman and Mt. Cook. Sing along with Australian tour group. Fun. Thursday. 0Thru Haast Pass to Makarora Valley and Kawarau Gorge, and Lake Wakatipu. Incomparably beautiful sky: cobalt blue sky and water. Queenstown and Garden Court Motel. Friday. Drove to Arrowtown, Queenstown really tourist city. Saturday. to TeAnau, on to Milford Sound, first in line for 10 seats available on Paranuie-smaller boat. Unparalleled scenery to, from, and on Sound. Thousands of waterfalls because of recent rains. Sunday. to Dunedin, rolling hills, rainbows, sheep huddled for shipment. Monday. Very slow day. Tuesday. Dunedin to Mt Cook. Got chalet at Hermitage. 30 April-Wednesday. Wind howled and mist flew outside chalet. Fairly easy drive to CC. from Mt Cook. Good views of Mt Cook. Changed plans to go to Sydney-Honolulu skipping Fiji. 1 May-Thursday. Drove to St. Paul's Cathedral (Ang) and climbed bell tower for view - 133 steps. P.O. for more stamps. Museum,

great variety. South Pole exploration featured whale skeleton. One hour not enough. To park kiosk for cuppa. Walked gardens, tropical hothouse, rose garden, picked up cuttings. To Victoria Square. Flower clock moving. Bank for another $20. Scrambled eggs and "eat up" for dinner. Scarecrow and Mrs. King on TV. South Island mileage: 2836 km = 1763 mi.

2 May Friday. Early up: 0445, leave at 0600 for 0730 takeoff. Arrive over Melbourne early, too much fuel, circle awhile to burnoff excess. On ground as schdeduled. Budget AA car to small for luggage. Upgrade to CC. Very good. Automatic and roomy. Into town for money exchance after settling on City Garden apartments (Aus $46.50). 2 Br, 1 tub, 1 shower, share john. Laundry, very comfy. Visit market-big. Groceries for breakfast. Cecil buys vegetables. I find bedboard after maintenance says no got.

3 May-Saturday. Visit and tour State Theatre and opera- lose my cap. See St.Paul's church. Hear rock band. Back to State Theatre. At intermission find cap in box G. Drive to Fairy Penguin Parade. Wait two hours. Funny little creatures. First one shakes and waits for others, then groups of 20-30 come ashore and find burrows. Back home for salad, soup, toast and cheese. Sunday. Visit museum then hit the road. Some wine tasting, old airplane, hangar and museum at Wangaratta airport. To Merriwa Motel (Aus$40)and proceed to lock key in car as we go to inspect our rooms. After good land trout dinner, we have RAC man succeed in unlocking rear door and we can unpack. Take walk. Some day! Monday. Too bright. Good colors. Tobacco country. Turn at Yass for Canberra. Arrive after dark. Regency Flag Inn (Aus$48), but only one night. Lotsa driving. Toured town. 6 May-Tuesday. Moved to Forest Lodge Motel. Then to "i" office. Capital project. New parliament house plan and origins of Canberra. Visited present parliament museum (blah!) and lunch. To court Bldg, to bell tower and saw workings. Music teacher who is coming to Chicago. To War Memorial-outstanding. Peanut butter and jelly & cheese and milk. Walk, Bed. Cecil down with cold.

7 May-Wednesday. Off to Sydney. Took coast road for second leg- not worth the time of the winding road. Get petrol outside Sydney. Long drive thru city streets. Yuck! Downtown to New South Wales travel agency. Got rooms at Grantham Lodge for Wed-Thur-Fri but not Saturday: Ten pin bowling team coming in. Kay hit on head by gate in parking garage. Bloody. Doctor put butterfly bandage. Stopped flow. Walked streets after dinner. Honky-tonk and sex places. Thursday. Busy driving day. To travel office and airlines for info on Barrier Islands. Parked front of old mint museum. To Parliament Bldg. and Opera House. 9 May-Friday. Last night we realized we had reservations leaving 19 May!. This puts us in Hawaii on 19 May, one day

268

later than planned.. Try to change to 18th on New Zealand Air. No go. Can make 17 May. Means one extra day in Hawaii. Ansett can get us on morning flight 10 May to Cairns. Arranges TAA. We go to TAA and girl Judd has awful time trying to get things straight. Parking $13. Home lunch. Taxi to Quay. (Polish driver) Harbor tour very good. Harbor is immense. Never saw so many sailboats - many different locations. Expensive (5-10 million) homes. Nude beach below naval installation. City Centre Tower for beer. Girls window shopped. Dinner in basement - cafeteria style. Good. Taxi home with Tanzania man studying municipal engineering. More of an English accent with rhythm of Barbados. Repack for flight to Cairns. Store extra luggage in closet near laundry. 10 May-Saturday. Turn in car ($333.03) & 0830 flight to Cairns. OK. Bus to Acacia. Good rooms - we 2nd, P 3rd). (Aus $41 nite) Walked to town after making reservation for reef & train. Motel gal said all trips alike - got second choice for reef. Reef Sunday, rest and drive Mon, train to Kuranda on Tues. Wed? Home to change. Dinner at The Fathoms. Only 1 sitting. Paramundi (?) fish excellent! Nice surroundings. Cecil bought wine. Also rented Martin car for Monday. Sunday. P's walked. Ride twin hull to Green Island. Little rough. Around Michaelmas Island to Hastings. Submerged viewing, then glass bottom. Fish, fish, fish. Coral viewing better on glass bottom. Then for snorkeling. Kay and I. Monday. To Bay village motel for 3 nites @ $41 with kitchen. Got car. Drove thru Cairns. To Port Douglas. Waltzing Matilda. To Mossman and grove. Stuck my feet in mountain stream. Back to Port Douglas for beach walk and ocean splash. 13 May-Tuesday. Tropic Tours bus pickup at 0800. Drove around town until @ 0845, picking up others. To train station and waited for train. Old coach, but diesel engine, and fumes in tunnels not good. Wednesday. Lazy day. Walk into town, check for reservations. Swim. Thursday. Arrive Sydney. Friday. Out to Bush country zoo to see Kangaroos, koalas - at last! Feed 'roos. 3 different species, wallabies also. Dingo. Kukaburra, Melanesian Devil, ducks and geese. Out to the point - kukaburras in trees.

17 May-Saturday. Departure. Airplane to Auckland, 17 May when we arrive Honolulu AT 0730. Honolulu-Dallas, Dallas-Orlando. Auto home. VISA spent: a little over $5000 for food and lodging.

87 EurBenelux

Early in the year, Bud Hampton suggested we go to Holland, Michigan, for the Tulip Festival. That sounded interesting, but we changed the trip to Europe to see the tulips in Holland, the Netherlands, in May.

Landing in Frankfurt, we picked up a rental VW Fox – Kay talked the agent in changing for an Anscona, larger, with a trunk.

On to Rhein-Main, on the road toward Koblenz, we passed Bingen, where we visited the old castle Burg Rheinstein. Down the Mosel, heading to historic Trier, we detoured to Bitburg to find Spangdahlen Air Base, got a nice suite in VOQ.

May 1st: located Todd and Diane Downey at the base. In Köln we studied the cathedral (Dom) of Archbishops of Cologne since the 5th century. (In town we had a beer and stole the glasses!) Found a carnival at Speicher. German guide, Irml Collin, conducted a good tour of the two thousand year history of Trier from Roman times – baths with heated floors and circulated warm air. (Frau Collin bore striking resemblance to tennis wonder-girl Billie Jean King.)

In AAchen, of WW II renown, we saw the treasure room of the cathedral. Now some days of rain and cool weather.

In Huy, on way to Mons, transfer DM for Belgian francs. The cathedral in Mons has spectacular alabaster, large paintings of the masters, tombstones in the floor and on the walls.

Brussels: encountered American kids from Holland school, wife of Major heading for Wright-Pat assignment. Had guided tour of City Hall, cathedral, museum with large Reubens display, no messages at U.S. Embassy.

May 6: gave ride to SHAPE Hqtrs to young wife (E5), took country roads to Tournay. Cathedral, treasures, Museum of Fine Arts, many Reubens, VanDycks, an immense Gallait.

In Brugge found "T Zand and Hotel die Roya. Met Anastasia Tavernier whose parents have interesting shop with underground tunnels used during German occupation. Saw ladies making lace in the church, and Japanese girl using machine with 175 bobbins! Then to Church of Blood of Christ Cloth. (Did not kiss vial.) Dined at Quick, their answer to McDonalds. Town had underground parking.

May 8: Found Church of Our Lady with Michaelangelo's Madonna and Child, done in 1501 when he was 16. Boat ride through canals. Ready for Ghent.

May 9: Saw Van Eyck 'Blood of the Lamb' in Ghent and vast underground. On to Antwerp and museum of Reubens, et al. Norway great sailing vessel Cristian Radich in port. Took canal rides. Stayed Hotel de Gouden Leeuw (the Golden Lion). Absolutely unbelievable the size of the port (or ports), possibly largest in the world. Tremendous locks opening to sea. Go to diamond museum. Drive on past Rotterdam and Den Haag to Voorschoten, and to Hotel Bijhorts in Wasssenaar.

A drive along the seashore and then to Keukenhof: never equaled sight of flowers, mostly tulips, an expanding panorama of 'Bloemen,'

acres and acres, row upon row of tulips, all colors. An emotional experience. Then to the tiny town of Maduradam.

The Delft factory to see the beautiful blue emerging from the pieces as the cobalt brightens from the forging. Encountered young girl (18) who was worried about her coming exams in English, French, German, Dutch, Economics, Geography.

May 15: Cheese market at Alkmar. Men, slings over shoulders, carrying hundreds of pounds of cheese rounds at a trot to the scales. Sampled some of the wares. Off to Urk, a small fishing village over the 31 km dike. Sampled and bought the wine.

May 16-20: Germany: Followed signs to military hotel in Bremerhaven, Übersee Hotel on side street Böttenstrasse. Bremen Shakespeare Company presenting *King Lear*. Revolving panels of history of transportation and discovery. Statue of Roland, medieval warrior figure. Bremen Town Musicians in bronze (donkey, dog, cat, rooster) originally designed in 1043, rebuilt in 16th and 19th centuries. Stopped by polizei outside small town, by speed trap, ticketed for 68 dm (less than $2). Celle: oldest theater in Germany in the castle, ornate chapel with items hanging from ceiling. Very large factory in Wolfsburg. Bad Hartzburg: beautiful little city, hotel proprietor tried so hard to please. Drove along river and the wall separating E. Germany, passing small towns, as we came in to Bad Ems, a resort town with baths, water, etc. Finally we find our way to Wiesbaden and the American Arms Hotel for our last night.

Thursday, May 20: Flight Home!! Long 23 day trip.

88 England – Yorkshire, Trossachs, London

"Oh, to be in England,
Now that April's there." (Browning).

In England again and renting a car from the Ford Export-Import Company in London again. As explained earlier, they rent new autos cheaply because they can sell a used auto at a price higher than the controlled price of a new one.

From Sutton Hall, our timeshare, we covered Yorkshire, and the little towns, Peterborough, Spalding, Boston, Thirsk, Oswaldkirk, Kilburn, Coxward, Newburgh Abbey, Sproxton, Helmsley, Rievaulx Abbey, Sutton Bank.

May 2: To Thirsk for gas – the owner said James Herriot had just left. Twin ladies in the market place would not tell where he lived. To Leyburn, Grinton, Reeth, Langthwaite, Feetham, Low Row, Gunnerside, Muker, Keld, Butertube Pass, Hardraw, Askrige, Carperby, Redmire, Wensley, Bedale.

May 3: Pickering, Straites, drink ale at Cod and Lobster. Breakwater on the West side of River Esk- old ruins of abbey on East side, Whalebone Arch, Scarborough, toured old castle, Lastinghame (old crypt), Hutton-Le-Hole.

May 4: To Thirsk, Ripon and cathedral, and back to Thirsk. Join two American ladies in talking with James Herriot (J.A. Wight) in his surgery, and having him autograph our books.

May 5: good guided tour of York. We have barbecue for newcomers at Sutton Hall.

May 6: Horse show in Hovington at estate of Duke and Duchess of Kent. We meet and shake hands with the newlywed Duke and Duchess of York. Kay mortified when I address her as 'Fergie.' We go to Castle Howard, Malton, have tea at Betty's in Harrowgate.

May 7, Saturday: Leave Sutton for timeshare in Trossachs. Through Richmond, Penrith – had ale with nice couple.

May 8: Loch Lomond, Aberfoyle, Covenanters Hall, Kay did laundry. Kit called at 2200. Felecia in labor. Baby Blake at 0800 next morning (0300 her time.)

May9: tour the Trossachs: wool shops at Callander, Lochearnhead, Killin, Crianlarich, Balquihidder and grave of Rob Roy. Down west side of Loch Lomond – view across the lake to Insersnaid, Balloch, Drymen. Dinner at Covenanters Hotel. Snow covered mountains.

May 10: Stirling Castle- Tudor history, King Robert the Bruce, Rob Roy, good tour guide.

May 11-12: shopping in Callander, through Stirling to Perth, church where John Knox preached the sermon that started rioting, Earl's palace, Glamis Castle (Macbeth). Walked first hole of famous St. Andrew's.

May 13: sampled various Scotch whiskies at Glengoyle distillery.

May 14: located Walton Hall outside Stratford, Lake Windermere, Birmingham, beds too soft at home.

May 15-26: toured backstage of *Macbeth* set; to Fransborough, Shutford, Butchers Arms pub, lined up for tickets to *Macbeth* and next week's *Much Ado About Nothing*, to Tetbury and find home of Charles and Diana, Cirencester,Fairford, Bitbury, Hathertop, Burton-on-the-Water. Excellent performance of Macbeth. Bull Hotel(bull prints moved since previous trips.) Colleges at Oxford, Wellesbourne, library, Eddington, Warwick, personal guided tour of St. Mary's church, Loxley, Whatcote, and Royal Oak pub. Stoke-on-Trent, toured the Wedgwood and Royal Doulton factories, Chipping Camden, Evesham, Worcester, Royal Worcester and Spode factories, exceptional Cathedral. Good performance of *Much Ado About Nothing*.

May 27-31: to the Barbican in London for *Merchant of Venice*, Oboe, bagpipe and Celtic dance group. London Philharmonic concert: Queen Mum came in and was seated in front of us.

May 29: Happy Birthday for Kay. Westminster Abbey, sat in choir, Piccadilly, Mme Tussaud's Wax Works, Planetarium, British Museum.

June 1-2: Home Guards Massed marching bands, Kensington Gardens and Royal Apartments. Wandered through town, Fleet Street, Flanagan's pub.

June 3: Taxi to Victoria Station and British Airways checkin – slick operation. Some wait at Gatwick. Good flight,

Arrived Orlando at 1845. Home looked good.

On previous trips we had seen most of the 'tourist' attractions. These thirty-six days were for getting the flavor of England. It worked!

89 France, Switzerland,Venice

A week in Paris: Springtime, Easter in Paris, Last Time I saw Paris. First time was 1969, returning to America from Thailand, via India, Pakistan, Saudi Arabia, Spain, Germany. Cold November Armistice Day, le Grand Charles De Gaulle has died, throngs fill les Champs d'Elysee, I buy beret. American Cathedral for 0900 Episcopal Easter service, fourteen people, Canon is Cynthia Taylor, young woman from South Carolina. Small version of Statue of Liberty in Seine river. Walk to *Place de Concord* – large obelisk from Egypt to France, to *les Invalides,* Rodin museum, metro to *Ste Michel place,* eat *croquet monsieur* (Welsh rarebit). To *Notre Dame* for 1900 mass. Back to Louvre to see new entrance – never realized how large the Louvre is. Stroll Tuileries (tiles) and many statues. Next day: magnificent view of city from atop Arc de Triomphe. Metro to Isle de Cite and Ste Chappelle church surrounded by Palais de Justice: watched emotional lawyer in civil suit. Ste Severine, a quietly beautiful church. Eiffel Tower. Throngs at Versailles, castle interesting, gardens not yet ready, immense stretch of gardens and water – over a mile. Stroll to hotel through Montmarte area. Six or seven hours in Louvre: many paintings, Mona Lisa, Winged Victory, Roman statuary, Egyptian relics and mummies, colorful tapestries.

April 1: on the TGV (Trés Grand Vitesse) very fast train to Geneva after stop at Bellegarde, short wait to change trains to Vevey, Montreux, and Brig. Stopped at Montreux, "I" closed and hurried to catch train to Brig. Now we see snow on the mountains. Conductor points out we could change at Sion and get faster train to Brig, where we found nice hotel Channa, with firm beds and feather pillows.

About 1-1/2 train ride Brig to Zermatt, looks like a tourist town, but the "I" is closed 1200-1600. Autos not allowed into Zermatt. We walk toward the Matterhorn, return to town after 30-40 minutes. Ride the ski train up to Gornagrat, over 10,000 feet, spectacular views, hundreds of skiers, all sizes ages 20-70. All kinds of ski boots. Ski train back down, some skiers get off at different spots. Brig to Kandersteg, to Spiez and good boat ride to Thun. found old castle after dinner, wet streets, misty rain. Train to Italy: helpful volunteer who speaks English, and official languages of Switzerland: French, Italian, German. Delayed for 'technical' at Domodossola, then passports and Army with German Shepherd dogs sniffing for drugs. Train roadbed much rougher in Italy. Train 20 minutes late in Milano, only 5 late in Padua – took taxi to San Antonio Hotel. Walked to old marketplace from 12th century. Terrible beds. Next day move to Terminus Hotel in Venice.

San Marco Square, took pictures from balcony. Walked the bridges, boat to Lido, back to Terminus Hotel. San Marco has bones of St Mark and fabulous gold altar, picture in stone that took 700 years to complete. Boat to Murando to see the making of glass in all shapes. Small church of St. John the Evangelist has large Tintoretto dated 1576, church dates from year 970. More Tintoretttos, primitive by Donatello in Basilica di Maria Glorioso Dei Frari.

Water bubbling up through gratings in San Marco Square as time comes in, orchestra playing old favorites. Interesting on canals at night-lotsa people. Finally found market stall that would sell two apples and two bananas – others insisted on a kilo! Down little side street located gondola maker Tramantino – one looked finished but had a date of 15 May 1990. Met couples from Australia and New Zealand.

Decided to spend a little money and take the Orient Express to Austria. Nice private cabin. Arrived Verona at 1157. Fancy lunch in luxury. Through Brenner Pass at 1540, stop for Austrian customs. Snow peaks, High Alps. Now served tea by Laurent who has Brazilian wife. Arrive Innsbruck and make good connection to Seefeld, then taxi to time share Hochegg – we are only ones in hotel, not expected. Everything closed or closing in town for the season. No laundry at hotel. Train to Innsbruck, found remembered places. The mountains are spectacular, formidable, thrusting into the clear blue heavens with their snowy peaks glistening.

In town to buy food for lunch, then train to Mittenwald, little town of interesting buildings painted with famous scenes : *trompe l'oeil*. Back to hotel tow watch Nick Faldo win The Masters in tiebreaker.

To Mittenwald, Garmisch, Linderhof Castle, Obergammergau, which we had seen before (1984?) but this time on a guided tour we saw more of the castle and the Grotto, like an Eastern seraglio. Then the Benedictine monastery, where the liquor is made.

Salzburg: took funicular to the schloss, took tour, led to torture room, state rooms, tower. Many steps! In town, museum had excellent display of medieval armor. People working on Mozart's house. Walked to station from Mozartplatz, cherry trees in magnificent bloom! Kay spotted Swarovski crystal factory as we passed through town of Wattens.

Tried to call Kit by direct dialing: telephone company had heard of this, but had never made a connection that way. Walked to the ski lifts; ski jumps really look high from the ground. Bought snow boots – later found they just don't fit.

Wattens: could watched glass blowers fashion vases of different colors and crystal workers in the small shop – factory itself closed because of 'sabotage.' Home to watch Mats Wielander lose to young Austrian Boris Becker. Pack for leaving tomorrow.

Trains to Innsbruck, Buchs, St. Gallen. Hotel Elite beds too soft. To Weissenstein with better beds. After dinner at Moevenpik (fast food) to operetta of Franz Lehar music.

Morning: calls to Nicole Wolters - no answer. Train to Romanshorn, watched ferry from Germany unload, little sailboats launch and start to sail for a race, along with larger boats. Saw Buick sedan bought by a couple from St. Gallen in Ft. Lauderdale and shipped to Switzerland. All ports have many sailboats, very extensive, strong breaking breakwaters. Ate in Rohrschach overlooking the Bodensee. Tried again for Nicole, spole to Theo Wolters:

arranged to call about arrival time in Lucerne and spend night with them. In church: what is significance of Christ nailed to the cross and the thieves tied?

Train to Zurich: long parade of guilds, custom 600 years old of burning snowman to celebrate end of winter: big bonfire and explosions until 'snowman' blew to pieces, tremendous crowd. Kay's shoe came apart at the toe. (Easy Spirit replaced with new shoe.)

April 18: married 47 years ago in California. I've had a great life with this woman I love. Found Swarovski crystal ball for gift to Henie.

Theo met us in Lucerne. Good chat with Henie and Theo in their home. Slept well in son's bed. Many medals for Theo and many guns.

Gave crystal ball to Henie – she has a small collection of Swarovski. Theo conducts special city tour: panoramic painting in circular building of French retreat into Switzerland during Franco-Austrian war (1870?) . Then to glacial holes and boulders and the stone lion symbolizing all Swiss guards who died defending the Pope.

Met with Henie for lunch at Schweiserhof Hotel – plush! Saw Theo's modern office for Hunter-Douglas Co. makers of aluminium sheeting with baked enamel finish. With the company for 24 years Theo made about $150,000 a year salary. When new management decided to let him go, to cut costs, he formed an independent company selling the same product, now making two and three times as much from his commissions. He is a real character, great flair for languages. Nicole showed up and her parents went home. She shows us 'old town' in a pouring rain, and then to her apartment for dinner. She has a collection of items from China, India, Tibet: a well-traveled young girl. Next day: Visited several churches in Lucerne .

Spent two days in New York with Lynne, home on April 23, 1989.

94 Scandinavia 2

May 31-Tuesday

Melbourne, Atlanta, New York, Copenhagen .

June 1-Wednesday. Arrive **COPENHAGEN** 1010 local (0410 EDT) and taxi to Imperial Hotel (DK 90=$15). Boy found boards for soft beds. Watched Paris Open

on TV. Took 1600 City Tour and view of castle complex. Walked.

June 2-Thursday. 0855 train/ferry/train to *Odense* (ó-dn-zuh). Walk to Hans Christian Anderson House and museum. HCA had strange life: wanted to be an actor but could never make it. His mark made in poetry and his tales for children. Long walk around town.

June 3-Friday. Gray day. Long walk on walking street and old churches. *Hamlet Tour,* go past university: students enter after taking exam following 12 years of school. University is free and students receive Kr 4,000 per month (@$660). See Fredericksborg Museum and castle. Should take 7 hour tour for this. We hurry thru church & rooms on to *Elsinore -Hamlet Castle* - see only from outside. Go to *Tivoli* - Tivoli overrated: a collection of restaurants and carnival-type rides and games.

June 4-Saturday. Feeling miserable. Got to boat early, had to wait for boarding at 1530 (our paper said 1500). Had help with luggage. Coupla walks around deck. Lie down in cabin. Stayed until 0700 Sunday. Kay had some dinner alone.

June 5 Sunday. Word is we're docking at 1000. Have been in an inlet for two hours. Dock in *Oslo* and take taxi to railroad station - Oslo to Lillehammer. taxi to hotel. Very nice. June 6-Monday. Spend hours at Maihaugen Outdoor Museum - almost whole village transplanted here. Most homes from 17th century. Pretty girl guide-will be senior in college. Saw older woman carding and spinning wool-interesting. 1400 Olympic Tour of skiing, hockey arena, downhill, slalom, ski jumps. Walk pedestrian street back to hotel. Good dinner.

June 7-Tuesday. Thru nice vistas and countryside. Snow on mountains. Waterfalls. Arrive Trondheim at 1440. Royal Garden Hotel after taxi wait. Cathedral closed 1500 but walked anyway. Kay not feeling good. Her turn.

June 8-Wednesday. Breakfast good-full like all other hotels-this hotel is fanciest. Short tour of cathedral.. taxi waiting-to hotel & luggage, to coastal steamer. Cruise harbor until 1153 checking RDF. OK and on the way. We sat on deck awhile, got cool and went to deck 7 and found portside chairs. Kristiansund at 1800. Interesting docking on spring lines. Stay just long enough to unload and load. Never stays longer, man says. Sun high and bright at 1800. Air cool. Arrive Älesund at 1230 a.m. Hotel Scandinavie had sold our room when we did not appear by 1800. Nothing to be had in town. Slept in conference room on the floor. This was at 0130. We were tired and angry.

June 9-Thursday. Breakfast and told by manager and ass't manager that we would be moved to a "nice" room. Ran for the bus to connect with the

Geiranger Fjord steamer. Missed the bus. Manager of Information center took us in his car to meet up with the bus at its first stop. Completed bus/ferry/bus,ferry/etc tour of fjord. Waterfalls and towering mountains.

Hotel had moved us into a suite - and letter of apology. Found little pub. Beer and large hamburgers with too much french fries and salad, but good. Nice place. Had soft ice cream when we left. Back to Scandinavie Hotel at 2200. Broad daylight. Luggage still there. Taxi to boat at 2340. Long wait, then no record of us on the boat. Mixup of boarding day vs sailing day. Narrative calls for boarding Friday 6/10, arriving Bergen on 6/11, but ticket indicates Friday departure and Friday arrival in Bergen. But got two berths. Did not call Sally.

June 11-Saturday. Due to dock in *Bergen* at 1400. Luggage has been taken someplace. Debarking OK. Had bought tickets on ship for bus to hotel. Made several stops. *Neptune* is first class hotel. Had expected us yesterday and efficient woman, assistant manager, made several phone calls to check on our late appearance. Ticket was for only three nights, short narrative calls for four.

Notes lost for remainder of travel through Norway, Sweden, Denmark, Finland, and St. Petersburg Russia. The mixups of the first days and nights of travel were not repeated. Most were the result of poor planning by travel agents.

The trip from Finland to St. Petersburg on a Russian cruise ship: the ship was not in good condition, the cabin was worn, the furniture torn, the service execrable.

The tour through the Hermitage, viewing the Czarist treasures was worthwhile.

ADDENDA

The Fated Mixer

She was a hostess at the Freshman mixer. Even now sixty-eight years later, I can remember the soft, black, Jersey knit wool dress, very plain, topped with a small, brown "dog collar." Tall and oh so poised, she seemed to be either much sought after or very adept at "mixing."

The woman I had been searching for, I told myself. Beautiful, willowy, slender, great legs, slender ankles. Kind of a honey-blond, with laughing eyes, the intoxicating aura of *Tabu,* and that certain easy aloofness of position, confidence, and a sense of identity.

Although I had been out of high school for some time, had been to college, had worked on different jobs, had developed what I thought was an air of sophistication and jauntiness, never had I encountered a girl who had so obviously 'arrived.' No doubt she was a BWOC, big woman on campus.

And dance! She could and did dance with all — all comers and all kinds of dancers. Every partner left reluctantly and with the assurance that he was the most important male in the group. She made them feel that way — just as she made me feel that way, and I couldn't resist finding her in the crowded gymnasium to enjoy the feeling time after time until it became obvious that I was smitten. But I was just a freshman (a sophomore in the eyes of the university), and she was outasight: a senior, president of her sorority, Mortar Board the senior women's honorary, a leader in several campus activities, sought after by many of the senior men, but firmly attached to a recent graduate who was a 'real' newspaper reporter. All this I learned later — at the time all I knew was her name, Kay Hampton, and that I had finally met 'the one girl.'

After I persisted in cutting in to dance with her, about four times, she said: "What are you doing? You're supposed to be mixing."

I replied: "I'm just getting acquainted with the girl I'm going to marry."

"You're crazy," she said.

It was several weeks before I encountered her again. She was coming out of the bookstore just as I was coming in and I forgot all about buying books. I blocked her way and began to introduce myself, quite clumsily, because

279

I was sure she had forgotten me from the dance — and she just about had, much to my annoyance.

Annoyance was also what she obviously felt, but it was still tinged with amusement at my persistent blocking tactics which she evaded finally as the bell rang for the next class. But not before I had asked for a date, which she refused by reason of a previous engagement.

Several more chance meetings, that became less and less 'chance' on my part, and several more refusals on the basis of previous engagements. That ran on and on into the future of Saturday nights, led me to change tactics and the locale of these 'chance' encounters.

So, I tried for Sunday night and took her to our Sunday night young people's group meeting at Second Presbyterian Church. We always had 'tea' (ice cream, cookies, bite sandwiches) at seven, followed by a short devotional. We would then go to someone's house and sit around and talk. Kay was immediately accepted by everyone in our group: *Roemer Wilbas, Billie Ruth Mechling, Tom Kirkpatrick, Anne Moore, *Charlie Knaus, Sally King, Frances Bradley, Knox Taussig, Jean Browning,*Ben Butler, *myself. (* "South St. Louis guys," the others were "West enders.")

After a number of 'Sunday nights' and scattered other dates (I sneaked a quick kiss after our third date), Kay invited me to her Christmas party at her home. I spent all my money on two dozen long-stemmed roses. That impressed Kay's mother who displayed them on the grand piano at the entrance to the living room. I was making progress. Got my foot in the door. (My mother had said to me: "Bud, since you met that Kay Hampton you can't seem to think of anything else." She was right. I had met the "love of my life.")

Summer, 1938. Kay's father and mother had reserved a cottage in Macatawa, Michigan. An important business problem arose and he couldn't leave the day they were supposed to leave. I volunteered to drive Mrs. Hampton (Mamomma) and bring the car back for Mr. Hampton (Pop). I was really making inroads now.

The next two years passed rather uneventfully. Byron Herbert, the former boyfriend, had been called to the army early in the draft, and I had assumed a greater role in Kay's life.

During 1940-41 I was a hotshot disk jockey and radio announcer at 'WJPF, the Voice of Egypt, Herrin, Illinois,' commuting on weekends to St. Louis for a date with Kay.

280

In the summer on vacation from the WU bookstore, Kay and her friend, Helen, drove out West to meet and visit with relatives in California. She wrote letters to me almost every day, recounting their travels. I still have, and treasure those letters after all these years.

Earlier in the year, I had passed all the requirements for entry into the Aviation Cadet program. I was ordered to report to Thunderbird Field in Phoenix, Arizona, in October 1941. Kay was sure she would never see me again. Cadets could not be married, but that rule was changed after the Japanese attacked Pearl Harbor. I wrote to Kay's father that I desired to marry his daughter.

We were married in the chapel at Gardner Field, Taft, California April 1942 as I finished basic flying school. We honeymooned in Hollywood and went on to Advanced flying school in Chandler, Arizona. *(Follow up in Chapter 13-14 in my "Biography.")*

My "magnificent obsession" with that beautiful woman persists after more than sixty-five years, and three years after her death April 13, 2003.

This is the true measure of love,
    when we believe
        that we alone can love,
        that no one could ever
            have loved so before us,
        and that no one
            will ever love in the same way
        after us.
        Goethe

My Lovely Women

I have been able to write freely about my parents, my brother and sundry others in my life, but it is difficult to be dispassionate about those closest to me. My father had rather little to do with my progress through life. My step-father certainly had more effect upon my life. My mother did affect me in many ways, but only until I left home "for good" to join the Air Force. I say "for good" because after college I was still a "resident," even though only periodically while I had a couple of blue collar jobs, and my year long stint at "WJPF the Voice of Egypt, Herrin Illinois" as a hot-shot news announcer and disk jockey. ('Egypt' because of proximity to Cairo, Illinois.)

Looking back at Chapter XVII, and pages 105 and 113, I can see that Kit got less attention than flying and poker. I would like to think that the "neglect" was in my writing about my life, rather than in the living of my life.

Lynne got really short shrift in Chapter XXI, page 135, 136. Our new house and Pabco floor coverings got a lot more attention.

Kay got better press in Chapter X, pages 56-59, but I would fail miserably if I attempted to paint a realistic picture of her and how she has affected my life in so many ways — no, in all ways.

But, after all the disclaimers, all I can do is try. I cannot now, in 1994 (and continued in 1999, updating in 2006), put on paper the complete effect these three girls, these three women, have had on me, because it is still happening — yesterday, today, and tomorrow. I cannot adequately describe them, for I am too close to be objective. At best, I will attempt to recollect salient points in their development, their trials, achievements, and perhaps an amateur analysis of their personna.

Kit, Kathryn Greer Barbee, Hampton, Wright, Lawrence. Kathryn for her mother, Greer for her grandmother, Kate Greer Hampton. Subject to the attention and care of the first child. Maybe that's why she always insisted she could do it "by self." And a surprising number of times she could. She liked to play "dressup" and liked to be dressed up in pretty clothes. Still does, fifty years later. Be dressed nicely, not play dressup. A very particular person. A very competent, intelligent person. At times a very difficult person to please. I have not felt that I received any degree of real affection from her since her teenage years when she became sexually active. After graduation from high school in 1960, at age seventeen, she became pregnant during the summer and gave up her opportunity to go to college. She eloped with her Sunday school teacher, the prospective father, and went to California where her first child was born.

Occasionally I detect a feeling of regret that she did not go to college. It has not been, and is not, a handicap to her. Kit has an inquiring mind, a desire to learn, and a firm appreciation that education and learning is a continuum, never completed. She can more than hold her own in her circle of friends, some of whom may have a few more years of academic experience.

Kit is a complicated person, and as she goes beyond her 63rd birthday (this is 2006), she suffers more acutely from the psychological disorder referred to as the "pack rat" syndrome. This must have developed at some point during the time of her first marriage, to Art Hampton, who proved to be incapable of providing the lifestyle that Kit was accustomed to. Her fetish about saving old newspapers was apparent during her second marriage, to Sam Wright.

This bothersome affliction became full-blown during the years she lived in Westport. Her garage became the repository of old newspapers, discarded records and clothing, rusted and useless food stuffs, animal feces, packages of new kitchen items, and other kinds of trash. We, her father, her sister, and her own children, had tried to help her clean up the mess. Finally, when it was apparent that something had to be done about the fire and health hazard that existed, Lynne and I made an attempt to bring some order to the mess.

This resulted in repeated vituperative accusations of theft and robbery and my being told by her husband that he "will deny" my entry into "his" home. Kit's reaction convinced me that she harbored very little affection for her father. This caused a rift in the family which may never heal. Someday there may be a post script to this situation.

It would not be inappropriate to review a few items in Chapter XVII. We were in Ainsworth, Nebraska, and the little town did not offer the medical facilities available in St. Louis, and my wife's mother was in St. Louis, as another consideration for Kay to go to the big city to have her (our) first baby. Kay claims I never missed her because I was playing poker all the time she was gone. We re-united when our little girl was about five weeks old and went to Rapid City, South Dakota, where our squadron had rejoined the group. That was where I sat up the night rocking our first-born when she was suffering from the six-week colic. Phenobarbitol was prescribed, but without the admonition to force liquids. This dosage knocked her out completely and we found ourselves wishing she would cry again.

We worried for a long time, and tried various "cures" to get her to stop sucking her thumb. Then one day, without any urging she declared "I'm not going to suck my thumb anymore." And she didn't. She is a positive woman. Kit married E. Swift Lawrence in February 1980. It appears to be a compatible, happy union.

Lynne is her sister — they have strong facial resemblances to their mother. Beyond that facial similarity, these two girls (women, Lynne says) are entirely different. Lynne is realistic, pragmatic. Some of the obvious differences would be observed naturally in any siblings, others might be thought to be a result of vastly different experiences in their later teen years. Kit from seventeen to twenty had three children and something less than financial security. During approximately the same period in her life, Lynne was exposed to a country club life style in Rio de Janeiro, followed by admission to a relatively exclusive female college, Mount Holyoke. She did not graduate *magna cum laude* but she is very bright, a 'quick study,' has developed strong leadership qualities. Her confidence may need some constraint occasionally. At times we regret her having chosen an "Eastern" school. But, perhaps it was the times, the Vietnam era, as much as the exposure to the leftist professors. Lynne majored in Political Science and, in my opinion, absorbed too much socialistic tendency. Naturally, we do not discuss politics.

She is a skilled, good photographer, writes well, and is well read. She could have been a successful photo-journalist had she kept an open mind, reporting and photographing without politicizing. Lynne seems to enjoy her present work as a union organizer, which is consistent with her dedication to 'causes.'

I deeply love my wife and our two beautiful daughters with an abiding affection and respect.

284

The stroke & Therapy

I died a little bit on Wednesday May 13, 1998, about four in the afternoon, enroute to St. Louis for Kay's Wash U. 60th reunion class of '38. My life will certainly never be the same again.

We had made good time and had come about 400 miles from home; earlier in the day Kay had driven about two hours and I had had a nice rest, anticipating spending the night in Montgomery, Alabama, another 60 miles up the road. I made a sudden stop for traffic signal in the town of Ozark and our cooler fell from the rear seat to the floor.

Kay turned around in her seat to put the cooler back on the seat, then stayed facing to rear, not moving. She did not respond to my voice.

I pulled into the parking lot of a large shopping center, moved her around and refastened the seat belt. When she showed no response whatsoever I knew it had to be a stroke. I had to get medical help so decided I had to get to Montgomery, the big city.

After driving 10 miles, I realized I should use our cell car-phone to call 911. The operator answered immediately, I explained what had happened. She established our position, had us turn around to return to Ozark where ambulance and rescue trucks were waiting to take us to Dale County Medical. It was now a quarter after five. I called Kit, who was still at our home in Florida, and told her where we were and what had happened. While waiting, it occurred to me to cancel our reservation in Montgomery. It was ten minutes before seven when the on-duty physician, a Dr Barlow, decided we should go to Flowers Hospital in Dothan (about 20 miles south of Ozark) where there was a neurologist.

Kay was admitted to Flowers just before 8:00 PM in the care of Dr David Davis, the neurologist, assisted by Dr James Sawyer, cardiology. A CAT scan revealed a bruised section of the left lobe of Kay's brain; the cause of the stroke.

Kay received some therapy at Flowers for eight days. Kit, Lynne and I were in constant attendance, but we were anxious to have her closer to home in Melbourne. By May 21, the Social Services office at Flowers (Patricia) had found a bed in two of the three choices we gave her, and we decided on The Arbors of Melbourne, the selection of Dr. McGrath.

When the nurse and others had Kay stand up to use the potty and check her undergarments, Lynne and I pulled the air-mattress off the bed, took it to the car, put on the fitted sheet and arranged the other covers. We had already provided a "level playing field" by filling up the floor of the back seat with luggage and soft packages to come to the level of the back seat.

Kit returned by air to Melbourne, Lynne and I left Dothan at 1110 am and drove straight through to Melbourne. Kay seemed to make the trip fairly comfortably. We arrived at 7:20 PM. They were ready for her, and it looked like a nice place. Actually, the best of a bad thing. Physical therapy, occupational therapy, speech therapy.

Over the next weeks, Kay progressed fastest in physical therapy, followed by occupational therapy — the use of her right hand and showed some progress in speech. The young speech therapist, Mary Bee, thought more highly of her skills than was justified.

Kay fell twice trying to get out of bed to go to the bathroom. A scratch and bruise on her right arm, a bump on her right forehead. We had the usual "not mes" and much apology. We questioned them at length regarding procedures, the number of people on duty at the time, and how many rooms they had to watch: two people to take care of eighteen patients. This resulted in a conference with all the staff and director heads where the only suggestion at first was to change to a lower bed with some pads alongside in case she got up again and fell. I asked about the warning thing placed under the bedding to alert the staff if she tried to get up. They did not know whether it was on or not.

The physical therapist appeared to be the only one who understood the problem. The others were busy with CYA. The speech therapist was especially defensive, wanting to have Kay's hearing aid checked by the doctor who installed it. I told her (Mary Bee) that she just didn't speak loudly enough. Miffed her a bit. They then came up with a schedule, which should provide better supervision. At first they said she had to be kept awake all day so she would sleep all night! I pointed out that people our age take naps during the day and that she was accustomed to do so. So they scheduled naptime for 1400-1500.

Earlier I had told the head nurse that we had been told that the Arbors was the best around, and that I wondered what the others were like. She said I should go see some of them. I replied that I was not interested in how bad the bad ones were, but how good the best ones could be if they really tried.

So I hired a "Kelly Girl" for a couple of days and then one of the young aides to stay with her during the night. Kay had almost a routine: she would go to the toilet around midnight, 2 AM, and 4 AM.

When Kay was walking a little more freely — with only slight touch of support — she rode in the wheelchair to Wal-Mart (which was across the street) and seemed to enjoy looking around. Bought little toys to use in therapy — items with texture and squeezable (like 'Ziggy' who has become a close bed-time friend), and fairly soft small volleyball. We could see some fatigue setting in so Lynne got the car to take her back. Before dinner she started to remove the Depend (diaper-type) which was

obviously bothering her, and did not want it put back on. Message seemed to be: "when I need to go to the bathroom, I'll get up and go."

Friday 5/29: Birthday! Staff members and patients came in with a big sign and a cake to sing Happy Birthday to my Kathryn. This brought that shy smile. Mary Bee, Speech therapist, had said that Kay had sung Happy Birthday and Row, Row Your Boat during her session. After dinner we had the birthday cake. Kim and Peter called and Kay sang Happy Birthday to them. Felecia called to wish Happy Birthday. Kit called 1930. Lynne left Sunday May 31, to return to Seattle. She had been invaluable.

We had brought Kay home a few times to have a small bite and there was no evident reluctance to return to The Arbors. Kay made gradual progress during June, and was scheduled to come home on July 8, 1998. Kit arrived — Kay came home. Kit stayed about 3 weeks, and then had to return home to arrange for renters. Just the two of us for about 3 weeks, then Lynne took unpaid sick leave and arrived August 19. Arrangements were made with the Visiting Nurses Association to provide home therapy: occupational on Tuesdays and Thursdays, and speech on Wednesdays and Fridays, and a weekly visit by a nurse to check "vital signs" and a young woman to help assist Kay in taking a bath.

With a doctor's prescription, we were able to have a month of therapy twice a week at Health South Sea Pines on outpatient basis. When Kay reached a "plateau" she could not continue as a Medicare patient. We continued having Mario Zinna twice a week at home for speech therapy. Slow, but some progress.

Kay can walk very well, ride the exercycle for fifteen minutes at a time, will play in the pool when Kit and Lynne are here and insist. Kay reads fairly well, seems to enjoy TV, can set the breakfast table, make her sandwich at lunch, load and put away the dishes from the dishwasher. Without assistance, she handles her dental hygiene and her body functions.

(I brought this narrative up-to-date in late May, 1999.)

Much, much later – about 5 years.

Saturday, April 12, 2003 – Kay in Charlton Hospital

Kay died gently and quietly at 0310, April 13, 2003.

Lynne was at her bedside.

No more pills or food to force.

My Sorrows & My Failures

(This was begun in May 2004, brought up again and again. The date now is September 20, 2006 and I will try to pick up near the time where I left off.)

Now I go back with hindsight, with regrets, with such anguish and suffering for the things I did not do, which I could have done, for things I did which I should not have done, following Kay's stroke. I must write of these things, because I cannot speak of them without breaking down in tears sobbing.

Earlier, I had noted that Kay was able to do some of the occupational things: setting the table, making a sandwich. But I did not work with Kay to stay with these accomplishments and urge more things to accomplish. In retrospect, I realize that I did not take the time to work with Kay. Did I give up on her before she gave up on herself? Why did I think I had to do the simple things that Kay could have done had I the patience to guide and direct and assist her? I can do nothing now but regret my impatience and neglect.

Physical therapy is never easy. Following my surgery in February 2003, the chemo and radiation therapy left me weak and unsteady and led to my falling and injuring my back. I can reasonably and clearly understand the importance of the exercises I must do to regain a more active life. When trying to get Kay to do the exercises she needed to do to improve her overall physical condition, especially the movements of her right side and the use of her right hand, it just seemed easier to let her learn to use her left hand. She could have made some progress writing or printing with her right hand had I worked with her regularly and conscientiously.

She would tire and want to stop. Why didn't I come back later and try again and again? What did I have to do that was more important than helping my dear wife in her recovery? What, what, what?

Kay was able to read some simple children's books and other readings, and comprehend the text. I did not urge her and spend time reading to her and with her. She would watch the TV program 'Animal World' and enjoy it. I did not urge her to watch the news and other programs, which she would understand. I did not urge the mental stimulation, even at that level. That neglect may have hastened the onset of Alzheimer's disease.

Lynne did find a children's book about learning to tie shoes. Kay succeeded and was able to master the task, but so often, it seems, I did not "have the time" to let Kay do these little things for herself. After awhile she forgot how again.

Then one day she came into the kitchen with a bright little smile on her face and I saw that she had tied her shoes by herself again. She was so proud.

What kind of excuse did I use to not walk with her and see that she would get the exercise she needed? One day Maury brought Kay home. She had wandered, in her bra and slip, into Maury's garage workshop. I had made very little effort to find someone to come and stay with Kay for a few hours when I had to go out.

When it was apparent that I could not leave her alone in the house, I took the easy way out and arranged for Kay to be admitted to Autumn House in Melbourne. Kay appeared to be happy there. She engaged in some of the activities, but mostly sat in her chair, passively, wearing her little blue cloth hat with the brim turned up in front and a pin attached. I can remember, I can actually picture, how Kay would smile when I came to visit. She just looked so happy. Now I can understand that my visits were short, no more than two hours, once a day, generally before dinner. That sort of schedule was strictly for my own selfish desire to be able to leave easily while Kay was eating.

(I had to stop for a day at the above point – I was sobbing and crying so hard I could not continue.)

Now I can recount so many ways that I failed my dear wife. It seems that I felt I was willing to die for her, but not willing to live with her and for her and help her in so many ways, in so many little ways.

June 11 '04: watching the pomp and ceremony of Ronald Reagan's state funeral, the touching eulogies by such notables as former prime minister of Canada Brian Mulroney, Lady Margaret Thatcher, former president George Bush, and his son President George W. Bush.

All day, Nancy Reagan controlled her grief. She was by his side during his last ten years of suffering with Alzheimer's disease. Seeing her, I felt ashamed of myself.

(Can't write anymore right now.)

June 12: Went for a walk today. Everything is a memory – a memory of some sort. Memory of walking down the hall, following two little women, squatty build, who swayed from side to side as they shifted their weight from one leg to the other. Kay would begin to imitate their walk and look at me and smile. After a meal, with Kay in a wheelchair as we walked back to our apartment, she would pick a small bit of food from her mouth and rub it on the handrail. And I would scold her. I could have just wiped the rail with tissue and gone on. Why make a big deal out of something so small?

Oh, I became quite good at picking on everything thing Kay did – taking a small crumb from her mouth and putting it on the table, instead of on her plate, taking out her teeth and putting them on the table during a meal, picking up food with her fingers instead of a the fork. If she hated me for picking on her, she never showed it.

Now, I can only hope that I can be a better person, be more tolerant of the small things I have criticized in others. I fretted about Kay standing too far away from the sink as she brushed her teeth. I scolded her about getting water on the floor. What difference did it make? (Can't write any more right now.)

(Picked up a photo of Kay, me, Kit and Lynne at Kit's. It is dated April 13, 1998, exactly one month before the stroke.)

When Kay was in the Health Care Center, I would occasionally bring her to the apartment. She would follow me from room to room, sit and watch me and sometimes doze off. Why would that bother me? Could I not see that she just wanted to be with me? I will never be able to forgive myself for my insensitivity. Too late now. (Have to quit again.)

June 14: Over the years we had tried to remember the advice about disagreements given us by Mamomma (Kay's mother): "Don't go to bed at night angry with each other." Only on very, very few occasions did we break that rule. And then, frequently, we would reach a hand out to touch each other before going to sleep and say: "I'm sorry."

Twice, during the last years of my inadequacy, I went to bed angry with my dear wife. She was upset and did not come directly to her bed. I heard her fall in the darkened room. She was bleeding from several gashes. I rushed her to the hospital where the doctors stitched up the gashes. Yes, I think I caused the fall and the injury. Had I been gentle and loving and understanding, she would not have been upset and would have come directly to bed.

Worst of all: One night I was trying to get her to bed and she wasn't ready. She got angry. I pushed her down onto the bed. She got up clawing and biting at me and I slapped her. She looked at me, and I could see the surprise and shock and hurt in her eyes that I, her loved and loving husband, would strike her. That incident lives with me every day I live, days that I no longer care whether I live or die. I have read of 'private grief.' A grief that cannot be shared. This is one of mine, the worst of several.

I pray daily that Kay will forgive me all my failings. From the time our children were old enough to understand, I frequently pointed out to them that many times we do wrongs and when we do we have to be prepared to suffer the consequences. Now my anguish and sorrow are the consequences of my failure to understand and assist in Kay's failing years. (Have to stop here.)

I must stop what I have been trying to say. Kit and Lynne, darling daughters, you may find it difficult to forgive your father for all his failings, but you know your dear, loving mother, and I think she will, out of love, forgive me.

I can't now, and I think I never will be able to forgive myself.

Goodbye and may God bless you.

September 20, 2006

EPILOGUE

After Kay's stroke in 1998 and the onset of Alzheimer's disease, it became clear that we would have to find an assisted living facility. The Autumn House in Florida was very good, but obviously a similar accommodation closer to our daughters would be a better choice.

To be nearer to Kit and Lynne, we moved to Sakonnet Bay Manor, in Tiverton, Rhode Island, December 18, 2001.

We had a three-room apartment: actually a one bedroom apartment with a connecting studio apartment, in the independent living section of the complex. There is also a section of Assisted Living, and a Health Care Unit.

Kay was doing fairly well for about a year, but began to weaken rather rapidly after suffering two bouts of pneumonia.

After Kay died on April 13, 2003, just five days before our sixty-first wedding anniversary, I have continued living in the apartment, playing bridge, trying to finish this biography, enjoying the visits from Lynne every two weeks, just waiting to join my beautiful, loving wife.

Bud Barbee

ISBN 142510966-7

9 781425 109660